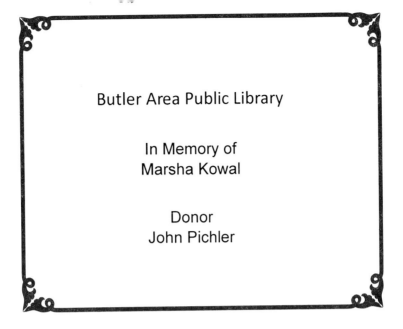

Religion and Culture
in Early Modern Russia
and Ukraine

Religion
and Culture

IN EARLY MODERN
RUSSIA AND UKRAINE

Edited by Samuel H. Baron and Nancy Shields Kollmann

rm

NORTHERN

ILLINOIS

UNIVERSITY

PRESS

DEKALB

1997

© 1997 by Northern Illinois University Press
Published by the Northern Illinois University Press,
DeKalb, Illinois   60115
Manufactured in the United States using acid-free paper ∞
All Rights Reserved

Library of Congress Cataloging-in-Publication Data
Religion and culture in early modern Russia and Ukraine /
edited by Samuel H. Baron and Nancy Shields Kollmann.

p.   cm.

Includes bibliographical references and index.
ISBN 0-87580-218-4 (alk. paper)
1. Religion and culture—Russia—History—17th century.
2. Religion and culture—Ukraine—History—17th century. 3. Russia—Church history—17th century. 4.
Ukraine—Church history—17th century. I. Baron,
Samuel H. II. Kollmann, Nancy Shields.
BL65.C8R442   1996
306.6'0947—dc20   96-22921
                                                  CIP

Sponsored by the Joint Committee on the Soviet Union
and Its Successor States of the American Council of
Learned Societies and the Social Science Research Council.

CONTENTS

Preface   vii

Introduction
   Religion and Cultural Studies in Russia, Then and Now
   Samuel H. Baron and Nancy Shields Kollmann   3

SOCIETY AND CULTURAL PRACTICE

"Backwardness" in Russian Peasant Culture
   A Theoretical Consideration of Agricultural Practices
   in the Seventeenth Century
   Janet Martin   19

Concepts of Society and Social Identity in Early Modern Russia
   Nancy Shields Kollmann   34

Ukrainian Social Tensions before the Khmel'nyts'kyi Uprising
   Frank E. Sysyn   52

RELIGION AND BELIEF

Court Ceremony in an Age of Reform
   Patriarch Nikon and the Palm Sunday Ritual
   Michael S. Flier   73

Supplicatory Prayers as a Source for
Popular Religious Culture in Muscovite Russia
   Eve Levin   96

Muscovite Miracle Stories as Sources for
Gender-Specific Religious Experience
   Isolde Thyrêt   115

The Miracle of Martyrdom
   Reflections on Early Old Believer Hagiography
   Robert O. Crummey   132

IMAGE, IDENTITY, AND MENTALITÉ

Misrepresentations, Misunderstandings, and Silences
    Problems of Seventeenth-Century Ruthenian and
    Muscovite Cultural History
    David A. Frick   149

Simon Ushakov—"Historicism" and "Byzantinism"
    On the Interpretation of Russian Painting from the
    Second Half of the Seventeenth Century
    Engelina S. Smirnova   169

**Religious Reform and the Emergence of the Individual
in Russian Seventeenth-Century Literature**
    Victor M. Zhivov   184

Afterword
    Orthodoxy and Heterodoxy
    Edward L. Keenan   199

Index   207

PREFACE

These articles are the fruit of the second workshop in Early East Slavic Culture, which was held June 19–24, 1993, at Stanford University, and by and large represent the core concerns of the workshop on religious and cultural life in seventeenth-century Russia and Ukraine. The workshop was sponsored by the Joint Committee on the Soviet Union and Its Successor States (JCSSS) of the American Council of Learned Societies and the Social Science Research Council and was supported by a grant to the JCSSS from the Andrew W. Mellon Foundation. Additional support was provided by the Center for Russian and East European Studies and the Department of History at Stanford University. The workshop was organized by a committee composed of Nancy Shields Kollmann, Michael S. Flier, Daniel H. Kaiser, and Daniel Clarke Waugh and gathered together twenty scholars from the United States, Canada, Russia, and Ukraine.

This was the second workshop sponsored by the JCSSS with the goal of developing the field of early East Slavic studies. The organizers of each workshop believed that the field would benefit from breaking down the barriers created by established historical paradigms or by disciplinary or generational boundaries. Thus the workshops were designed to promote interdisciplinary and comparative perspectives, fresh theoretical paradigms, or new methodologies. The first workshop took place in June 1990 at the University of California, Los Angeles, and was devoted to East Slavic culture through the sixteenth century. The papers presented there may be found in *Medieval Russian Culture,* volume 2, edited by Michael S. Flier and Daniel Rowland. The second workshop focused on East Slavic culture in the seventeenth century; authors were asked to consider such themes as the physical environment, war and society, orthodoxy and heterodoxy, the concept of self, and so on. Although most of the research focused on Muscovy, we tried to look at seventeenth-century Russia in the broader cultural context of its interactions with other East Slavs; in some cases papers addressed other East Slavic cultures independent of a Russian connection. Fourteen scholars from various disciplines (art history, literature, history) were invited, and seven advanced graduate students or young faculty were chosen by international competition. The competition winners at the second workshop included emerging scholars from Ukraine, Russia, Canada, and the United States.

Each workshop also benefited from the critiques of outside specialists. For the first workshop, for example, two scholars of Kievan Rus' and Petrine Russia provided a diachronic perspective from their various chronological viewpoints. The second workshop was fortunate to have the stimulating contributions of Natalie Zemon Davis of Princeton University, whose insights into new methods and issues in early modern French history pushed us to examine our period with fresh eyes. We also appreciated in this capacity the penetrating comments of a specialist in our field, Edward L. Keenan of Harvard

University. This volume ends with his provocative array of propositions regarding the early modern East Slavs and the process of historical inquiry itself.

That process is indeed a continuous one, of assessment, interpretation, and reassessment. We hoped that these two workshops would make scholars more self-conscious of the ways in which they conduct their historical analysis, broadly conceived; we hoped that the workshops would encourage scholars to try new approaches and to cross the boundaries of disciplines in our common endeavor. Similarly we hope that this collection might inspire others to think again—whether more deeply, more broadly, more theoretically, more comparatively, with more complexity—about the process as well as about the content, about analysis and about the cultural world of the East Slavs in the seventeenth century.

Religion and Culture
in Early Modern Russia
and Ukraine

S A M U E L   H .   B A R O N   A N D

N A N C Y   S H I E L D S   K O L L M A N N

INTRODUCTION

RELIGION AND CULTURAL STUDIES IN RUSSIA,
THEN AND NOW

SINCE RUSSIA in the popular mind is often associated with fervent spirituality and deep cultural identity, it is a paradox that religion and culture have been so selectively—some would say even shabbily—treated in historical literature. We take the word of Slavophile publicists and modern philosophers on the communal essence of Russian spirituality; we get our theology from *The Brothers Karamazov;* we are enlightened by Tolstoi on the cultural rift between noblemen and peasants in nineteenth-century Russia. Meanwhile, historians have not created an edifice of scholarly knowledge comparable to that which exists for the medieval Latin West, about the church or about premodern cultural life, about theology and religious practice, religious dissent, social values and mores. This, despite the fact that Russia remained a nonsecular, principally religious society significantly longer than did Europe. This relative neglect makes all the more striking the contemporary turn toward religion and culture in historical studies broadly conceived (not just in the discipline of history), which this book itself exemplifies. So it may be instructive to explore the treatment of religion and culture in Russian historiography briefly to put this volume into context.

Religion and culture were inextricably intertwined in Russia through at least the seventeenth century, since the Russian Orthodox church provided the vocabulary for ethics, creative expression, political ideas, and for most social mores, ritual, and symbolic activity. (Non-Christian ideas and practices endured but were often subsumed into Orthodoxy.)[1] Given its ubiquity in cultural discourses in particular, the church's feeble representation in historiography—especially in the nineteenth century when Orthodoxy was the Empire's official religion—is striking. One scholar declared: "The history of Orthodoxy in Old Russia is perhaps the least known aspect of the history of the country in the entire pre-Petrine era." Another goes further:

> One of the most striking—and lamentable— characteristics of Russian historiography has been its unmitigated secularism: only the barest attention is given to the Church and religion, particularly in the eighteenth and nineteenth centuries. Such neglect is all the more salient when compared with the *Forschungsstand* in European historiography.[2]

This is not to say that no work was done on the history of the Russian church, but that it was selective and even tendentious. Official church historians, for example, focused on political and institutional history, not culture and belief. George Fedotov speaks of scholars who treated Orthodoxy as "eternal and changeless": "external forms and the data of religion were studied . . . but the depths remained unstirred."[3] Or, they infused their work with a nationalist or anti-sectarian zeal. Secular historians meanwhile looked for the most political moments: V. O. Kliuchevskii depicted the church as colonizer and patron of Moscow; others examined the role of the "non-possessor"/"possessor" debate in building autocracy; many construed the Old Belief as a clash between church and state or as a struggle of obscurantism with Western influence. Studies of premodern high culture (such as icon painting) flourished in the nineteenth century, but conspicuously lacking was any serious treatment of piety, spirituality, and the practice of religion.

Several explanations can be put forward for such neglect. The liberal intelligentsia and most of the scholarly community were overwhelmingly secular in the nineteenth century and were uninterested—even actively hostile—to religion. Religion did not fit well into the dominant historical paradigm of the nineteenth century (or, for that matter, the twentieth). This paradigm was the "statist" presumption that political power was the primary mover in Russian history and that Russia followed the European path toward centralization and secularization and away from obscurantist religion and feudal disarray. Thus scholars pushed religion and thereby culture to the margins, relegating the study of religion, as Bushkovitch says, to a "theological ghetto."[4]

In this "ghetto" conservative scholars—ecclesiastical as well as secular—either construed their task narrowly or responded to the dominant secular intellectual trends by reducing "the content of Old Russian Orthodoxy to national ideology."[5] The legacy of this trend was a kind of romanticization of the official church, and a fierce denunciation of the Old Belief. Compounding the absence of religion and culture in scholarly study was the fact that religious themes were taken up by circles outside the historical profession: the original Slavophiles were publicists more than scholars, and it was novelists and symbolic poets who popularized versions of Russian spirituality.

Finally, historical study of Orthodoxy was specifically slighted by scholars' and religious thinkers' tendency to Europeanize and universalize the vision of Russian religion and spirituality. Bushkovitch persuasively shows how, for example, early studies of Old Russian literature (and thus religion) by the philologist S. P. Shevyrev depicted early Russian church and belief on the model of nineteenth-century European Catholicism, turning Orthodoxy into a bulwark of social order and hierarchy and discounting aspects such as monasticism that were antithetical to this view.[6] The fascination with religious themes in turn-of-the-century poetry and literature and the renaissance in Russian Orthodox religious philosophy in the early twentieth century also abjured a historically based examination of Russian Orthodoxy and depicted it as a generalized universal Christianity, devoid of local specificity.[7]

The legacy of selective study of Russian Orthodoxy in the premodern period is that modern students implicitly share "the notion that Russian history can be written and understood with minimal attention to the Church and religion."[8] Paul Bushkovitch gives a telling example. He argues that the traditional picture of the Muscovite landed gentry that has become the canon since Kliuchevskii is excessively secular. It emphasizes the gentryman as "serviceman," loyal to the tsar, bound to service, defined by his military lifestyle, and primed for the westernizing influences so dear to the hearts of liberal historians.[9] But scholars have recently put us on notice that these "servitors" were also religious men who marked their lives' various passages with religious rituals and understandings.[10] In sum, despite the misleading ponderousness of multivolume histories of the church (Metropolitan Makarii, A. P. Dobroklonskii, E. E. Golubinskii) and various and sundry encyclopediae of theology, nineteenth-century scholars barely scratched the surface on what spirituality meant to early Russians and what kind of culture they lived in.

The legacy of twentieth-century scholarship is somewhat more encouraging. Because Soviet Marxism encased all historical—and to a lesser extent literary—research in a framework that systematically slighted religion, Soviet scholarship necessarily slighted religious topics. Ideological imperatives dictated the primacy of socioeconomic formations, and accordingly socioeconomic historical investigations prevailed. It was essential somehow to fit Russia's history into what was said to be a universally operative Marxian historical scheme. The overemphasis on premodern socioeconomic history in Soviet historiography inevitably made for a relative neglect of cultural history and an active hostility to religion. To be sure, studies could be carried out on church support of an oppressive autocratic system, and on monastic institutions as great landowners and exploiters of the peasants. But serious attention to religious thought and practice—and their role in the life of the elite, the masses, and society as a whole—was discouraged. After all, if religion was nothing but "the opium of the people" and culture merely a superstructural element, they hardly merited consideration. At the same time religion did duty as a bearer of the state principle and of the national ideology in the mélange of nationalism and cosmopolitanism that was Soviet Marxism. Such biases were bound to produce a ludicrously one-sided picture of medieval Russia.[11]

All was not gloom here, thankfully. In the interstices of these extremes some excellent work was done. In the Soviet period many perspicacious scholars fit between the frames of the requisite quotes from Marx, Lenin, or Stalin excellent monographic studies of monastic landholding and libraries and carried out fundamental textual analysis of religious literature, hagiography, and publicistic writings. Thus, a good deal of sound information can be culled from Soviet works on religion and the church by sifting the contents of these monographs with discrimination.[12] Also, as a rule, in the Soviet period literary scholars fared better, exemplified by either D. S. Likhachev's welcome comparative focus and emphasis on the human element of early Russian literature, or the Tartu-Moscow School of Semiotics. This school's approach has oriented studies of religion and culture away from the study of Orthodoxy as institutional religion, analyzing it as a mythical system that provided an enduring worldview for Russian culture.[13]

In twentieth-century European and American scholarship on Russia, religion played a greater role, but interpretations were problematic. Echoes of Chaadaev's condemnation of Orthodoxy's suffocating effect on civil life and the public sphere in Russia emerged during Cold War years, as well as a popularized tendency to lump Orthodoxy into Stalinism as "Russia's Byzantine heritage" and to describe Russia as a theocratic and messianistic enemy of Western values.[14] In the émigré community the intelligentsia and scholars were completing the turn toward spiritual issues that had begun in Russia in the late nineteenth century. Disillusionment with positivism was exemplified by the philosophy of Vladimir Solov'ev and before the 1917 Revolution found expression in the *Vekhi* (1909) and *Iz glubiny* (1918) collections, all of which called for spiritual regeneration. Emigré scholars continued this search for the spiritual side of Russianness. But much of their work maintained the universalistic Christianizing trend mentioned above, as is evident in the national-religious ideas of the Eurasianists or the popularity of Berdiaev's theosophic vision of the Russian soul.[15]

It is very significant, however, that the Russian emigration spawned two historians who purposely gave historical grounding to their quests for Russian spirituality. These were Georges Florovsky (1893–1979), author of influential studies of Russian religious thought and theological debates from the fifteenth through the nineteenth centuries, and George Fedotov (1886–1951), whose work is particularly germane to current interests in spirituality and religious life. Fedotov, perhaps inspired by his scholarly training in European medieval studies while in St. Petersburg, in emigration set himself the task of defining the "Russian religious mind," by which he meant the whole content of consciousness . . . the subjective side of religion as opposed to its objective side. . . . This wholeness of the religious personality is the invisible center out of which the main phenomena not only of religious but of cultural life in general have their origin and receive their meaning. . . . The history of Christianity is the history of [the human response to Grace]; its culture is the culture of this experience.[16]

Here Fedotov enunciates a vision of "culture" akin to the modern concept of cultural studies. Although betraying a universalistic predilection common to the Orthodox renaissance of the twentieth century and in keeping with his passionate commitment to Christian socialism, Fedotov nonetheless focused on the specifically Orthodox content of Russian religious life. Although his work on "the Russian religious mind" was unfinished, Fedotov's studies of saints as spiritual exemplars and his posthumously published essay on "normal Christian ethics" broke new ground in the use of sources (hagiography, unpublished moralizing texts such as the *Izmaragd*) and in its focus on daily life. Marc Raeff, noting that Fedotov did not have immediate influence on studies of Russian religiosity, likens Fedotov's approach to Clifford Geertz's "thick description" and puts his *Russian Religious Mind* in the same camp as the work of *Annales* school historians Emmanuel Le Roy Ladurie and Carlo Ginzburg.[17] Raeff's comment is on the mark: the postwar period saw excellent scholarly work done by non-émigré historians on the church, but primarily on traditional topics such as institutional history and monasticism.[18]

Fedotov, who died in 1951, would probably be pleased, and even bewildered, at current enthusiasm for studying the "wholeness" of Russian spiritual and cultural experience. Since the 1980s or so, American and European scholars have been delving deep into the nexus between religion, culture, and society. Recent work, much by authors in the present collection, has focused on topics as diverse as sex and society, Old Believer spirituality, the spiritual and social interpretation of hagiography, the clergy as a caste, the rise and fall of miracle cults, almsgiving and practices of charity, and pietistic literature and theological debates in their own rights.[19] Meanwhile historians in post-*perestroika* Russia are rediscovering religion and mentality but generally are taking traditional political approaches.[20] In the West the decided break with a stodgy historiography probably owes as much to trends in American and European social science as it does to Florovsky, Fedotov, the Moscow-Tartu school, and other influences internal to the field. Trends since the 1960s in the social sciences (law, anthropology, sociology, and history) have pushed scholars toward an engagement with "lived experience," with how people thought, lived, and interacted on a local level. Such a focus has evolved not as a flight from the macrohistorical theories that had dominated social sciences until then (be they Marxism, neoMarxism, structuralism, modernization theory, or so forth) but rather as a way to test such broad paradigms of social structure and change. The hallmark of the new cultural approach is its focus on human agency in the context of the institutions, ideas, and other "discourses" that shape human action but do not predetermine it: hence the focus on "praxis," how individuals negotiate and manipulate the discourses within which they are situated, and on "culture," seen not as "some subjective or idealized world view that is to be distinguished from behavior but as a form of behavior in itself and as the tangible results of that behavior."[21] Thus scholars are taking microhistorical tacks, delving into mentality, exploring minority or historically underrepresented populations (women in particular), analyzing the symbolic and ritual world of daily life, and getting at the deepest personal level in the study of the body and sexuality.[22]

"Cultural studies" is fast assuming the primacy that "social history" enjoyed through the 1960s and that political and diplomatic history had enjoyed in generations before that. Cultural studies are profoundly interdisciplinary and inclusive, cutting across traditional ways of looking at traditional problems. One could, for example, do a "cultural" history of a political problem, if one looked not narrowly at institutions and laws but at people's experience of the law, at their manipulation of and negotiation with legal institutions, at their concept of the law in theory and practice. Such exploration then might be applied back to broader paradigms about the relationship of state and society. The point of a "cultural" approach is ultimately to elucidate, reframe, or expand the traditionally central questions of a given field. Getting at "lived experience," as Sherry Ortner terms it, is not mere "human interest" respite from the work of writing real history, it is indeed real history. It gives new perspectives on the old problems—periodization, social structure, conflict and change, power and hierarchy—at a more authentic level than institutional, biographical, elitist, diplomatic, or other approaches might previously have been able to do.

In the case of early Russia such currents, as they penetrated this field in the past decade or so, struck a welcome note. Among literary scholars they were familiar, since the Tartu-Moscow school had long put Russian literary and cultural studies on the cutting edge of theory. Many historians were familiar with new directions through Edward L. Keenan's bold challenges to the statist paradigm of Russian politics, applying structuralist and anthropological analysis to the "system" of court politics.[23] One can also see a shift in some historians' interest in line with new trends. Eve Levin's work on sexuality and prayers exemplified here, for example, follows her earlier, more traditionally conceived work on the social and political role of women in Novgorod. Robert Crummey's study of Old Believer spirituality, included here, represents a return to material that he had earlier approached from a social and political viewpoint. Cross-fertilization among fields is common, with scholars using methods and comparisons drawn from comparable fields. Isolde Thyrêt brings classical training in Western medieval studies to her analysis of Russian hagiography, particularly the "form-critical" mode of analysis earlier developed and applied to the synoptic gospels by Gerd Theissen; Gail Lenhoff has applied a *Sitz im Leben* approach to hagiography; Nancy Shields Kollmann has in the past ventured into symbolic anthropology and here takes a comparative approach, implicitly contrasting early modern Russian with European social consciousness, without condemning the differences.[24]

We are definitely not out of the woods yet, as Keenan's trenchant critique apropos the prevailing configuration of ideas about Orthodoxy and Russian spirituality declares. The heavy weight of old assumptions about Russian culture, national character, and religious belief will take a while to analyze and assess. Clearly it will help, as Bushkovitch has suggested, for us to develop a critical awareness of what we know and how we know it, so that we can more self-consciously pick our way through the minefield of received wisdom.[25] This call to self-criticism is the great contribution of Keenan's afterword. Meanwhile, research such as that included here continues the work of asking new questions, breaking new ground, and reflecting back again on issues of long-standing importance.

The essays included in this volume represent new directions in a variety of ways. Some, for example, try to see the interconnectedness of the East Slavic cultural world in the early modern period, specifically dismissing modern national sensibilities and looking for the commonalities of belief and social structure among Orthodox Slavs from Ukraine to Moscow. Thus, David Frick explores identity on the boundaries of Russia and Ukraine, and Engelina Smirnova, David Frick, Victor Zhivov, and Michael Flier assess the fertile interplay of European, Byzantine, and Ukrainian Orthodox elements in the religious and cultural life of the seventeenth century. Frank Sysyn takes a structural approach to Ukrainian political change, endeavoring to explain how and why the Khmel'nyts'kyi uprising in Ukraine succeeded—when many other social upheavals failed—in overthrowing the existing social order and replacing it with another. His inquiry takes us into the intricacies of the social and confessional structures of Poland-Lithuania and various Ukrainian territories and shows how changing demographic and economic patterns produced tensions in a rigid and inflexible structure, ultimately leading to the undoing of the small privileged elite by Cossack forces.

An interdisciplinary content also epitomizes the cultural approach. For example, Michael Flier's study of change in a major Russian religious ritual draws upon literary and historical sources and reflects as well upon semiotics. Flier, earlier having deciphered the inner meaning of a central but perplexing feature of the annual Palm Sunday ceremony in sixteenth-century Moscow,[26] here tackles a related puzzle: how to account for the significant change in the ritual introduced in 1656. Displaying both an impressive mastery of several disciplines and painstaking attention to detail, Flier convincingly argues that it was Patriarch Nikon who, for complex reasons, added and subtracted various elements from the ritual. Nikon's intention was not just to exalt his own position, as one might expect; at the symbolic level he aimed to bring the ceremony into closer correspondence with the purportedly historical entry of Christ into Jerusalem, while retaining certain traditional Muscovite elements, and thus reenforce the image of Muscovy—the new Jerusalem—as God's instrument for the redemption of the Orthodox world.

Engelina Smirnova's piece on the "historicism" (and Byzantinism) of the major artist Ushakov's icon paintings is itself historicist, as is Viktor Zhivov's piece on the emergence of the individual in literary texts. Zhivov argues that the seventeenth century was an era of radical literary and cultural change, brought on not so much by westernization as by an internal dynamic triggered by the Zealots of Piety *(Bogoliubtsy)* in response to the harrowing Time of Troubles, a fifteen-year period of dynastic crisis, social upheaval, and foreign invasion from 1598 to 1613. Their reform efforts—in reality involving a reappraisal of Orthodox culture, although represented as its restoration—led to the famous church schism. But Zhivov contends that their activity also produced a schism within the country's literature (and culture), bringing forth diverse genres where the distinction between the sacred and the secular had been rudimentary at best and where none whatsoever had existed between prose and poetry. Provocative too is this author's proposal that the reform movement made alternative cultural values available and thereby fostered individualism. The reform movement led to "the emergence of the individual as an autonomous cultural value," with writers approaching their texts as individuals for the first time and creating individual literary characters (Avvakum and Neronov). A private sphere began to take shape, and with it literary and artistic autonomy.

These essays also bring new sources into service, such as religious material, which earlier scholars had largely ignored because of an elitist bias or for want of appreciation that historical truths might be mined from fabulous stories. Eve Levin considers supplicatory prayers—composed by or on behalf of ordinary people, and possessing many characteristics different from the official "cognitive religion"—as vehicles for gaining access to popular religious culture. She treats us to a selection of fascinating pleas to the forces of a mythological "otherworld" (partly pagan, partly Christian) for everything from protection of herds, to the excitement of sexual desire, to the banishment of drunkenness. Isolde Thyrêt explores little-appreciated miracle tales that illuminate the role of gender in the spiritual life of the Muscovites. She shows that, in three different religious environments, women's participation in the cult of several saints varied in extent, but that, although Russian saints had a greater appeal among females than males, because of the misogynistic attitudes of the clergy, in all three milieux, women had a lesser part than men.

Other essays here show how modern cultural studies draw on new theoretical approaches or methodologies. Janet Martin examines entrenched notions about the Russian peasantry—that it was backward, inefficient, and uninterested in improving its modes of work—in the light of Ester Boserup's theory of peasant economies. Her analysis leads to the arresting suggestion that peasant practice represented a successful adaptation to conditions prevailing in seventeenth-century Russia as opposed to the normative judgments of modern commentators critical of peasant "backwardness." She invites further research to test her thesis: it might be well also to consider whether successful adaptation might be advantageous in the short term but harmful in a longer perspective. Nancy Shields Kollmann explores Muscovite concepts of self and society, applying a *Begriffsgeschichte* method. Recognizing that premodern societies were localistic, she sensitively teases out of well-known sources a whole array of subgroup self-identifications: kinship, regional, professional, rank and network related. Interconnections and "negotiations" among such groups at local levels, she argues, were much more important for constructing "lived experience" than were relations with the distant centralized state.

And in what is perhaps the most methodologically and interpretively subtle essay in the collection, Frick canvasses the difficulties of studying the formation of cultural identities in Europe's eastern borderlands, Rus' in particular. At a time when Rus' was trying for the first time to come to terms with the West, individuals manifested complex and ambiguous identities. Ethnic and confessional identities were in flux, loyalties were opaque, and there were often great discrepancies between the public programs and private consciousness of major figures. Deconstructing a number of public pronouncements of Archbishop Meletij Smotryts'kyi and others, Frick shows how inapplicable modern concepts of national consciousness are in the multicultural "borderland" between Rus' and Muscovy. He suggests that "misrepresentations, misunderstandings, and silences" may offer better access to the "possibly ineffable core" of early modern identity than the prevailing structural approaches.

Implicitly following Clifford Geertz's concept of religion as a "cultural system," Robert Crummey examines the place of martyrdom in its hagiography through a nuanced analysis of two historically based tales. He finds (as in Thyrêt's essay) differences in this religious experience in the lives of men and women, as exemplified by Avraamii and Boiarynia Morozova. Also notable is the vivid portrayal of Morozova as a powerfully individualistic personality, adding weight to one of the ideas that Zhivov emphasizes. There is little one might expect in these religious tales of miraculous elements; rather than the intercession of God in human affairs, the greatest miracle the tales convey is "the strength to endure martyrdom for the Old Faith," thus demonstrating its truth.

These essays sparkle with complexity and variety. They resist the impulse to press data into binary oppositions, to see things in terms of either/or. Inasmuch as reality is too complex and too multifaceted to be encompassed by fixed categories, unconditional resort to such categories is bound to distort reality. Zhivov is especially emphatic on this point. He takes to task scholars who divide ancient Russian texts into sacred and secular when, he insists, no such distinction actually existed. He bridles at the predilection he perceives to divide Russian cultural history into pre- and post-Petrine eras, which obscures the significance of the seventeenth century. Smirnova discounts a prevalent inclination to see Ushakov as either a traditionalist or an innovator, arguing instead that his work combined both tendencies: he borrowed some devices from European painting but depended more on traditional subject matters and forms. These essays tend to discount Western influence as a force driving change in Russia (and thereby the bipolarity between Russia and the West), emphasizing instead internal developments such as the seventeenth-century religious reform movement. Levin's work shows that the dichotomies "pagan/Christian" and "elite/popular" are faulty, for the popular mentality did not distinguish between the first of these polarities, and there was more than a little overlap between elite and popular religious culture.

Frick's essay is especially sensitive to the hazards—noting that we are apt to employ unequivocal concepts in discussing figures, movements, and events that are themselves ambiguous. In alerting readers to the dangers of rigidly binary oppositions (a point emphasized by Iurii Lotman and Boris Uspenskii), this collection performs a valuable service.[27]

The bipolar way of seeing the early modern period mainly in terms of "continuity" and "change" (focusing on Peter I and his reforms) is put to rest here. Our authors have found major cultural continuities in some areas of Russian life and portentous innovations in others. In the economic sphere, for example, some peasants adopted improved methods of cultivation, but most evidently preferred to stick to the traditional ways. Kollmann's paper portrays a social structure within which shifts could occur, but on the whole the picture presented is one of stability rather than significantly changing relations. Crummey, Thyrêt, and Levin show how religious practice and belief were dynamically reshaped within a continuous idiom; each group studied— women, lay people, and Old Believers—presented innovations responding to changing spiritual needs and communities as tradition. Flier's investigation of the Orthodox ritual change of 1656 epitomizes the tension between new and old so characteristic of the seventeenth century. Nikon's changes represented a development of previous efforts to establish Muscovy as the new Jerusalem and the source of redemption for the Orthodox world, and nevertheless they can be perceived as radically changing Muscovite religious norms. Zhivov's case for the rise of individualism may seem insignificant because it was primarily a literary phenomenon, but cultural historians such as Lotman and Uspenskii contend that Russian literature has produced socially significant effects, in that readers have often fashioned themselves on literary models. In the matter of individuation (as is definitely the case in genre differentiation, and perhaps some other items as well), seeds were planted in the seventeenth century that came to full development only much later.

Cultural studies provide the means to study what these various authors implicitly demonstrate: different aspects of a society wherein change was occurring at different rates, on different levels, for different groups simultaneously and eclectically. These essays demonstrate the importance of human agency in historical change, as well as the shaping force exerted by ideas, institutions, and other discourses and cultural practices. They highlight the rich complexity of social and cultural reaction when a tradition-bound society encounters indigenous and exogenous stimuli to change; they go well beyond the old cliché that represents early modern Russia and Ukraine as societies in "transition" to modernity. To understand early modern religion and culture in Russia and Ukraine, these authors suggest, is to embrace complexity and dynamism, contingency and volition. Perhaps most important, in light of the anachronizing and universalizing trends in traditional scholarship, they show us how different the past was from our lives today, how deeply social and symbolic life was permeated with discourses far unlike our own and far unlike any romanticized vision of Orthodox Christianity. Early modern people in these areas dynamically shaped their social reality from the many sources open to them, and they did so continually; their actions may be discernible as broad cultural patterns, but we do well to recall that individuals experienced and applied the shaping discourses of their time differently. The essays in this volume do us the service of demonstrating the creativity of early modern East Slavic cultural life. The challenge now for scholars is to integrate the "macro" and the "micro" historical perspectives, to generate new broad understandings of religion and culture that are grounded in the bracing complexity of lived historical experience.

NOTES

1. Here one might mention the intermingling of pre-Christian and Christian ritual and belief (the so-called *dvoever'e*), the somewhat secular symbolic world of the minstrels *(skomorokhy),* and the curious phenomenon of "holy fools," perhaps sharing elements of indigenous belief systems. On minstrels, see Russell Zguta, *Russian Minstrels: A History of the "Skomorokhi"* (Philadelphia, 1978). On holy fools, see Ewa M. Thompson's book and Nancy Shields Kollmann's review of it: Thompson, *Understanding Russia: The Holy Fool in Russian Culture* (Lanham, Md., 1987); review in *Slavic Review* 47, no. 2 (1988): 320–21.

2. Paul Bushkovitch, "Orthodoxy and Old Rus' in the Thought of S. P. Shevyrev," *Forschungen zur osteuropäischen Geschichte* 46 (1992): 203; Gregory Freeze, "Russian Orthodoxy in Prerevolutionary Historiography: The Case of V. O. Kliuchevskii," *Canadian-American Slavic Studies* 20, nos. 3–4 (1986): 399. Robert F. Byrnes also notes Kliuchevskii's remarkable neglect of religion: "'Between Two Fires': Kliuchevskii on Religion and the Russian Orthodox Church," *Modern Greek Studies Yearbook* 6 (1990): 157–85. Marc Raeff notes the neglect of "the spiritual or religious component" in traditional historiography of Russian intellectual history through the Soviet period in "Enticements and Rifts: Georges Florovsky as Historian of the Life of the Mind and the Life of the Church in Russia," *Modern Greek Studies Yearbook* 6 (1990): 187–244.

3. George P. Fedotov, *The Russian Religious Mind: Kievan Christianity. The Tenth to the Thirteenth Centuries* (1946; reprint, New York, 1960), xii.

4. Paul Bushkovitch, "V. O. Kliuchevskii as Historian of Religion and the Church," *Canadian-American Slavic Studies* 20, nos. 3–4 (1986): 365. Raeff gives an extended explanation of why the intelligentsia's emphasis on social problems led to a neglect of spirituality in "Enticements and Rifts."

5. Bushkovitch, "Orthodoxy and Old Rus'," 203.

6. Ibid.

7. V. V. Zenkovsky, *A History of Russian Philosophy,* trans. George L. Kline, 2 vols. (New York, 1953), chaps. 6, 10, 13 (vol. 1); chaps. 16–17, 26 (vol. 2).

8. Freeze, "Russian Orthodoxy," 416.

9. Bushkovitch, "V. O. Kliuchevskii," 365–66.

10. Paul Bushkovitch, *Religion and Society in Russia: The Sixteenth and Seventeenth Centuries* (New York, 1992), chap. 2; Robert O. Crummey, *Aristocrats and Servitors: The Boyar Elite in Russia, 1613–1689* (Princeton, N.J., 1983), chap. 6; Daniel H. Kaiser, "Death and Dying in Early Modern Russia," *Kennan Institute for Advanced Russian Studies: Occasional Paper no. 228* (Washington, D.C., 1988). Even recent treatments of two figures traditionally considered "westernizers" emphasize

their adherence to traditional Muscovite religious and cultural practices: Abby Finnogh Smith, "Prince V. V. Golitsyn: The Life of an Aristocrat in Muscovite Russia" (Ph.D. diss., Harvard University, 1987); and Lindsey Hughes, *Sofiia, Regent of Russia, 1657–1704* (New Haven, 1990).

11. Since the advent of *perestroika,* and then the collapse of the Soviet regime, efforts have begun to restore religion and the church to their important places in Russian history. Wonderfully symbolic is a scene witnessed in St. Petersburg in May 1994, when a great crowd gathered to watch a helicopter lower a cross onto the top of the Kazan Cathedral, which had been converted during the Soviet era into an anti-religious museum.

12. John Meyendorff praised some Soviet work: G. P. Fedotov, *The Russian Religious Mind: Kievan Christianity,* vol. 2, *The Middle Ages: The Thirteenth to the Fifteenth Centuries,* ed. John Meyendorff (Cambridge, Mass., 1966), x–xi. See also the journal *Kritika,* 20 vols. (Cambridge, Mass., 1964–1984), published by historians at Harvard University specifically to review those works of Soviet scholarship deemed worthy of serious attention.

13. But see E. L. Keenan's criticism of Likhachev's nationalism in *Russian History* 20 (1993): 274–77. On the Tartu school, which endured intense criticism in the Soviet Union before winning broad acceptance, see Boris Gasparov, "Introduction," in *The Semiotics of Russian Cultural History,* ed. Alexander D. Nakhimovsky and Alice Stone Nakhimovsky (Ithaca, N.Y., 1985), 13–29; Peter Seyffert, *Soviet Literary Structuralism: Background, Debate, Issues* (Columbus, Ohio, 1983); Henryk Baran, "Introduction," in *Semiotics and Structuralism: Readings from the Soviet Union,* ed. Peter Seyffert (White Plains, N.Y., 1974), vii–xxvi. Thanks go to Michael Flier for bibliography and stimulating comments on the Tartu-Moscow School of Semiotics.

14. See, for example, Richard Pipes, *Russia under the Old Regime* (New York, 1974), chap. 9; Arnold J. Toynbee, "Russia's Byzantine Heritage," in his *Civilization on Trial* (New York, 1948), 164–83; and Dimitri Obolensky's response to Toynbee in *Oxford Slavonic Papers* 1 (1950): 37–63.

15. On Eurasianism, see Nicholas V. Riasanovsky, "The Emergence of Eurasianism," *California Slavic Studies* 4 (1967): 39–72; G. E. Orchard, "The Eurasian School of Russian Historiography," *Laurentian University Review* 10, no. 1 (1977): 97–106; Jane Burbank, *Intelligentsia and Revolution: Russian Views of Bolshevism, 1917–1922* (Oxford, 1986), 208–22. On Berdiaev, see Zenkovsky, *History,* chap. 26, and Burbank, *Intelligentsia,* 193–208. Raeff in "Enticements and Rifts" also describes the setting in which Eurasianism flourished.

16. Fedotov, *The Russian Religious Mind: Kievan Christianity,* ix, xi.

17. See ibid., and Marc Raeff, *Rossiia za rubezhom: Istoriia kul'tury russkoi emigratsii, 1919–1939* (Moscow, 1994), 228–32. Other sympathetic comments: George Ivask, "George Fedotov (1886–1951)," *Russian Review* 12, no. 1 (1953): 79–82; K. Naumov, "Georgy Petrovich Fedotov, 1886–1951," *Slavonic and East European Review* 31, no. 76 (1952): 254–56; Serge Zenkovsky, review of *The Russian Religious Mind,* vol. 2, in *Russian Review* 26, no. 3 (1967): 296–98.

18. See, for example, work by Igor Smolitsch, Albert Ammann, and A. V. Kartashev: Smolitsch, *Russisches Monchtum: Entstehung and Wesen, 998–1917* (Würzburg, 1953) and *Geschichte der russischen Kirche, 1700–1917,* 2 vols. (Leiden, 1964–1991); Ammann, *Untersuchungen zur Geschichte der kirchlichen Kultur und des religiosen Lebens bei den Ostslawen* (Würzburg, 1955) and *Abriss der ostslawischen Kirchengeschichte* (Vienna, 1950); and Kartashev, *Ocherki po istorii russkoi tserkvi,* 2 vols. (Paris, 1959).

19. Eve Levin, *Sex and Society in the World of the Orthodox Slavs, 900–1700* (Ithaca, N.Y., 1989); Robert O. Crummey, "The Origins of the Old Believers' Cultural Systems: The Works of Avraami," *Forschungen* 50 (1995): 121–38, and "Old Belief as Popular Religion: New Approaches," *Slavic Review* 52, no. 4 (1993): 700–12; Gail Lenhoff, *The Martyred Princes Boris and Gleb* (Columbus, Ohio, 1989); David B. Miller, "The Cult of St. Sergius of Radonezh and Its Political Uses," *Slavic Review* 52, no. 4 (1993): 680–99; Bushkovitch, *Religion and Society;* Ludwig Steindorff, "Klöster als Zentren der Totensorge in Altrussland," *Forschungen* 50 (1995): 337–54; Georg Bernhard Michels, "Myths and Realities of the Russian Schism: The Church and Its Dissenters in Seventeenth-Century Muscovy" (Ph.D. diss., Harvard University, 1991); Cathy Jean Potter, "The Russian Church and the Politics of Reform in the Second Half of the Seventeenth Century" (Ph.D. diss., Yale University, 1993); Gregory L. Freeze, *The Russian Levites: Parish Clergy in the Eighteenth Century* (Cambridge, Mass., 1977), and *The Parish Clergy in Nineteenth-Century Russia* (Princeton, 1983).

20. For example, R. G. Skrynnikov, *Sviatiteli i vlasti* (Leningrad, 1990), and *Gosudarstvo i tserkov' na Rusi XIV–XVI vv.* (Novosibirsk, 1991); V. A. Kuchkin, "Sergii Radonezhskii," *Voprosy istorii,* no. 10 (1992): 75–92.

21. Robert Wuthnow, *Communities of Discourse: Ideology and Social Structure in the Reformation, the Enlightenment, and European Socialism* (Cambridge, Mass., 1989), 15.

22. For interpretive overviews, see Sherry B. Ortner, "Theory in Anthropology since the Sixties," *Comparative Studies in Society and History* 26 (1984): 126–66; Robert W. Gordon, "Critical Legal Histories," *Stanford Law Review* 36 (1984): 57–125; Ben Agger, "Critical Theory, Poststructuralism, Postmodernism: Their Sociological Relevance," *American Review of Sociology* 17 (1991): 105–31; Gabrielle Spiegel, "History, Historicism, and the Social Logic of the Text in the Middle Ages," *Speculum* 64 (1989): 59–86; and Richard Johnson, "What Is Cultural Studies Anyway?" *Social Text: Theory, Culture, Ideology* 16 (1986–1987): 38–80.

For specific studies, see Robert Wuthnow, James Davison Hunter, Albert Bergesen, and Edith Kurzweil, *Cultural Analysis: The Work of Peter L. Berger, Mary Douglas, Michel Foucault, and Jürgen Habermas* (London, 1984); Wuthnow, *Communities of Discourse;* Lloyd S. Kramer, "Literature, Criticism, and Historical Imagination: The Literary Challenge of Hayden White and Dominick LaCapra," in *The New Cultural History,* ed. Lynn Hunt (Berkeley and Los Angeles, 1989), 97–128; Anthony Giddens, *A Contemporary Critique of Historical Materialism,* vol. 1, *Power, Property, and the State* (Berkeley and Los Angeles, 1981) and vol. 2, *The Nation-State and Violence* (Berkeley and Los Angeles, 1987); and Michael Mann, *The Sources of Social Power,* vol. 1, *A History of Power from the Beginning to AD 1760* (Cambridge, England, 1986).

23. Works by Edward L. Keenan: "Muscovite Political Folkways," *Russian Review* 45, no. 2 (1986): 115–81; "Royal Russian Behavior, Style, and Self-Image," in *Ethnic Russia in the USSR,* ed. Edward Allworth (New York, 1979), 3–16; and "Ivan the Terrible and His Women: The Grammar of Politics in the Kremlin" (Unpublished lecture, 1980).

24. Eve Levin, "The Role and Status of Women in Medieval Novgorod" (Ph.D. diss., Indiana University, 1983); Robert O. Crummey, *The Old Believers and the World of Antichrist* (Madison, 1970); Gail Lenhoff, *The Martyred Princes,* "Canonization and Princely Power in Northeast Rus': The Cult of Leontij Rostovskij," *Welt der Slaven* 37 (1992): 359–80, and "The Ermolin Chronicle Account of Prince

Fedor the Black's Relics and the Annexation of Iaroslavl' in 1463," *Russian History* 19, nos. 1–4 (1992): 155–68; Nancy Shields Kollmann, "Ritual and Social Drama," *Slavic Review* 45, no. 3 (1986): 486–502.

25. Bushkovitch, "Orthodoxy and Old Rus'," 203.

26. Michael S. Flier, "Breaking the Code: The Image of the Tsar in the Muscovite Palm Sunday Ritual," in *Medieval Russian Culture,* vol. 2, ed. Michael S. Flier (Berkeley and Los Angeles, 1994), 213–42.

27. Iurii M. Lotman and Boris A. Uspenskii, "Binary Models in the Dynamics of Russian Culture (to the End of the Eighteenth Century)," in *The Semiotics of Russian Cultural History,* ed. Nakhimovsky and Nakhimovsky, 30–66. Although it takes binary models seriously, this piece also shows that polarities are deceptive, and that they should therefore be used critically.

Society and Cultural Practice

JANET   MARTIN

"BACKWARDNESS" IN RUSSIAN PEASANT CULTURE

A THEORETICAL CONSIDERATION OF AGRICULTURAL PRACTICES IN THE SEVENTEENTH CENTURY

ONE OF THE THEMES that dominates historical investigation of seventeenth-century Russia is "westernization." An assumption that Russia was "backward" commonly underlies studies that approach the issue of westernization. A corollary to this assumption is that in order to overcome its "backwardness," to modernize and compete effectively with European states, Russia had to imitate Western institutions, technologies, and cultural norms.

Russian society was indeed receptive to foreign influence. By the seventeenth century it had borrowed from religious, political, and military models offered by neighboring cultures.[1] Muscovite society in the seventeenth century was also adopting foreign technologies in the area of manufacturing. Yet Russia's borrowing was selective. Despite a prevailing historical judgment that it should have adopted them as well, Russia ignored or rejected some concepts and technologies even though they were providing other societies with distinct and perceptible economic advantages.

Agriculture was one sphere of Russian economic activity that remained traditional. As was the case in other pre-industrial sedentary societies, agriculture was the most widespread economic activity in seventeenth-century Russia. The bulk of its population was engaged in the process of raising food products for themselves and for those smaller segments of the society that dwelled in towns and cities or were engaged in government, military, or other non-agrarian occupations. The agricultural sector was thus essential to the maintenance and development of all other sectors of the society. Its task was difficult. Agricultural producers or peasants used relatively primitive tools to cultivate relatively poor soils in the forest zones of the Muscovite state. They had little defense against natural catastrophe and resultant poor harvests. High transportation costs for bulk products, such as edible grains, inhibited the dispersal of this responsibility for food production, even though more favorably endowed areas were being added to the country's territories.

Scholars studying Russian agriculture have described the basic methods employed during the seventeenth century. Peasants typically used a three-field rotation system. They generally planted a winter crop in one field, a spring crop in the second, and allowed the third to lie fallow. They supplemented the cereal grains normally grown in this fashion with production of vegetables and livestock and, when possible, with fish and forest products. This system had, by most accounts, been adopted in the Russian lands from the late fifteenth century; through the sixteenth century it replaced other field systems as well as the slash-and-burn and long fallow methods of farming that had been widely used in earlier centuries. In some areas, however, peasants continued to practice the older methods.

Researchers have also discussed another dimension of the agricultural system, the methods used by elite members of Muscovite society to extract the items required for their own support from the agricultural producers. These impositions on the peasantry, which took the form of taxes, rents, and labor obligations, were increasing during the seventeenth century.[2] Commerce provided an alternate means by which non-agrarian commoners were able to obtain food supplies from the surpluses produced by the peasantry.

Standard studies of the Russian agrarian system yield several generalizations. Using primitive methods, the system managed to feed one of the most populous countries in Europe, and it did so successfully enough to support a growing bureaucracy, army, and urban sector (except during successive years of widespread poor harvests, which resulted in famine and for which no contemporary system was able to compensate). The operation of this agrarian system, however, is associated with the forceful exploitation of the agricultural producers, a factor that was epitomized by the enserfment of the peasantry in 1649. The conclusion generally is that all levels of Russian society, from the peasantry itself all the way up to the tsar, failed to adopt the more advanced, efficient, and productive methods of agricultural production and corresponding forms of social organization that were beginning to be employed in western Europe. But the system employed in Muscovy was also, as R. A. French described it, a durable and long-lasting one.[3] Other than legal compulsion, however, little is offered to explain how this "primitive" system survived. The question of why Russian society preferred its traditional agricultural practices to the more "advanced" methods that were becoming known elsewhere in Europe remains insufficiently explored.

One deficiency of standard descriptions of Russian agriculture is that, despite their concern with the changes from one system to another, they do not fully acknowledge the flexibility of the peasant producers or appreciate the implications of their flexibility. They do not, therefore, attempt to explain why the peasantry, which had been fully capable of shifting from long fallow to field rotation and was subject to increasing rents and taxes, made no noticeable effort to intensify its agricultural practices in order to increase output. Neither do these descriptions account for the behavior of government officials and large landowners. Although their demands for increased revenue from the peasantry suggest they had an interest in improving agriculture, they neglected to use their direct contacts with westerners to facilitate the introduction of improved agricultural methods as they did for selected manufacturing and military technologies. Instead of imitating "advanced" Western models in the agricultural sphere, officials and landowners adopted the "archaic" system of serfdom, which restricted the mobility and initiative of Russian agricultural workers. Standard discussions do not explain why the peasantry as well as estate owners and the government remained satisfied with the "backward" three-field system.

To better understand the durability of this system, it is useful to identify factors that appear to stimulate the replacement of one method of organization with another. Studies of pre-industrial European agriculture point to several. Carlo Cipolla, for example, stressed the availability and choice of crops as critical factors in the determination of a society's agricultural system. He argued that, despite the inefficiency of agricultural systems dependent upon fallow, medieval and Renaissance Europe relied on one of them, a "primitive form of rotation," in order to preserve land fertility in the absence of sufficient fertilizers. Consequently, for centuries before the modern era, from one-half to one-third of the arable land in Europe lay fallow. This "constraint" was "particularly severe," he observed, because yields were low, only three to six times the quantity of seed of sown. Beginning in the seventeenth century, however, food production levels improved slowly in response to the introduction of new crops, which, when included in the rotation cycle, replaced nutrients in the soil and made it possible to reduce or abandon the period of fallow.[4]

Fernand Braudel also recognized the importance of land use and crop selection but considered them closely related to other factors, most importantly, population size. Placing greater emphasis on the effectiveness and flexibility of pre-modern agricultural systems, he noted that some societies preferred meat to vegetable products, others had the opposite preference. The choice between eating meat or cereals (that is, between focusing on herding livestock or focusing on growing grains) depended upon the number of people in the society or community. Grain production tended to be favored over stock-raising as the human population grew because a given unit of land, when used for agriculture, could support from ten to twenty times as many people than when it was used for stock-raising. In this context, according to Braudel's assessment, the European practice of leaving large portions of arable land fallow was not a constraint but an advantage, at least for a meat-eating population. Europeans were able to continue to raise livestock precisely because "the European countryside, beyond the Mediterranean shores, had long remained half empty with vast lands for pasturing animals. Later on, its agriculture left ample facilities available for stock-raising." Land left fallow was used for pasturage; stubble remaining in fields after harvest could similarly be used to feed grazing livestock. These lands, in addition to forests, mown meadows, and parcels of wasteland, all supported livestock. The relative sizes of the human population, its herds of livestock, and its crops were thus all interrelated.[5] But, Braudel observed, Europe's "advantage" declined after the seventeenth century in conjunction with its population growth.

Although there is no consensus among them, it is possible to use European studies of this nature as guides to identify the factors influencing the choice of one agricultural system over another, that is, the factors that trigger the adoption of new agricultural methods. Cipolla considered the awareness and availability of new crops as the main factor responsible for the shift from field rotation to a system of permanent cultivation, in which crops such as turnips and clover were rotated with cereal grains. Unaccountably, however, "these practices . . . spread only very slowly and throughout the preindustrial period land remained largely unexploited." Despite the presence of this triggering factor, the established system, field rotation with fallow, continued to be practiced.[6] Braudel, in contrast, pointed to population size as the factor that prompted the change from long fallow to field rotation, and again from field rotation to systems that abandoned fallow (that is, crop rotation).

In Russia, however, the three-field rotation system did not give way to a more intensive system of annual cropping. To determine whether the factors identified by Cipolla and Braudel similarly activated change in the Russian environment, it is instructive to examine the transition from slash-and-burn (a form of long fallow) to the three-field rotation system.

For centuries the slash-and-burn method was widely used in the forested regions of the Russian lands. This method involved selecting a forested area for cultivation. Preparation of the land entailed ringing the trees, that is, cutting rings around their trunks deeply enough to penetrate the layers of tissue beneath the bark and kill the trees. Once the trees died and dried, the area was burned. Tree stumps and heavy roots were left in the ground. The fire, however, left a layer of ash on the soil, in which seed could be sown for several years. When the nutrients were depleted, the plot was abandoned and cultivation was transferred to another that had been similarly prepared. An alternative but similar system left the abandoned area fallow for lengthy periods (perhaps twenty years) but eventually reused it for cultivation; this practice is referred to as a long fallow system *(perelog)*.[7]

The second system was a form of field farming. It involved clearing major encumbrances such as tree stumps and roots from the areas intended for cultivation. Crops were then sown in the fields, but on a rotational basis. In the three-field system, which became the favored system in the forest zones of the Russian lands, cultivation was rotated in three-year cycles among three fields; each year two fields were sown with crops and the third was left fallow. Livestock, as Braudel suggested, was not only compatible with this system, but virtually a requirement; draft animals were necessary to haul heavy objects from the fields, and their manure added nutrients to the soil. These practices allowed regeneration of the soil and thus enabled farmers to cultivate the same parcels of land repeatedly.[8] Other types of field rotation have been identified as alternatives to the three-field rotation method or as intermediate stages in the perceived evolution toward it.[9] But it was this form of cultivation that predominated and to which the Russian peasantry clung in the sixteenth and seventeenth centuries.

The transition from the slash-and-burn system to the three-field rotation system has attracted scholarly attention. Studies of Russian agricultural development have attempted to determine when and why peasants selected one system over another. One school of thought found the answer in technology. Its adherents regard farming implements, especially those used to prepare the soil for sowing seed, as the key factor determining the type of agriculture practiced by a given community at a given time. Technological improvements, such as the advance from simple digging sticks to ploughs, this school asserts, marked the transition.[10]

R. E. F. Smith rejected this interpretation. He considered field rotation to be a natural, although not a necessary, outgrowth of the slash-and-burn and long fallow methods. The combined result of continued use of those methods, of slow rates of soil regeneration, and of population growth was a reduction in the amount of land suited to a long fallow system. As suitable land diminished, it became more advantageous for farming communities to complete the process of creating fields by removing tree stumps and roots and to initiate rotation cycles.[11] The factors determining which agricultural system was selected were the availability of suitable land for the slash-and-burn method and the presence of draft animals. R. A. French similarly concluded that, "as population density increased, as average settlement size increased, giving greater labour resources per settlement, and as the amount of intervening forest shrank, . . . the majority of peasant lands adopt[ed] the basic three fields." The transition, which he regarded "if not an agrarian revolution, an agrarian transformation and an advance in efficiency," was occurring in the Russian lands from the late fifteenth century.[12] French, like Braudel, regarded population growth and population density as critical to a shift from one agricultural system to another.

Although they qualify the point, most investigators who approach the issue of agricultural development in Russia regard the reorganization from the slash-and-burn or a long fallow system to a field rotation system as a mark of progress, a social and economic advancement. But just as Cipolla noted in relation to Europe's shift to the crop rotation system, French indicated that the practice of slash-and-burn and long fallow "continued side by side with three-field cultivation for some considerable time." Smith, too, made the point that, although the systems appeared to be adopted in "a series, in which the possibility of the existence of any one arises from the achievements of the preceding one," there was no strict chronological succession, nor did the introduction of a new, advanced system automatically result in the abandonment of the old, less efficient one. Jerome Blum noted, furthermore, that in times of social and economic stress, notably in the late sixteenth century, there was a reversion to the less advanced systems.[13]

The observation that systems deemed better, more efficient, or more advanced were not automatically or rapidly adopted after their initial introduction to Russia suggests either that Russians were short-sighted or that factors other than modern conceptions of efficiency and productivity were influencing their decisions. Before accepting the first interpretation, it is appropriate to explore the second. Studies made by economists who have examined developing societies and the circumstances under which they tend to adopt more modern agricultural methods are instructive. The insights into the dynamics operating within seemingly static traditional systems that they provide are helpful in understanding when and why population growth in traditional agricultural communities prompts the abandonment of one agricultural system for another, and, importantly, when and why they do not.

Theodore Schultz, for example, asserted that traditional agriculture is characterized by an equilibrium, in which farmers or peasants, using long-established practices and technologies, maintain a balance between the allocation of their resources, including their labor, and the return or yield they achieve. He argued that durable traditional systems of agriculture were highly efficient: farmers obtained the maximum yield possible from their labor and other investments. The systems remained stable because farmers also understood that any additional increase in yields would require a disproportionately large increase in investment and was, therefore, deemed to be unwarranted. In other words, according to Schultz, traditional agriculture, having only its relatively primitive tools and equipment available, is incapable of growth except at high cost. Once they reached equilibrium, additional inputs resulted in such relatively small increases in output that the incentive to work more became minimal.[14]

Even earlier, A. V. Chaianov made similar observations, which he discussed in terms of an "equilibrium between family demand satisfaction and the drudgery of labor itself."[15] He explained that the peasant family worked just enough to produce the goods it required. Once it developed a suitable method to meet its requirements and achieved the desired levels of production, it maintained this system and these levels. Beyond this point of equilibrium there was, Chaianov argued, a disincentive to alter the system or produce more; the peasant family did not regard the increased returns it would gain from such changes to be worth the extra drudgery or burden that the additional labor needed to make the changes would involve. As long as equilibrium between the elements is not reached, "the [peasant] family . . . has every cause to continue its economic activity. As soon as this equilibrium point is reached, however, continuing to work becomes pointless, as any further labor expenditure becomes harder for the peasant . . . to endure than is foregoing its economic effects."[16]

Neither Chaianov nor Schultz, however, regarded the equilibrium as absolutely stable. Factors contributing to it may shift; the resulting imbalance may, in turn, stimulate peasant farmers to compensate by altering various components of their agricultural system and even by adopting a new one. Population size, more particularly population density, as Braudel and French indicated, is one factor that can upset the equilibrium traditional farmers strive to maintain.[17]

The Danish economist Ester Boserup has gone further. From observations drawn mainly from twentieth-century underdeveloped societies but also from European historical experience, she advanced a set of theoretical principles of economic development.[18] For Boserup, population density is the central factor that stimulates pre-industrial societies to change their agrarian systems. When, in response to an increase in its density, a community does change its agricultural system, the critical factor that it adjusts is the length of the time period land is allowed to lie fallow. Not unlike Braudel, Boserup maintained that, as populations become denser, they tend to shorten the periods of fallow in their agricultural systems. At one extreme, very low density populations allow their land to remain fallow on a permanent basis; in other words, they do not cultivate the land but engage in nomadic herding of livestock or in hunting and gathering. At the other extreme, highly dense populations cultivate their land continuously; they employ systems of multiple cropping and completely eliminate fallow periods. The slash-and-burn, long fallow, field rotation (short fallow), and crop rotation systems (annual cropping), mentioned earlier, all represent intermediate alternatives to these two extremes. Factors such as tools and crops do not determine a society's form of land use; they are functions of that form.[19]

But, Boserup added, agricultural producers must work more to operate agricultural systems designed around reduced periods of fallow. When the size of a population in an area increases and fallow periods are shortened in favor of more frequent cropping, "more and more labor-intensive methods must be used to preserve soil fertility, reduce weed growth and parasites, water the plants, grow fodder for animals, and protect the land." Some of the additional labor, such as that applied to draining land or building fences, is labor investment. "If these investments are made with human and animal muscle power, the necessary input of human labor is large. Even animals cannot reduce the work burden much, if fallows and other grazing lands have been reduced so much that the cultivator must produce their fodder." More frequent cropping, as defined by Boserup, constitutes a more intensive agricultural system.[20]

As communities adopt more intensive systems, their output per labor-hour declines. In Boserup's words:

When a given population in a given territory shortens the fallow period and changes its agricultural methods and tools correspondingly . . . output per man-hour is more likely to decline than to increase. This means that in typical cases the cultivator would find it profitable to shift to a more intensive system of land use only when a certain density of population has been reached. In a region where this critical level of density has not yet been reached, people may well be aware of the existence of more intensive methods of land use and they may have access to tools of a less primitive kind; still they may prefer not to use such methods until the point is reached where the size of the population is such that they must accept a decline of output per man-hour.[21]

Boserup thus joined Chaianov and Schultz in the observation that at some level peasant producers recognize that "improvements" in their agricultural system require additional investments, mainly in the form of their own labor. But the expected increase in output, not to mention the added risks and uncertainty associated with using different approaches, is not sufficient to warrant the extra work. It is this insight that explains a community's reluctance to adopt more intensive systems of agriculture despite their potential for enhanced output; more intensive systems require added labor but do not produce a proportionate increase in output. Traditional agrarian communities tend to make the change only when they have to, when food or other necessities become scarce relative to a growing population. It is noteworthy, however, that it is precisely the additional labor resources of the denser population that also make it possible for a community to operate the more intensive system.[22]

These and other related theories have interesting implications for the study of Russian agriculture and economic development. Viewing Russian economic history from the perspective of the theories of Chaianov, Schultz, and Boserup, the following outline of development emerges. Agrarian producers in the Russian lands, as in others, used slash-and-burn techniques when and where relatively small communities cultivated land. This concept contradicts the assertion that slash-and-burn (forest fallow) methods required large population concentrations to carry out various tasks involving heavy labor. Boserup maintains that, although "the time used for clearing forest for one or two years' cultivation varies widely with differences in climate, type of vegetation and make of the axe, . . . fire does most of the work and there is no need for the removal of roots, which is such a time-consuming task when land has to be cleared for the preparation of permanent fields."[23] There would, therefore, be no need for large numbers of people to conduct this form of agriculture. This view may account for the ability of very small hamlets and villages, such as those in the northern Russian countryside in the fifteenth century, to support agriculture.[24]

By the end of the fifteenth century, long fallow methods were being abandoned in favor of the three-field rotation or short fallow system. The latter method, as it was adopted by the larger, more densely populated communities, co-existed with the long fallow systems, which were still in use in less densely populated communities. The preference for the three-field method coincided with an increase in the Russian population, whose rate of growth had previously been stalled by successive plagues and wars.[25] Communities that successfully adopted the new methods had the labor resources as well as the knowledge of techniques for raising livestock and fertilizing land that those methods required.

Conversely, if and when those factors were absent or disappeared, the theories predict that a population would opt for a simpler, less labor intensive system of agriculture. That situation describes the critical period of late sixteenth-century Russia, when population density decreased as a result of the Livonian war, disease, crop failures, the effects of the *oprichnina*, and residents' flight. During this period entire estates and districts were devoid of peasant populations; others were left with much reduced working populations. It would be expected that under such circumstances the remaining population would revert to less labor intensive agricultural methods, that is, they would crop the land less frequently. Blum pointed out that at this time the Russian peasantry did tend to resort to "more primitive" methods.[26] Alternatively, members of the remaining populace might cluster together to maintain a few pockets of relatively dense population groups. Data contained in Novgorodian *pistsovye knigi* from the 1580s indicate that both these strategies were used.[27]

These behaviors are consistent with the theoretical principles that suggest the agricultural producers would have adopted methods most appropriate to their resources. When population growth resumed after the Time of Troubles, densities reached levels that once again made the short fallow method of farming advantageous.[28] The choice between a short fallow system and an annual cropping method may also be regarded as a function of population density. In this case, however, the durability of the three-field system, the Russian peasants' preferred form of short fallow, suggests that the ratio of peasant producers to land did not increase to the point that peasant communities had both the means and the incentive to shift to a more intensive agricultural system. The theories outlined above thus provide a basis for understanding when and why communities in Russian society adopted or selected their agricultural systems.

Although increased population densities enable and pressure communities to adopt more intensive agricultural systems, this is not necessarily the only option available to them. One possibility is to reduce population density. When land resources and political-economic circumstances allow it, at least some members of the community may opt to leave, settle in other territories, or cultivate other lands:

> it may [therefore] be sound economic reasoning rather than indolence [or ignorance] which induces a community of cultivators under the system of long fallow to refuse to abandon fire and axe . . . [in favor of the plough], and instead to move to another place in the forest, where there is still room for the system of long fallow. Conversely, sound economic reasoning may persuade another community, which is unable to find suitable land for continued cultivation under long fallow, to . . . take to ploughing of permanent fields.[29]

The same reasoning applies to shifting from short fallow (field rotation) to annual cropping (crop rotation).

Territorial expansion can provide opportunities for members of an agricultural community to migrate. If they do so in sufficient numbers, population growth would not necessarily result in higher density levels, and the pressures to adopt more intensive agricultural methods would be modified. The extension of Muscovy's borders to the southwest, south, and east during the seventeenth century offered such opportunities. Selection of this option allowed the peasants to apply their traditional methods to a broader area and reestablish an equilibrium without increasing their labor investments.[30]

Another option is to divert labor into non-agricultural activities that bring greater returns than those anticipated by an intensification of labor in the agricultural sphere.[31] The growth of non-agrarian sectors in a society can thus also have the effect of curbing an increase in the density of the agrarian population while the size of the total population is rising. The enlargement of government bureaucracies, military forces, and commercial and manufacturing operations, according to Boserup, all tend to draw population away from agriculture. This phenomenon may occur without risk to the food supply for urban and other non-agrarian elements of the population provided that population density is generally increasing and transportation networks are being improved. If these conditions are met, then there is a rise in the potential value of the increase in yield resulting from additional work. Agricultural producers located at greater distances from towns gain both incentive and opportunity to intensify their agricultural practices and use the additional output to supply foodstuffs and other agricultural products to the growing non-agricultural sectors of the society. The food provided by distant communities compensates for any decline in output and food supply created by the transfer of agricultural producers from nearby communities to non-agrarian occupations.[32]

If population growth is stagnant, however, an "increasing demand for manpower for the army and for nonagricultural occupations" may reduce "the absolute size of the agricultural labor force. The remaining agricultural population ha[s] to reduce the area under cultivation, and the supply of food . . . [falls] short of demand." Even if the total population is expanding, departure of a large portion of the rural population may also "cause food supply to fall short of demand." The development of other sectors of an economy and the diversion of agricultural producers to non-agrarian occupations thus affects rural population densities, agricultural systems, and food supply. "Food . . . [may become] scarce either because the nonagricultural population . . . [grows] more rapidly than the agricultural labor force, or because the agricultural labor force . . . [declines] in periods when the overall population size remain[s] constant."[33]

The last alternative is for peasants to cultivate their land more intensively, that is, shorten the fallow period at the expense of more work and a decreased output per unit of labor. This option may be selected when the first two are unavailable and, as Chaianov expressed it, "the concern to meet the year's needs forces the family to turn to an intensification with lower profitability. They have to purchase the increase of the total year's labor product at the price of a fall in income per labor unit."[34] The "needs" of the peasant family include not only the products for its own sustenance but also those required to meet rental and state obligations.

As suggested by the preceding discussion, factors other than a growing population can affect the density of agrarian populations and the choice of agricultural system. The concepts outlined above may thus be useful in analyzing the implications of a host of developments in seventeenth-century Russia. They lend a new dimension to the significance of state policies that resulted in territorial expansion, the growth of the government bureaucracy, military reform, and a related need for increased revenue. These concepts similarly suggest different ways to understand the effects of the expansion of commerce and manufacturing and the imposition of serfdom. Population density and therefore the selection of a community's agricultural system, the theories suggest, are interconnected with all these other developments. Some of the central government's policies, for example, would have retarded an increase or even reduced the density of rural communities, especially those nearest towns and cities. The extension of the country's frontiers and military reform measures that drew heavily upon the peasant population are two examples. Both offered means of curbing an increase in population density of agrarian communities. It may be postulated that such policies would, accordingly, have slowed the formation of conditions motivating peasants to adopt more intensive agricultural methods.

The imposition of serfdom, however, would be expected to have had the opposite effect. By reducing peasant mobility it inhibited the peasants from exercising the option of dispersing and thereby recreating conditions appropriate to less labor-intensive agricultural systems. The adoption of serfdom should have promoted an increase in the density of established peasant communities. Such political, legal interference might be an example of the type of situation Boserup describes, in which "governments took steps to prevent too much labor from being drawn out of agriculture" in order to avoid leaving the countryside shorthanded and threatening the food supply of both rural and urban populations.[35] Alternatively, by artificially maintaining or even increasing rural population density levels, the policy may have allowed the government to remove larger numbers of peasants from agricultural communities to satisfy military needs, for example, without disrupting the effectiveness of the agricultural system and the production of food supplies. Especially under conditions of restricted mobility, increases in taxes and other obligations imposed on the peasantry would, by adding to the amounts required to satisfy the peasants' total needs, also create pressures favoring the adoption of a more intensive system.

The effects of competing opportunities and pressures, generated by various state policies and non-agricultural economic developments, and their net impact on peasant agriculture, both generally and regionally, can all be examined. Yet, any research designed around the theoretical principles discussed

here, which are themselves derived from observations of patterns of economic behavior in a variety of twentieth-century and historical societies,
would have the advantage of guiding students of Russian economic development away from simple comparative approaches resting on assumptions that
label certain systems and methods "advanced" or "superior" and inevitably
lead to conclusions that Russia was relatively "backward."

The incorporation of these principles into their research will, in contrast,
direct investigators beyond questions of why Russia remained "backward"
despite its society's awareness of the more "advanced" and "superior" tools,
technologies, methods, crops, and social arrangements that had been
adopted in western Europe. It will lead them past the issue of what Russia
should have done to achieve the "best" or "most productive" or competitive
economy. It will allow them to suspend the simple, yet unrevealing premise
that it was ignorance, short-sightedness, or stubbornness that led Muscovite
society to reject innovations that other societies found attractive and demonstrated to be effective. It will instead draw attention to factors that prompted
Russian society to select the methods and technologies it did. Inquiries into
these factors will highlight conditions within Muscovy itself and seek more
meaningful insights into the dynamics underlying the seemingly stable, traditional surface of the Muscovite agrarian economy.

The suggested line of research thus emphasizes Muscovy's own resources,
traditions, and goals; it focuses as well on the society's own economic experi-
ences and choices. Pursuit of this line of research requires examination of demographic and economic data. Most primary sources containing appropriate
materials for the seventeenth century remain unpublished, but a variety of
studies based on them include statistics and summaries concerning agrarian
populations, demographic changes, agricultural output, and a range of related issues.[36] Additional quantitative analyses of these data will provide the
information on population growth and density, on the relative growth of
agrarian and non-agrarian sectors of society, and on relative densities of rural
regions near and distant from growing towns, all of which are necessary to
address issues such as the adequacy of food production and supply systems as
they operated under the pressures of competing demands for labor.

Results of such analyses will provide the bases to test the hypotheses generated by the theories discussed above. They might confirm, for example, that
the net result of the competing pressures and opportunities was to prevent a
rise in the population densities of Muscovy's agricultural sector to a level that
would motivate peasants to adopt a more intensive agricultural system. Peasant communities would, therefore, have continued to be able to balance the
satisfaction of their needs, that is, their own sustenance, rents (in cash, kind,
or in labor obligations), and taxes, with an amount of work or "drudgery"
sufficient to operate the three-field system. They would have been able to
feed their population and meet their legal obligations, and do so without increasing the amount of "drudgery" in their work lives, that is, without inten-
sifying their labor input and accepting a lower return per unit of labor.

Studies based on this approach thus offer both a fresh understanding of why Muscovite peasants retained their traditional agricultural methods as well as new interpretations of the interrelationships between economic and political developments and policies in seventeenth-century Russia. Verification of the theoretically generated hypotheses would accordingly support the following set of propositions. Muscovite peasants remained attached to their traditional agricultural practices and refused to imitate methods and technologies adopted abroad because there was little incentive to upset the equilibrium balanced around the established system. Traditional techniques made the most efficient use of Muscovite resources and successfully met the needs of the society. The adoption of "advanced" or "superior" methods and technologies, on the other hand, required additional labor resources that the Muscovites did not have and elevated the cost of agricultural activities higher than the peasants were willing to pay. If research validates such premises, then the "failure" of the Russian peasantry to adopt the "more advanced" crop rotation methods of agriculture might be interpreted not as a sign of backwardness, but as a sensible response to the realities of the demographic, social, and economic conditions in seventeenth-century Muscovy.

NOTES

1. On the borrowing of Muscovite political structures from Tatar societies, see, for example, Donald Ostrowski, "The Mongol Origins of Muscovite Political Institutions," *Slavic Review* 49 (1990): 525–42; for Muscovy's adoption of military technology and tactics from western Europe, see Richard Hellie, *Enserfment and Military Change in Muscovy* (Chicago, 1971), 152–57, 170, and 182–83.

2. See, for example, A. Ia. Degtiarev, *Russkaia derevnia v XV–XVII vekakh* (Leningrad, 1980), chap. 5.

3. R. A. French, "The Introduction of the Three-Field Agricultural System," in *Studies in Russian Historical Geography*, 2 vols., ed. J. H. Bater and R. A. French (London, 1983), 1:79.

4. Carlo M. Cipolla, *Before the Industrial Revolution: European Society and Economy, 1000–1700*, 2d ed. (New York, 1976, 1980), 170–71.

5. Fernand Braudel, *Capitalism and Material Life, 1400–1800*, trans. Miriam Kochan (Evanston, 1967), 66–67, 76, 78, 82.

6. Cipolla, *Before the Industrial Revolution*, 171.

7. R. E. F. Smith, *The Origins of Farming in Russia* (The Hague, 1959), 52, 54; R. A. French, "Russians and the Forest," in Bater and French, *Studies in Russian Historical Geography*, 27–28. Variants of the slash-and-burn method have also been described. Jerome Blum understood it to involve cutting down the trees and hauling them away from the site; fire was used merely to burn remaining brush and debris; see Blum, *Lord and Peasant in Russia from the Ninth to the Nineteenth Century* (New York, 1964), 21. Colin Clark considered it to involve chopping down trees with axes, allowing the felled trees to dry, and then burning them; see Clark, *Population Growth and Land Use* (New York, 1968), 132.

8. Smith, *Origins*, 87, 91–92; French, "Three-Field Agricultural System," 65.

9. A. L. Shapiro, *Problemy sotsial'no-ekonomicheskoi istorii Rusi XIV–XVI vv.* (Leningrad, 1977), 50–52, and "O podsechnom zemledelii na Rusi v XIV–XV vv.,"

in *Ezhegodnik po agrarnoi istorii vostochnoi Evropy 1963 g.* (Vil'nius, 1965), 122–23; French, "Three-Field Agricultural System," 67–70; Smith, *Origins,* 74–75, 87–88; Iu. M. Iurginis, "O zemledel'cheskoi sisteme, predshestvovshei trekhpol'iu," in *Ezhegodnik po agrarnoi istorii vostochnoi Evropy 1962 g.* (Minsk, 1964), 95–100. A. V. Chaianov described a number of cultivation systems, including several field rotation variants, that were in use in the late nineteenth and early twentieth centuries; see A. V. Chayanov (Chaianov), "Peasant Farm Organization," trans. R. E. F. Smith, in *The Theory of Peasant Economy,* ed. Daniel Thorner, Basile Kerblay, and R. E. F. Smith (Manchester, 1966, 1986), 134–53.

10. For a summary of this school of thought, see Smith, *Origins,* 87–92; also Degtiarev, *Russkaia derevnia,* 59.

11. Smith, *Origins,* 51, 71, 149.

12. French, "Three-Field Agricultural System," 70–72, 79. See also Blum, *Lord and Peasant,* 22–23. For discussions of when the three-field system was adopted, see Shapiro, *Problemy,* 50–57; G. E. Kochin, *Sel'skoe khoziaistvo na Rusi kontsa XIII–nachala XVI v.* (Moscow, 1965), 232–48; R. E. F. Smith, *Peasant Farming in Muscovy* (Cambridge, 1977), 27–29, 107, 109–10.

13. French, "Three-Field Agricultural System," 79; Smith, *Origins,* 51; Blum, *Lord and Peasant,* 66–67. See also Shapiro, "O podsechnom zemledelii," 121–31, and Degtiarev, *Russkaia derevnia,* 50–57.

14. Theodore W. Schultz, *Transforming Traditional Agriculture* (New Haven, 1964), 5, 24, 29–30, 37; for equilibrium, 28, 31–32.

15. Chayanov, "On the Theory of Non-Capitalist Economic Systems," trans. Christel Lane, in *The Theory of Peasant Economy,* 6, and Chayanov, "Peasant Farm Organization," 81–82.

16. Chayanov, "On the Theory of Non-Capitalist Economic Systems," 6, and "Peasant Farm Organization," 73–85, especially 81.

17. Chaianov also identified population density as a determinant of the agricultural system; see his "On the Theory of Non-Capitalist Economic Systems," 12, and "Peasant Farm Organization," 61–64. Smith and Blum, recognizing the relevance of this factor, repeated the widely accepted assertion that large population concentrations were required for the application of slash-and-burn methods. Blum, *Lord and Peasant,* 22; Smith, *Origins,* 55, 123, 126.

18. Ester Boserup has discussed her theories in several books: *The Conditions of Agricultural Growth: The Economics of Agrarian Change under Population Pressure* (Chicago, 1965); *Population and Technological Change: A Study of Long-Term Trends* (Chicago, 1981); and *Economic and Demographic Relationships in Development* (Baltimore, 1990). A summary of the concepts enunciated in the first of these books is presented by Colin Clark, *Population Growth and Land Use,* 133–35.

19. Boserup, *Conditions of Agricultural Growth,* 23–27.

20. Boserup, *Economic and Demographic Relationships,* 13; Boserup, *Conditions of Agricultural Growth,* 43.

21. Boserup, *Conditions of Agricultural Growth,* 41. See also *Economic and Demographic Relationships,* 58.

22. Boserup, *Conditions of Agricultural Growth,* 26, and *Economic and Demographic Relationships,* 58.

23. Boserup, *Conditions of Agricultural Growth,* 29–30.

24. For discussions on small agrarian settlements, see, for example, A. L. Shapiro, *Agrarnaia istoriia severo-zapada Rossii XVI veka* (Leningrad, 1974), 248; and I. L. Perel'man, "Novgorodskaia derevnia v XV–XVI vv.," *Istoricheskie zapiski* 26 (1948): 147–49.

25. Population figures for the Russian lands are imprecise, but George Vernadsky, for example, estimated that the size of the population at the end of the fifteenth century (following the Mongol invasions, the Black Death, and the civil wars of the mid-fifteenth century) was not much larger than it had been at the beginning of the thirteenth. See his *Kievan Russia* (New Haven, 1948), 104. See also Lawrence N. Langer, "The Black Death in Russia: Its Effects upon Urban Labor," *Russian History* 2 (1975): 62. During the first half of the sixteenth century, however, the population was growing once again. Lawrence N. Langer, "The Medieval Russian Town," in *The City in Russian History,* ed. Michael Hamm (Lexington, Ky., 1976), 30; Blum, "Lord and Peasant," 120. Studies on specific regions confirm their generalizations. See, for example, I. L. Perel'man, "Novgorodskaia derevnia," 164–65 (tables).

26. Blum, *Lord and Peasant,* 166.

27. Janet Martin, "Economic Survival in the Novgorod Lands in the 1580s," in *New Perspectives on Muscovite History,* ed. Lindsey Hughes (New York, 1993), 103–4. One method such relatively large peasant communities used to supplement crops grown on their village lands was to cultivate additional land associated with vacated villages and estates. For the practice of cultivation *naezdom,* see ibid., 116–18. V. I. Kuznetsov discussed the use of a similar strategy in the 1620s, in "K voprosu ob evoliutsii sel'skikh poselenii v Rossii poslednei treti XVI–nachala XVII v.," *Vestnik Moskovskogo universiteta,* ser. 8, no. 5 (1986): 95. See also his articles "Pashnia 'naezdom' v sisteme pozemel'nogo nalogooblozheniia russkogo gosudarstva v XV–pervoi polovine XVI v." *Vestnik Moskovskogo universiteta,* no. 5 (1987): 79–84, and "Pashnia 'naezdom' v sisteme pozemel'nogo nalogooblozheniia russkogo gosudarstva vo vtoroi polovine XVI–XVII v.," in *Vestnik Moskovskogo universiteta,* no. 2 (1988): 69–82.

28. A. L. Shapiro, ed., *Agrarnaia istoriia severo-zapada Rossii XVII veka* (Leningrad, 1989), 11; Kuznetsov, "K voprosu ob evoliutsii sel'skikh poselenii," 85–96.

29. Boserup, *Conditions of Agricultural Growth,* 66–67; see also *Economic and Demographic Relationships,* 16–17.

30. Chaianov, who observed a correlation between the number of agricultural workers and the amount of land under cultivation, provides evidence that Russians in a later period selected this method of responding to increases in population density. Chayanov, "Peasant Farm Organization," 69.

31. Ibid., 101, 106–9, 113.

32. Boserup, *Economic and Demographic Relationships,* 33, 60.

33. Boserup, *Population and Technological Change,* 99; Boserup, *Economic and Demographic Relationships,* 33.

34. Chayanov, "On the Theory of Non-Capitalist Economic Systems," 7.

35. Boserup, *Population and Technological Change,* 100.

36. Such secondary studies include those conducted, for example, by A. L. Shapiro et al. and V. I. Kuznetsov and are published in their works cited above. For a study that approaches issues of agricultural production and distribution and their relation to military demands on society, see Carol Belkin Stevens, *Soldiers on the Steppe: Army Reform and Social Change in Early Modern Russia* (DeKalb, Ill., 1995).

N A N C Y   S H I E L D S   K O L L M A N N

CONCEPTS OF SOCIETY AND SOCIAL IDENTITY IN EARLY MODERN RUSSIA

A STRIKING ASPECT of early modern Russia is how individuals represented themselves in public discourse and how they conceived of society. The terminology they used suggests the boundaries and bonds that structured individual experience and shaped people's understanding of how they belonged to a society. So we shall explore that vocabulary, keeping as close as possible to sources involved in day-to-day political life. This is a different and more limited task than exploring how individuals constructed their identity in practice, a process of interplay between received social categories and personal experience. Unfortunately, the most appropriate sources for such inquiry—personal correspondence, diaries, and ample documentation of an individual's activities and views—are virtually nonexistent in the pre-Petrine period.[1] Litigations often reveal the raucous world of social values in practice,[2] but here we shall look at formal ways of describing self and society in the belief that even formulaic public discourse holds valuable clues to the kind of social integration early modern Russia enjoyed.

Muscovy produced no social theory explicitly defining the social order. Some narrative texts that could be called theoretical touch on the issue (the Kurbskii-

Groznyi correspondence, the *Secreta secretorum,* Peresvetov), but they were narrowly dispersed and not widely influential.[3] Other sources with apparently wider appeal and less theoretical intent might also be used to extrapolate a vision of social hierarchy and the social whole: the scales of punishment and compensation for various crimes; narrative descriptions of public ceremonials such as coronations, pilgrimage processions, other liturgies; chronicle descriptions of collective gatherings.[4] But the best source for individuals representing themselves and the social order are petitions *(chelobitnye),* both from individuals and from groups, because they represent the entire social range: they were the standard means of addressing the government and thus were used in day-to-day interaction. Most that I have collected date from the seventeenth century and are largely from Russian and Orthodox individuals. This is not surprising given that most non-Russian areas were governed relatively independently from the central administration, in many cases preserving local institutions and elites.

Petitions prescribed a personal form of address: their formulaic salutations ("To Tsar, Sovereign, and Grand Prince Mikhail Fedorovich of all Russia, your slave Ivashko Ivanov petitions") and conclusions ("Tsar and sovereign, have pity, grant your favor") conjure up an image of intimate, if unequal, relations.[5] They do not mention the chancery or court jurisdiction through which the petition was processed; they simply make a direct and subservient request for "favor." Through most of Muscovite history, individuals had the right to petition the sovereign directly, paralleling the "petitionary order" that Geoffrey Koziol describes at the heart of early medieval French politics.[6] Only beginning in 1649 were Muscovites enjoined from submitting petitions to the tsar, and the frequent repetition of this directive suggests how ingrained was the expectation of direct, physical access to the ruler.[7]

Because the language of petitionary address was formulaic, skepticism is immediate at attempts to generalize internalized sensibility from prescribed catchphrases. Certainly that some people called themselves the tsar's "slaves" in petitions does not mean that they, or the whole social group that did so, felt themselves to be slavish and powerless—far from it. See, for example, a boyar from a major princely clan, Prince Ivan Petrovich Pronskoi, presenting himself as "clanless and helpless Ivan Pronskoi" in 1675.[8] That people used diminutives in the prescribed address to the tsar does not mean they personally felt like a child. These words were a marked discourse, setting social boundaries and establishing the ritual and ceremonial framework of the exchange. What I am taking literally here is not the emotional content this terminology might have implied for the individuals, but rather the implicit social ordering that petitionary formulae demonstrate and the supplementary information given by petitioners. Broad conceptions of the social order are implicit in this language, and whether or not individuals internalized it for themselves, the language in turn provided a distinct and commonly invoked idiom for understanding the social order.

Petitions were couched in a language of submissiveness and personal connection to the tsar. Individuals underscored their childlike or subordinate relationship to the tsar by referring to themselves with diminutives, a form of name customarily used for children, dependents, and loved ones (Ivashko for Ivan, Aninitsa for Anna, Bogdashko for Bogdan). The referent and social hierarchy is thereby made clear: the tsar is addressed as superior to the entire populace, which presents itself as equal in personal dependency on him. Large collective social distinctions were also couched in humble language.[9] Servitors of all sorts—Moscow-based and provincial gentry ranks, military units that did not enjoy landownership (musketeers, Cossacks, new-model infantry troops, and so on), high-ranking merchants, even artisans in the tsar's ministries or properties—called themselves the tsar's "slaves" *(kholopy):* "your slave Petrushka Volynskoi,"[10] "your own slave Mikitka Boriatinskoi,"[11] "your slave Bogdashko Dubrovskii,"[12] "your slave the humble undersecretary Volodka Nikitin."[13] The term conjures up the theme of personal service, a lord and his retinue, a master and his man. Women of servitor ranks used a different term for "slave," *raba,* with an even more servile connotation.[14] By contrast, taxpaying individuals from city or country called themselves the tsar's "orphans" *(siroty),* a term suggesting rootlessness and an appeal for protection: "your own orphan, the communion bread baker *[proskurnitsa]* of Velikii Ustiug Ovdot'itsa, daughter of Filip," "your own orphan, past customs and alcohol warden *[tseloval'nik]* Nikita, son of Kalin Pykhov."[15] Here the implicit image of society is again patriarchal—the tsar is addressed as father and protector of his defenseless children. Sometimes petitioners specified their profession in lieu of a term such as "orphan": "Efimko the blacksmith, son of Mark," or "the humble elected judge Kalinka, son of Grigorii Mitinskii."[16]

Clerics identified themselves as "those who pray to God" *(bogomol'tsy),* underscoring their role as intermediary between secular and spiritual worlds: "your tsarist impoverished one who prays to God *[bogomolets]* of the town of Shuia, the priest of the Church of Saints Cosmas and Damian, Lukoianishche."[17] Completing the metaphor of the realm as patriarchal household, the real kinsmen of the tsar did not address themselves to him subserviently through petitions; they exchanged charters whose formulaic language reinforced the representation of the ruler as head of household. The ruler was to be the "elder brother" of the "younger brothers" with whom he was negotiating, regardless of exact kinship relations, and he was to stand "in the place of the father" or "as brothers" to those kin.[18] Thus a threefold social ordering emerges, one that in no way borrows medieval European ideas of the "three orders," but that reflects the basic social divisions in Muscovite Russia and the particular relationship each large social stratum in theory enjoyed with the tsar.

Less metaphorically, individuals chose very specific categories and information to further represent themselves. Probably since the Orthodox idiom dominated literate life and a majority of the populace that petitioned was Orthodox (non-Orthodox ethnic groups enjoyed local autonomies), religion was rarely specified in self-representation. Members of minority populations in the tsar's service used various terms to indicate their foreignness: "European foreigner" *(inozemets),* "taxed Tatar" *(iasachnyi Tatar),* "Tatar prince" *(murza)*. Rather than religion, family provided the central category of self-identification. Men used the patronymic to identify their father: "your own orphan, the tailor Shestachko, son of Pavl." Women identified themselves in terms of the men whose households were responsible for them, often adding subservient adjectives: "the poor widow, prisoner of war, from Roslovl', Luker'itsa, Aleksei Shumiatskii's humble daughter and humble wife of Stepan Makovnev"; "the impoverished and humble widow Avdot'itsa, daughter of Vasilii and wife of Kirill son of Sidor." Indentured people identified themselves in terms of their masters: "man of your own boyar, Prince Daniil Ivanovich Mezetskii, Ondriushka Ofonas'ev."[19] But the higher a man was placed in social ranks, the more likely he was to identify himself to the tsar by first name only, omitting patronymic, princely title, and rank. "Your slave Ofonka Lobanov-Rostovskoi" was Boyar Prince Afanasii Vasil'evich Lobanov-Rostovskii; "your slave Fedka Sheremetev" was Boyar Fedor Ivanovich Sheremetev.[20] This omission probably indicates no disrespect to fathers but more likely underscores the intimacy of the tsar's relationship with his closest advisors. Paralleling the dependency at the heart of a slave's identifying himself by his master, this usage places the accent on patronage and friendship in the elite, whereas the other usage underscores that people found the basis of social security in the patriarchal family. After all, woe to the orphaned child in this subsistence society without a network of kin for support.

Equally important self-referents were rank and region. Muscovites enjoyed little social mobility and their livelihood and life chances were embodied in their rank. Ranks in the broadest sense were de facto hereditary: it was difficult (although not legally forbidden and not out of the question) for an enserfed, tax-paying peasant to break into more privileged status. Such social mobility where it did exist took place at the edges of the state—physically, in frontier territories, and metaphorically, in the interstices between ranks. Carol Belkin Stevens, for example, shows the upward mobility of serfs' becoming frontier guards, and the blurring of the roles of traditional social groups on the southern frontier in the seventeenth century.[21] But as a rule, rank told who you were in a nutshell. In some cases, geographical location adumbrated one's rank. Provincial gentry, for example, enjoyed lower social status and economic prosperity than metropolitan gentry. Government policy explicitly used locality as a social ordering principle for many social groups. Provincial cavalrymen mustered in regional units;[22] the state summoned elected representatives to assemblies according to territorial units;[23] gentrymen demonstrated solidarity in regional communities.[24]

Taxed people in different regions enjoyed different political institutions and privileges. The peasants and townsmen of the North (the old Novgorodian lands, by and large, generally west of the Urals), for example, enjoyed a more independent local government than that of the increasingly enserfed and more bureaucratically controlled central and frontier parts of the realm.[25] Peasants and townsmen were enrolled by community in cadastres, which served as a central institution in fixing the taxed population to the land. Social categories were in great flux on the southern steppe frontier,

while non-Russian, non-Slavic areas enjoyed broad autonomies for traditional elites and ethnic institutions. Siberia, the middle Volga, the Urals, Belarus' cities, all governed themselves with different institutions and laws and
adapted Muscovite ranks to traditional groups. Muscovy's regional diversity
and toleration of local autonomies were more characteristic than the centralization and social regimentation that has often been stressed.[26] For many
people, only by identifying rank and geography could one fully express who
one was.

Thus people identified themselves in terms of locality and rank and family—a triad that pretty well encompasses operative visions of community.
Examples abound. Taxpayers identified the many coordinates of their town
or village: "your own orphan of Vazha province, Kokshenskaia district,
Spaskaia commune, the poor, destroyed man Ftorushka Stepanov Timo-
feeva"; "your orphans of the hamlet Veska of your own estate village of
Voshchazhnikov of Rostov province, the humble peasant Putilko Stepanov,
speaking for all the peasants." Indentured men added region to their reference to their masters: "man of Stepan Iakovlevich Miliukov of Suzdal'
province, Tumakov village, Ratmanko Samuilov."[27] Provincial gentry and
men of lesser servitor classes identified themselves as "man of Suzdal'" or
"man of Uglich," or by region and rank, as in "your slave the Cossack hundredman of the Siberian towns of Eniseisk Island Stenka Ivanov."[28] Musketeers or men in new-model army units did not enjoy the right to own land
and serfs and were mustered by regiment rather than by region. Their self-
identification reflects this: "musketeer of Mikita Dmitrievich Bestuzhev's regiment Gavrilko Faleev" or "your slave hundredman of the Moscow musketeers Ganka Bibikov."[29] These various communities—regiments, villages,
urban communes, masters—represented the variety of constituent communities that made up the Muscovite state. Only for the highest social ranks
was region and rank omitted in tacit assertion of personal acquaintance with
the tsar. Foreigners serving at the Kremlin cited their occupations: "your
slave, doctor Vendelinka Sibilist," and "the foreigner, master artisan of lace-
work, Ontoshka Tamsan [Anthony Thomson]." A boyar did not call himself
a boyar, but a "slave" on a first-name basis with the tsar. In 1695, for example, boyar Prince Boris Alekseevich Golitsyn petitioned the tsar, calling himself "your slave Borisko Golitsyn."[30]

The way individuals presented themselves in public discourse, then, reveals that they belonged simultaneously to several communities—kin group,
household, patronage network or indenture, village or town, social rank.
They demonstrate little unifying national consciousness, to be anachronistic.
This is not surprising in the premodern context. Scholars of the medieval
Latin West, for example, make the same observation: "In fact people were related to many different kinds of group: universal and local Church, kingdom, feudal domain, city, village, gild, confraternity, family. . . . There was
no single, all-pervasive, over-arching 'society,' but a wide variety of compul-
sory and voluntary groups."[31] Indeed, studies of Muscovite "national" consciousness find the root principle to be religious, rather than social—elite

writers depict the society as the Godly Christian community, not as a cohesive political unity of a common people.[32]

Nonetheless Muscovites were indeed part of a larger social unit that we would call a society, not only because modern Russian nationalism claims its roots in this historical experience but also because of unifying principles in the Russian language, Orthodox religion, or (most salient) political subordination and bureaucratic organization in an empire. When Muscovites did confront this problem in a nontheoretical context, they sensibly described their perceived community in terms of diversity. When groups of individuals submitted collective petitions for common needs, by and large they identified themselves by region and rank: "your slaves the *stol'niki, striapchie,* and Moscow gentry and *zhil'tsy* and men of all ranks and the holders of service and ancestral land *[pomeshchiki i votchinniki]* of Tula, Solov, Odoev, Dedilov, and other towns."[33] Many spoke in the name of broad social categories: "the provincial gentry *[dvoriane* and *deti boiarskie]* of various towns" or "of all towns," or groups of musketeers or merchants.[34] Here the defined community was confined to a certain estate because the goals of the petitions were estate-specific: gentrymen sought greater control over peasant labor, and merchants sought a monopoly on domestic trade.[35]

Just as in collective petitions, documentation for collective assemblies and other collective gatherings described the whole as the sum of its parts. At irregular intervals, for example, the tsar summoned representatives of most social ranks and territories (peasants and non-Russians were generally excluded) in what were later labeled "councils of the Land" *(zemskie sobory).* These assemblies offered counsel to the tsar on issues that affected all of society, such as increases in taxation or declarations of war. The summoning of such gatherings began by the mid-sixteenth century and was a response to changing political circumstances—territorial expansion, administrative reform, social differentiation. In form and symbolism they were consistent with Muscovite ideology, an ideology that mandated personal consultation between the tsar and his people. They should probably best be regarded as a consultative process rather than as formal institutions, particularly of a protoparliamentary type.[36]

Sources for these assemblies generally envision society as a compilation of ranks *(chiny),* some at the top of the social hierarchy very narrowly defined and others quite generally defined in composition. Here, for example, is the description of what most scholars consider the last such gathering, in 1653:

> The Great Sovereign Most Holy Patriarch of Moscow and all Rus' Nikon, the Krutitsa Metropolitan Sylvester, the Metropolitan of Serbia Mikhailo, archimandrites and hegumens with all the Holy Council, boyars, *okol'nichie,* men in other council *[dumnye]* ranks, *stol'niki, striapchie,* Moscow-based gentry, *zhil'tsy,* provincial gentry *[dvoriane and deti boiarskie],* merchants *[gosti]* and trading people and people of all other ranks of the merchant and textile guilds and of the taxpaying hundreds and of the tsar's tax-exempt neighborhoods and musketeers.[37]

Often a document would avoid repetition of such a long list by substituting the phrase "people of all ranks" *(vsiakikh chinov liudi)* for the lesser social strata.[38]

Significantly, other similar enumerations of the "body politic" included non-Orthodox subjects, indicating that visions of the social whole crossed confessional and ethnic lines. The forces assembled to defend Muscovy from the Poles in the Time of Troubles are enumerated in this salutation from a letter of 1611:

> Greetings to Lord Ivan Ivanovich and Piatoi Faleleev and to the elders and swornmen and urban taxpayers and all resident *[zhiletskie]* people of the Perm' land *[zemlia]* from Vasilii Morozov, Nikonor Shulgin, Stepan Dichkov, and captains and gentry and musketeer hundredmen and musketeers and gunners and defense artillery and all servitor and resident people and princes and *murzy* and newly-Christened servitors and Tatars and Chuvash and Cheremis and Votiaki and all people of the Kazan' state *[gosudarstvo].*[39]

Less well developed but significant was the tendency to see society as composed of a few aggregate social ranks. When participants responded to the issue at hand in an assembly, for example, they spoke "in ranks" *(po chinam),* dividing the gathered into three, five, eight, or more social groups.[40] The threefold social identification we have seen in petitions separated society into intercessors, servitors, and taxed dependents.[41] An unprecedented collective petition of 1657 even explicitly makes a fourfold social division and enunciates a hierarchical social philosophy:

> so that in your own realm all the people of God and your own people each from the great and four ranks *[chiny]*—clerical, service, trade, and agricultural—by their own discipline *[ustav]* and by your tsarist order would stand strong and unhesitatingly and not a one would be harmed by any other and so that all people would live according to the word of God and from their own direct labors and so that all men in all ranks, great and small, when they are at home, be satisfied with God's gifts to them and your tsarist grants and their own direct earnings *[obroki]* and [would not covet] others' property and profits.

But this document is unique.[42] What is more salient is that all these sources proposed a different and multiplex vision of social ordering.

We can see a tension here between self-representation that is local and personal and political processes that push people to identify a collective whole. It was a common tension in premodern societies and one generally not resolved until the discourse of nationalism took hold much later on. In Russia, a single terminology did not supplant the available vocabularies even at a moment of national crisis, the Time of Troubles (fifteen years of dynastic crisis, foreign invasion, and domestic unrest, from 1598 to 1613), when military and political forces of the state did indeed mobilize to defend the whole. The word *"gosudarstvo"* or "state," which had been used since the late sixteenth century to indicate the realm as the tsar's territory rather than as his authority, was one recourse.[43] In 1606, for example, Tsar Vasilii Shuiskii declared that Moscow's higher ranks had elected him to act "as all the Muscovite state *[gosudarstvom]*"; in 1610 the boyars and representatives of servitor classes and the northern towns declared that they all "stand as one, as all the state"; later in 1610 the boyars declared that they, "acting as all the Muscovite state," had elected the Polish heir Wladyslaw as Russian tsar. But at the same time the term "state" also could refer to frontier regions that retained cultural and political autonomies: "the Novgorod state," "the Kazan' state."[44]

Other documents resorted to a more multifold description of the social whole that people were being called to defend. In 1608, for example, Tsar Vasilii Shuiskii asked the people of Galich to defend "the Muscovite state, the Orthodox faith, and their own fatherland." In 1612 Prince Dmitrii Pozharskii declared that he was fighting "for the icon of the Most Holy Mother of God of Vladimir, and for the miracle-working relics of the great Miracle Workers and for the ruling town of Moscow and all the towns of the Muscovite state."[45]

The concept of "the Land" *(zemlia)*—which occurs in our sources as a noun, an instrumental phrase ("acting as all the Land" *[vseiu zemleiu]*), and an adjective *(zemskii)*—was also available from of old to connote the social whole.[46] But it also had variant meanings. In 1610, for example, the assembled ranks—from boyars to urban taxpayers and towns of the North—are said to have beseeched Tsar Vasilii Shuiskii "as all the Land" to relinquish the throne.[47] In 1613, similarly, the Time of Troubles was attributed to "the universal sinfulness of the Land *[obshchii zemskii grekh]*" (the document elsewhere speaks of "the sins of all Orthodox Christians"). After the Time of Troubles the usage continued: in 1619 an assembly was called to "set the Land in order" *(zemlia ustroit')* after the Time of Troubles; in 1639 merchants at an assembly referred to the tsar's orders "for the whole Land."[48] These are the most inclusive usages of the term, but they are the exception.

Generally "the Land" was envisioned as being separate from the tsar, the privileged military ranks, and the apparatus of government. The usage of the term "Land" fairly explicitly distinguishes between the tsar's realm and a perhaps vestigial public sphere; this distinction is evident since the mid-sixteenth century.[49] Delegates to assemblies, for example, were summoned to discuss the "affairs of sovereign and Land."[50] A document of 1611 distinguished the "boyars and military commanders" from "all the Land"; another of 1612 speaks of "all ranks of servitor and Land *[sluzhilye i zemskie]* people"; in 1615 Tsar Mikhail Fedorovich issued a directive saying "by our order and by the agreement of all the Land."[51] Similarly, in lists of attendees at assemblies, the shorthand phrase "and all the Land" indicated ranks below the privileged landholding elite, such as the non-landed military servitors, trading people, and urban and rural taxpayers.[52]

But the picture was more complicated. The terms *"zemlia"* and *"zemskii"* could also refer more broadly to local or public concerns not directly associated with tsar's decrees and directives; thus gentrymen in 1648 spoke of their grievances as "our *zemskie* concerns," and in 1641 provincial gentry of various towns petitioned the tsar speaking "as all the Land" *(vseiu zemleiu)*, yet seeking satisfaction of fairly narrow class interests: help in recovering runaway peasants, protection from oppressors (wealthy landlords, corrupt officials— *sil'nye liudi*), and a more locally responsible juridical system. Similarly in 1648 "elected people of all ranks" petitioned "from all the Land" to end tax-exempt neighborhoods.[53] Similarly, the "Land" could connote the self-governing, taxed, but not enserfed, urban and rural communes in the North. These communities elected officers such as "land judges" *(zemskie sudeiki)* and "land elders" *(zemskie starosty)* who oversaw local issues and executed Moscow's policies such as tax collection.[54] Or "the Land" could refer to the populace of a given territory, as in *"vsia zemlia kazanskaia."*[55] Here the import of the phrase "acting as all the Land" is not only a distinction between state and society but also an affirmation of local collective action, on the part of a village, a town, or a "corporation" of local servitors, or a general uprising. Such underscoring of collective unanimity is seen in many contexts: in 1611 men of all ranks swore allegiance "as all the Land of the Kazan' state"; in 1614 the urban taxpayers of Ustiug elected local officials "as all the Land"; in 1622 the peasants of the Ust'ianskie communes elected officials "as all the Land." Of parallel meaning is the phrase "as the whole town" *(vsem gorodom)*.[56] So the society is envisioned as bifurcated, although composed of fairly large aggregate groups.

Thus Muscovites used myriad ways to describe the social community larger than their local and familial world. They were driven to seek broader terminology by the exceptional circumstances of the seventeenth century: not only what we would call national crisis in the Time of Troubles, but also the chronic social tensions arising in response to the state's bureaucratic and imperial growth, which forced some social groups to mobilize for collective concerns. Nevertheless the need for a word or a concept for society was not sufficiently compelling to generate new social concepts that lasted. Note, after all, that Muscovy had no tradition of legal discourse to generate theory about society. For historical reasons, Muscovy did not experience the tension between canon or Roman law and customary law out of which much European debate about society developed; it lacked the university tradition that gave physical space for theoretical inquiry. In the late seventeenth century, cultural innovations at court forced some action on this front: while paraphrasing Plutarch's civic verse, the Belarus' scholar Semeon Polotskii coined the word *"grazhdanstvo"* for "society." But neither the usage nor the civic philosophizing (derived from Renaissance humanism via the Kievan Orthodox revival) caught on in this generation.[57] The modern Russian word for "society" *(obshchestvo)* finally gained currency in the late eighteenth or early nineteenth century, again first appearing in translations of European political theory and given staying power by social receptivity to such theory and to Enlightenment-inspired concepts of national consciousness.[58]

There are many possible interpretations of this evidence about social terminology. One very traditional angle (and one with which I would like to take issue) would take literally the metaphors of submission implicit in some of the terminology discussed here. As I have pointed out, much of the language we have explored—diminutives, the triad of "slaves, orphans, and intercessors"—envisioned the state as a godly community on the model of a patrimonial household, headed by a grand prince who treats his subjects as members of an extended family: his fighters and officials are metaphorically his domestic servants; his taxpayers, wards he adopts into the fold; his clerics, spiritual intercessors. To take this language literally might support claims of the literal autocracy of the tsar and the passivity of society. This approach would complement the "statist" tradition of Russian historiography but would miss the point of how ethnically, administratively, and socially diverse and how minimally centralized pre-Petrine Russia was.[59]

If that interpretive angle privileges the political center, a second equally risky one privileges a European comparison. This one would lament the "absence" of a self-conscious discourse on society in Muscovy, as evidenced by the lack of terminology and theory.[60] Even in the medieval period, after all, Europe had at its disposal various theoretical discourses about society—Peter the Chanter's work, the theory of the "great chain of being," Catholic political theory, the idea of the three orders.[61] And later, in the early modern period, theory about state formation ran rampant.[62] But, as noted in passing, Russia developed out of very different influences from those in Europe, and although the differences from Europe may be noteworthy, they are not to be considered moral failings (as they have often been). This is all the more the case not only because medieval Europe was (despite the theoretical discourses) just as localistic as Russia but also because no historical experience can be held a normative milestone for any other. The temptation to do so here is great, because comparing Russia to Europe to Russia's detriment has been a preoccupation of the Russian intelligentsia since at least the nineteenth century ("when will the new day come?" Dobroliubov lamented) and has occurred since the late fifteenth century as Russia began to enjoy increasing political and military contact with Europe. But these historical circumstances do not deny that Russia's development followed a complex and independent path, in which many foreign influences participated and not one of them alone set the pace or direction.

This evidence can best be construed as indication of early modern Russia's social cohesion. But even here there is a potential pitfall imbedded in the very idea of social cohesion, which, as commonly understood, has a presentist, as well as European, bias. Asking whether a society possesses a concept of itself as a unified whole—bound by homogeneous values, laws, and institutions—betrays a preconception of what historical development should have been like. For Russia in this era, searching for cohesion means looking for a centralizing "national monarchy," the mobilization of resources, the emergence of national consciousness, growing political pluralism and social differentiation, as in the rise of the "modern" European bureaucratic monarchy.[63] Some, but not all of this was happening in Russia, and neither in reality nor in terminology was Russia terribly well integrated. Looking for cohesion might be a misguided effort on comparative grounds, and at a deeper theoretical level.

For the pursuit of cohesion as it usually is construed (homogenizing and

unifying, implicitly harmonizing) betrays our hopes and dreams about ideally integrated communities; images of society as organically unified wholes
have proliferated from the Romantics and Slavophiles to Durkheim and Tal-
cott Parsons. Even social theory that makes cohesion the result of conflict
and coercion, such as Marxism, looks forward to a utopian future devoid of
conflict, pure "communism," with the emphasis on community. The sort of
self-conscious, unified, and cohesive society implicit in this quest is, even in
the modern period, illusory. Current theory suggests plausibly that social cohesion is a process, a continual push/pull of negotiation and interaction
rather than a fixed state, especially in premodern circumstances.[64]

As we have seen, premodern societies like medieval Europe and Russia
were localistic, loosely tied together by assertions of political unity or by a
common religion and language, but notable more for their regional autonomies and social divisions than for integration. The boundaries of identity in premodern times were not fixed but fluid, the content of identity was
not national but local and personal. And this was the case regardless of how
strong a learned discourse a given social body might have possessed about
community and society.[65] Even in modern circumstances of media and national discourse, cohesion and integration are contingent and changing. So,
in many ways the multifold vocabulary about individual and society in Muscovite documents accurately reflects the spirit of its social order.

Muscovite terminology of the self and society depicts a richly textured social cohesion. Individuals presented themselves as embedded in many networks—family, household, locality, social rank (Orthodox religion was perhaps implicit for most). These networks served the primary need of this
society, that is, the need for protection and mutual aid in a society of short-
age that lacked public institutions of social welfare. Family, patronage, depen-
dence, village or town, the comradeship of social rank gave sustenance and
stability to individuals in Muscovy, far more than did the central institutions
of the state or the myth of the tsar's patrimonial kindness. The centralizing
state may indeed have envisioned a greater degree of control, but premodern
conditions of means of communication, education, literacy, infrastructure,
population density, and so on, militated against it, particularly in Russia's far-
flung empire. Thus the cohesion of the state that was indeed perceived (if imperfectly described) by the writers of the various documents we analyzed was
the embodiment of a constant intertwining of many nexuses of personal
identity. Cohesion was to be found in managing, not necessarily resolving,
the tension between localistic identity and Muscovy's ambient sources of
community—religion, language, and imperial bureaucratic control.

NOTES

This research was supported by the International Research and Exchanges
Board, the Fulbright-Hays program of the Department of Education, and the Center
for Russian and East European Studies, Stanford University. My thanks go to my

anonymous reviewer for reference to juridical traditions, and particularly to Edward L. Keenan for specific citations and for persistently pointing my attention to the underlying tensions in this vexing topic.

1. Firsthand accounts are rare. Extant are a few letters among members of elite families or of boyars to their bailiffs, some poetic texts in the form of petitions by chancery officials, sermons by Polotskii and Slavinetskii, Avvakum's autobiography, and there is the generally recognized trend toward greater humanism in seventeenth-century literature. But nothing exists so revealing of individuals as the Inquisition records that Emmanuel Le Roy Ladurie and Carlo Ginzburg have plumbed or the pardon tales Natalie Zemon Davis has studied: Emmanuel Le Roy Ladurie, *Montaillou,* trans. Barbara Bray (New York, 1979); Carlo Ginzburg, *The Cheese and the Worms,* trans. John and Anne Tedeschi (Baltimore, 1980) and *The Night Battles,* trans. John and Anne Tedeschi (New York, 1985); Natalie Zemon Davis, *Fiction in the Archives* (Stanford, 1987).

2. See my articles: "Honor and Dishonor in Early Modern Russia," *Forschungen zur osteuropäischen Geschichte* 46 (1992): 131–46; "Women's Honor in Early Modern Russia," in *Russia's Women: Accommodation, Resistance, Transformation,* ed. Barbara Evans Clements, Barbara Alpern Engel, and Christine D. Worobec (Berkeley and Los Angeles, 1991), 60–73; "Honor and Society in Early Modern Russia" (manuscript), chaps. 2–3.

3. On the *Secreta secretorum* or Pseudo-Aristotle in Russia, see D. M. Bulanin, "Tainaia tainykh," in *Slovar' knizhnikov i knizhnosti drevnei Rusi,* 3 vols. in 5 parts to date (Leningrad, 1987–), vol. 2, pt. 2 (1989): 427–30. On Peresvetov, see A. A. Zimin, *I. S. Peresvetov i ego sovremenniki* (Moscow, 1958). On aspects of secular and church law, see Daniel H. Kaiser, "Law, Russian (Muscovite), 1300–1500," in *Dictionary of the Middle Ages,* ed. Joseph R. Strayer, 13 vols. (New York, 1982–1989), 7: 506–12; and Ivan Žužek, *Kormčaia Kniga: Studies in the Chief Code of Russian Canon Law, Orientalia Christiana Analecta,* vol. 168 (Rome, 1964). On the Domostroi, see Carolyn Johnston Pouncy, ed. and trans., *The Domostroi: Rules for Russian Households in the Time of Ivan the Terrible* (Ithaca, N.Y., 1994). For a survey of ideas about the ruler, see Vladimir Val'denberg, *Drevnerusskie ucheniia o predelakh tsarskoi vlasti* (Petrograd, 1916).

4. For scales of compensation for dishonor, see, for example, *Rossiiskoe zakonodatel'stvo X–XX vekov* (hereafter *RZ*), ed. O. I. Chistiakov, 9 vols. (Moscow, 1984–1994), 2: 101, art. 26 (1550), and 3: 106–12, chap. 10, arts. 27–99 (1649). Daniel Rowland has extrapolated political "ideology" from historical texts about the Time of Troubles: see "The Problem of Advice in Muscovite Tales about the Time of Troubles," *Russian History* 6, pt. 2 (1979): 259–83; and "Did Muscovite Literary Ideology Place Limits on the Power of the Tsar (1540s–1660s)?" *Russian Review* 49, no. 2 (1990): 125–56. For one interpretation of pilgrimages and similar public rituals, see my "Pilgrimage, Procession, and Symbolic Space in Sixteenth-Century Russian Politics," in *Medieval Russian Culture,* vol. 2, ed. Michael S. Flier and Daniel Rowland (Berkeley and Los Angeles, 1994), 163–81.

5. Examples are drawn from a database of over six hundred litigations on insult to honor and on women as litigants; the sources are described in my "Honor and Dishonor" and "Women's Honor."

6. Geoffrey Koziol, *Begging Pardon and Favor: Ritual and Political Order in Early Medieval France* (Ithaca, N.Y., 1992).

7. Valerie Kivelson discusses this point with reference to 1648 in "The Devil

Stole His Mind: The Tsar and the 1648 Moscow Uprising," *American Historical Review* 98, no. 3 (1993): 755. The texts are *Polnoe sobranie zakonov Rossiiskoi imperii* (hereafter *PSZ*), coll. 1 in 40 vols., with five vols. of indexes (St. Petersburg, 1830), nos. 1 (chap. 10, art. 20; see also chap. 1, arts. 8–9), 1707, 1748, 3261, 3838, 3947 (1649, 1699, 1700, 1718, 1721, 1722, respectively).

8. Rossiiskii gosudarstvennyi arkhiv drevnikh aktov (RGADA), f. 210, Prikaznyi stol, stb. 686, l. 64; also l. 63 ("Ivashko Pronskoi"). He was a boyar from at least 1652 to 1683: Robert O. Crummey, *Aristocrats and Servitors: The Boyar Elite in Russia, 1613–1689* (Princeton, 1983), 190.

9. This is not, however, a hard and fast rule. See examples of these usages omitted: *Russkaia istoricheskaia biblioteka* (hereafter *RIB*), 39 vols. (St. Petersburg, 1872–1927) 14: no. 226, col. 547 (1604), no. 253, col. 587 (1608), and no. 301, col. 673 (1626); *RIB* 25: no. 18, col. 19 (1626), and no. 87, col. 102 (1631).

10. *Pamiatniki delovoi pis'mennosti XVII veka: Vladimirskii krai* (hereafter *PDP*) (Moscow, 1984), no. 206, p. 220 (1618); reference to Petr Vasil'evich Volynskoi, cited as a *stol'nik* and regional governor from at least 1614 to at least 1633: *Dvortsovye razriady* (hereafter *DR*), 4 vols. (St. Petersburg, 1850–1855), 1: col. 152; *Knigi razriadnye, po ofitsial'nym onykh spiskam* (hereafter *KR*), 2 vols. and index (St. Petersburg, 1853–1856), 2: col. 752.

11. *RIB* 2: no. 164/2, p. 573 (1634). Probably a reference to Prince Nikita Mikhailovich Boriatinskoi, cited as a military commander *(voevoda)* from 1626 to 1639 in *DR* 1: col. 859, *DR* 2: 602, or possibly Prince Nikita Petrovich, cited as a military commander from 1614 to 1632 in *DR* 1: col. 123, 2: 292.

12. I. E. Zabelin, *Domashnii byt russkikh tsarei v XVI i XVII st.,* 4th exp. ed. (Moscow, 1918), 365 (1645), refers to Bogdan Minich Dubrovskii, *dumnyi dvorianin* and *kaznachei* by 1643, d. 1661/62 (Crummey, *Aristocrats,* 186).

13. *RIB* 25: no. 81, col. 95 (1630).

14. Zabelin, *Tsarei,* 354 (1642).

15. *RIB* 25: no. 9, col. 10 (1626) and no. 19, cols. 19–20 (1626). Other examples are in *RIB* 25: no. 10, col. 11 (1626).

16. On the idealized mores of a patriarchal household, see Pouncy, ed. and trans., *The Domostroi.* On the centrality of the metaphor, see my "Honor and Dishonor," 143–45. For profession instead of "orphan," see *RIB* 14: no. 259, col. 595 (1609–1610); *RIB* 14: no. 261, col. 598 (1610).

17. *PDP* no. 114, p. 154 (1621).

18. *Dukhovnye i dogovornye gramoty velikikh i udel'nykh kniazei XIV–XVI vv.* (Moscow, 1950), nos. 5 (ca. 1360s), 9 (1375), 27 (1433), 45 (1447), 73 (1481), 101 (1531). Such treaties between kinsmen do not survive after 1531 (*Sobranie gosudarstvennykh gramot i dogovorov* [hereafter *SGGD*], 5 pts. [Moscow, 1813–1894], vols. 2–4; *Gosudarstvennoe drevlekhranilishche khartii i rukopisei: Opis' dokumental'nykh materialov fonda no. 135* [Moscow, 1971]), due to restrictions on granting appanages to such relations and to the paucity of male heirs, particularly in the seventeenth century. For that matter tsars' wills do not seem to survive after the mid-sixteenth century, perhaps reflecting a new Romanov concept of the state.

19. For patronymic, see *RIB* 25: no. 2, cols. 2–3 (1624). For women, see *Akty moskovskogo gosudarstva* (hereafter *AMG*), ed. N. A. Popov, 3 vols. (St. Petersburg, 1890–1901), 1: no. 686, p. 628 (1634); *RIB* 14: no. 221, col. 540 (1603). For the indentured, see *RIB* 2: no. 244, col. 1035 (1625).

20. *AMG* 1: no. 74, p. 111 (1614); Lobanov-Rostovskii was a boyar by February 1615, d. 1628/29 (Crummey, *Aristocrats,* 181). RGADA, f. 210, Moscow stol, stb. 1037,

l. 243 (1640); Sheremetev was boyar by 1605, d. 1650 (Crummey, *Aristocrats,* 179).

21. Carol Belkin Stevens, *Soldiers on the Steppe: Army Reform and Social Change in Early Modern Russia* (DeKalb, Ill., 1995).

22. For examples see *Tysiachnaia Kniga 1550 g. i Dvorovaia Tetrad' 50–kh godov XVI v.* (Moscow, 1950); *SGGD* 3: no. 40, pp. 171–73 (1618); *KR* 1: cols. 781–85 (1621); *SGGD* 3: no. 113, pp. 381–84 (1642).

23. For summons to election representatives to state assemblies from Galich, Novgorod, and other towns, see *Akty, sobrannye v bibliotekakh i arkhivakh Rossiiskoi imperii Arkheograficheskoiu ekspeditsieiu Imp. akademii nauk* (hereafter *AAE*), 4 vols. and index (St. Petersburg, 1836, 1838), 3: no. 105, p. 144 (1619); Iu. V. Got'e, ed., *Akty, otnosiashchiesia k istorii zemskikh soborov* (Moscow, 1909), no. 10, pp. 35–36 (1636), and nos. 13–15, pp. 60–62 (1648); P. P. Smirnov, "Neskol'ko dokumentov iz istorii Sobornogo Ulozheniia i Zemskogo Sobora 1648–1649 gg.," in *Chteniia v Imp. obshchestve istorii i drevnostei rossiiskikh pri Moskovskom universitete: Sbornik,* 264 vols. (Moscow, 1845–1918), bk. 4 (1913), nos. 2–8, pp. 8–17 (1648); *AAE* 4: no. 27, pp. 40–41 (1648). For instructions of Vladimir gentrymen to their delegate, see St. Petersburgskii filial Instituta russkoi istorii Rossiiskoi akademii nauk (SPbFIRI), Collection of A. I. Artem'ev, no. 2 (1648).

24. On sixteenth- and seventeenth-century gentry communities, see V. B. Kobrin, *Vlast' i sobstvennost' v srednevekovoi Rossii* (Moscow, 1985), and Valerie A. Kivelson, *Autocracy in the Provinces: The Muscovite Gentry and Political Culture in the Seventeenth Century* (Stanford, Calif., 1996).

25. On more centrally controlled cities, see J. Michael Hittle, *The Service City* (Cambridge, Mass., 1979); on the North, see M. M. Bogoslovskii, *Zemskoe samoupravlenie na russkom Severe v XVII veke,* bk. 1 (1910) and bks. 2 and 3 (1912) of *Chteniia;* and Bogoslovskii, "Zemskie chelobitnye v drevnei Rusi," *Bogoslovskii vestnik,* 1911, nos. 1–4.

26. On Muscovy as having hermetically sealed social castes, see David MacKenzie and Michael W. Curran, *A History of Russia, the Soviet Union, and Beyond,* 4th ed. (Belmont, Calif., 1993), 193. Such is also the thrust of Marc Raeff's generally insightful interpretation of late Muscovy, *Understanding Imperial Russia,* trans. Arthur Goldhammer (New York, 1984), chap. 1. See also arguments that Muscovy was weakly centralized and tolerated local autonomies: M. N. Tikhomirov, *Rossiia v XVI stoletii* (Moscow, 1962); A. A. Zimin, "O politicheskikh predposylkakh vozniknoveniia russkogo absoliutizma," in *Absoliutizm v Rossii, XVII–XVIII vv.* (Moscow, 1964), 18–49; Andreas Kappeler, "Das moskauer Reich des 17. Jahrhunderts und seine nichtrussischen Untertanen" (paper presented at the Seventh International Conference on the History of Kiev Rus' and Muscovy, Berlin, 1992); and Kappeler, *Russlands erste Nationalitäten* (Cologne, 1982).

27. *RIB* 14: no. 284, col. 643 (1620); *PDP* no. 133, p. 168 (1631). For indentured men, see *PDP,* no. 132, p. 167 (1629).

28. *RIB* 2: nos. 176–77, col. 722 (1638); RGADA, f. 210, Prikaznyi stol, stb. 122, l. 122; *RIB* 25: no. 206, col. 271 (1654).

29. RGADA, f. 210, Prikaznyi stol, stb. 84, l. 21 (1632); *Moskovskaia delovaia i bytovaia pis'mennost' XVII veka* (hereafter *MDBP*) (Moscow, 1968), no. 34, p. 61 (after 1644).

30. For the doctor, see *Akty istoricheskie, sobrannye i izdannye Arkheograficheskoiu kommissieiu,* 5 vols. (St. Petersburg, 1841–1842), 3: no. 237, pp. 396 (1644). For the laceworker, see *Akty, otnosiashchiesia do iuridicheskogo byta drevnei Rossii,* 3 vols. and index (St. Petersburg, 1857–1901), 1: no. 104, col. 643 (1646). For

Golitsyn, see Zabelin, *Tsarei,* 393; he was a boyar from at least 1690 until at least 1713 (Crummey, *Aristocrats,* 210).

31. Antony Black, "The Individual and Society," in *The Cambridge History of Medieval Political Thought, c. 350–c. 1450,* ed. J. H. Burns (Cambridge, 1988), 589. Underscoring Muscovy's differences from the Latin West, however, is the continuation of Black's remarks: "and a corresponding variety of sentiments about social bonds and societal authority. Different intellectual traditions—Neoplatonic, Aristotelian and humanist, theological and juristic, realist and nominalist—produced divergent views on the individual and society."

32. Paul Bushkovitch, "The Formation of National Consciousness in Early Modern Russia," *Harvard Ukrainian Studies* 10, nos. 3/4 (1986): 355–76; Michael Cherniavsky, "Russia," in *National Consciousness, History, and Political Culture in Early-Modern Europe,* ed. Orest Ranum (Baltimore and London, 1975), 118–43; A. N. Nasonov, *Russkaia zemlia i obrazovanie territorii drevnerusskogo gosudarstva* (Moscow, 1951); David B. Miller, "The *Velikie minei chetii* and the *Stepennaia kniga* of Metropolitan Makarii and the Origins of Russian National Consciousness," *Forschungen zur osteuropäischen Geschichte* 26 (1979): 263–382.

33. A. A. Novosel'skii, "Kollektivnye dvorianskie chelobitnye o syske beglykh krest'ian i kholopov vo vtoroi polovine XVII v.," in *Dvorianstvo i krepostnoi stroi Rossii, XVI–XVIII vv.* (Moscow, 1975), no. 13, p. 340 (1694).

34. P. P. Smirnov, "Chelobitnyia dvorian i detei boiarskikh vsekh gorodov v pervoi polovine XVII v.," *Chteniia,* vol. 254 (1915), no. 3, pp. 38–50 (nos. 1–3), and Novosel'skii, "Kollektivnye," nos. 2–5, pp. 308–20 (gentry); Hans-Joachim Torke, *Die staatsbedingte Gesellschaft im Moskauer Reich* (Leiden, 1974), 104 (musketeers), 97–116 passim (merchants).

35. On collective petition campaigns in the seventeenth century, see Torke, *Die staatsbedingte Gesellschaft,* chap. 3; and Kivelson, *Autocracy,* chap. 7. Publications include Novosel'skii, "Kollektivnye," 303–43; and Smirnov, "Chelobitnyia," 1–73. Several of the documents in the Smirnov collection were translated by Richard Hellie in his *Readings for Introduction to Russian Civilization, Muscovite Society* (Chicago, 1967).

36. Rowland, "The Problem of Advice" and "Did Muscovite Literary Ideology Limit?" A standard view is L. V. Cherepnin, *Zemskie sobory Russkogo gosudarstva v XVI–XVII vv.* (Moscow, 1978). See critiques by Edward L. Keenan in *Kritika* 16: no. 2 (1980): 82–94, and Peter B. Brown, "The *Zemskii sobor* in Recent Soviet Historiography," *Russian History* 10, pt. 1 (1983): 77–90. For other less institutional approaches, see Richard Hellie, *"Zemskii sobor,"* *Modern Encyclopedia of Russian and Soviet History* 45 (1987): 226–34; Torke, *Die staatsbedingte Gesellschaft,* chap. 4, and "Reichsversammlung," in *Lexikon der Geschichte Russlands,* ed. Hans-Joachim Torke (Munich, 1985), 317–19; Kivelson, *Autocracy,* chap. 7. I will not use the term "council of the land," but will refer simply to assemblies.

37. *SGGD* 3: no. 157, p. 481 (1653). The presence of the Serbian metropolitan here indicates the growing Greek Orthodox presence in Muscovy following the establishment of the Patriarchate (1589) and the intensification of Muscovy's contacts with Ukraine in the seventeenth century.

38. *AAE* 2: no. 210, p. 368 (1612); *SGGD* 3: no. 2, p. 5 (1613); *AAE* 3: no. 31, p. 70 (1614); *KR* 1: cols. 561–62 (1618); *SGGD* 3: no. 99, p. 342 (1634); *SGGD* 3: no. 113, p. 388 (1642).

39. *AAE* 2: no. 188, p. 318 (1611). Thanks go to V. A. Kivelson for help in translating some of this terminology.

40. In 1566, for example, first the church hierarchs spoke, then the boyars and high officials, then gentrymen "of the first rank," then those "of the second rank," then *pomeshchiki* of Toropetsk, then those of Lutsk, then chancery officials, then merchants (Got'e, *Akty*, no. 1, pp. 1–10). In 1621, the clergy spoke, followed by all the service people, then the trading people (*KR* 1: cols. 779–80). In 1639, the order was first the clergy, then the boyars, *okol'nichie*, and counciliar ranks; the *stol'niki*, *striapchie*, and Moscow-based gentry; the provincial gentry; the *gosti* and trading people (V. N. Shumilov, "Delo zemskogo sobora 1639 g.," in *Dvorianstvo i krepostnoi stroi*, nos. 3–6, pp. 299–302). In 1642, it was first the clergy, then the *stol'niki*, the Moscow-based gentry, the Moscow musketeers, then many regional groups of provincial gentry, then *gosti*, guild merchants, and urban taxpayers (*SGGD* 3: no. 113, pp. 384–97). In 1653, the assembled groups responded "in ranks": the boyars, *stol'niki*, *striapchie*, Moscow-based gentry, chancery officials, *zhil'tsy*, provincial gentry, musketeer captains, *gosti*, merchant guilds, urban taxpayers, and musketeers (*SGGD* 3: no. 157, p. 489).

41. This may resemble the European scheme of three orders—those who pray, those who serve, and those who work. But there are significant differences. Here the vocabulary was personal and patrimonial, not legalistic or theoretical, and in none of these sources does a term for "order" emerge (the 1657 petition expands the familiar word for rank, *chin*).

42. Novosel'skii, "Kollektivnye," no. 2, p. 312; also published by V. N. Storozhev in "Dva chelobit'ia," *Bibliograficheskie zapiski*, no. 1 (1892), pp. 14–15. The document is *RGADA*, f. 210, Moscow stol, stb. 310, delo 3, ll. 1–10, but its author is unknown.

43. Zoltán András, "Polskie 'państwo' a rosyjskie 'gosudarstwo'," *Zeszyty naukowe wydziału humanistycznego uniwersitetu gdańskiego: Filologia rosyjska*, no. 10 (1982): 111–15.

44. Referring to Novgorod are *AAE* 2: no. 44, p. 101 (1606); *AAE* 2: no. 162, p. 277, and no. 164, p. 279 (1610); *AAE* 2: no. 210, p. 367 (1612). To the Kazan' state are *AAE* 2: no. 188, p. 318 (1611), and no. 203, p. 353 (1612). A document of 1610 speaks of the "Vladimir, Moscow, and all states of the Russian tsardom" (*AAE* 2: no. 164, p. 279).

45. *AAE* 2: no. 90, p. 183 (1608); *AAE* 2: no. 203, p. 355 (1612). On the cult of the Moscow miracle workers, see Günther Stökl, "Staat und Kirche im Moskauer Russland: Die vier Moskauer Wundertäter," *Jahrbücher für Geschichte Osteuropas* 29 (1981): 481–93.

46. Nasonov, *Russkaia zemlia*.

47. *AAE* 2: no. 162, pp. 277, 278. A similar usage occurs in a document of 1611, which uses the term *"zemlia"* in a more limited manner (*AAE* 2: no. 188, p. 319).

48. *SGGD* 3: no. 2, p. 5 (1613); *SGGD* 3: no. 47, p. 209 (1619); Shumilov, "Delo," nos. 5–6, pp. 300, 302 (1639).

49. E. L. Keenan pointed me to an early citation: V. I. Buganov, ed., *Razriadnaia kniga 1475–1598 gg.* (Moscow, 1966), 110 (7055/1547).

50. Numerous usages of this phrase: Smirnov, "Neskol'ko dokumentov," no. 1, pp. 6, 7 (1648); Got'e, *Akty*, no. 13, p. 60 (1648). Torke discusses the usage: Torke, *Die staatsbedingte Gesellschaft*, 44–46.

51. *AAE* 2: no. 188, p. 318 (1611). For other usages in 1606 and 1613, see *AAE* 2: no. 44, p. 101; *SGGD* 3: no. 6, p. 22. *AAE* 2: no. 210, p. 368 (1612); *AAE* 3: no. 68, p. 105 (1615).

52. *AAE* 2: no. 6, p. 15 (1598).

53. SPbFIRI, Collection of A. I. Artem'ev, no. 2 (1648); Smirnov, "Chelobit-nyia," no. 2, p. 41 (1641); *AAE* 4: no. 32/III, pp. 47–48 (1648).

54. On elected administration, see Torke, *Die staatsbedingte Gesellschaft,* chap. 2; Torke, "Zemlja," in *Lexikon,* ed. Torke, 419–20; Torke, "Continuity and Change in the Relations between Bureaucracy and Society in Russia, 1613–1861," *Canadian Slavic Studies* 5, no. 4 (1971): 457–63; B. N. Chicherin, *Oblastnye uchrezhdeniia Rossii v XVII–m veke* (Moscow, 1856), 504–73; Bogoslovskii, *Zemskoe samoupravlenie,* and "Zemskie chelobitniia."

55. *Sbornik Imp. Russkogo istoricheskogo obshchestva,* 148 vols. (St. Petersburg, Petrograd, 1867–1916), 95 (1895): 406 (1517) (citation from E. L. Keenan).

56. *AAE* 2: no. 188, p. 319 (1611); *AAE* 3: no. 37, p. 76 (1614); *AAE* 3: no. 126, p. 177 (1622). In 1636, Galich gentry elected men to an assembly "as the whole town" (Got'e, *Akty,* nos. 10–11, pp. 35, 36). In 1648 the Elets gentry petitioned "as a whole town" against corrupt officials (Got'e, *Akty,* no. 15, p. 61). Here *gorod* indicates the provincial gentry who mustered from a particular "service town."

57. Douglas J. Bennet, "The Idea of Kingship in Seventeenth-Century Russia" (Ph.D. diss., Harvard University, 1967), 244. The term was rarely used in Muscovite sources and in the eighteenth century tended to refer to urban citizenship: *Slovar' russkogo iazyka XI–XVII vv.* 4 (1977): 117, 118; *Slovar' russkogo iazyka XVIII veka* 5 (1989): 216–17; and *Slovar' Akademii rossiiskoi* 2 (1790): col. 303. On civil philosophizing, see Bennet, "Kingship," chap. 4, and Paul Bushkovitch, *Religion and Society in Russia: The Sixteenth and Seventeenth Centuries* (Oxford, 1992), chap. 7. See also L. N. Pushkarev, *Obshchestvenno-politicheskaia mysl' Rossii. Vtoraia polovina XVII veka: Ocherki istorii* (Moscow, 1982). Interest in social and political theory continued, but less strongly than interest in other areas: Gary Marker, *Publishing, Printing, and the Origins of Intellectual Life in Russia, 1700–1800* (Princeton, 1985), esp. 208–10, 230–31, and tables 1.1, 2.1, 2.2, 3.2, 3.5, 4.2, 5.1, 8.1.

58. Muscovite usages of *obshchestvo* were rare: *Slovar' russkogo iazyka XI–XVII vv.* 12 (1987): 193–95. There is no entry for either *grazhdanstvo* or *obshchestvo* in these studies of Muscovite terminology: A. L. Diuvernua, *Materialy dlia slovaria drevnerusskogo iazyka* (Moscow, 1894); G. E. Kochin, *Materialy dlia terminologicheskogo slovaria drevnei Rossii* (Moscow, 1937); A. A. Gruzberg, *Chastotnyi slovar' russkogo iazyka vtoroi poloviny XVI–nachala XVII veka* (Perm, 1974); H. W. Schaller et al., *Real- und Sachworterbuch zum altrussischen* (Neuried, 1985). In the eighteenth century, *"obshchestvo"* referred both to society and to organizations: *Slovar' Akademii rossiiskoi* 4 (1793): col. 601. But even in the nineteenth century, the meaning of *"obshchestvo"* as "society" may not have been deeply established: V. I. Dal', *Tolkovyi slovar' zhivogo velikoruskogo iazyka,* 4 vols. (Moscow, 1863–1866), 2: 1214.

On terminology for social estates in the eighteenth century, see Gregory L. Freeze, "The *Soslovie* (Estate) Paradigm and Russian Social History," *American Historical Review* 91, no. 1 (1986): 11–36; David Griffiths, "Of Estates, Charters, and Constitutions," in *Catherine II's Charters of 1785 to the Nobility and the Towns,* trans. and ed. David Griffiths and George E. Munro (Bakersfield, Calif., 1991), xvii–lxix; and Richard Pipes, *Russia under the Old Regime* (New York, 1974), 70–71.

59. This is an argument I have made in "Russia, 1450–1598," in *Oxford Illustrated History of Russia,* ed. Gregory L. Freeze, forthcoming. But cautionary voices about the tendency to exaggerate the centralization and power of the state in the sixteenth century have long been voiced: see works by Tikhomirov, Zimin, and Kappeler cited in note 26 above.

60. This discussion is reminiscent of the debate about the "silence" of medieval Russia: Georges Florovsky, "The Problem of Old Russian Culture," *Slavic Review* 21, no. 1 (1962): 1–15; Francis Thomson, "The Corpus of Slavonic Translations Available to Muscovy . . . ," in *Christianity and the Eastern Slavs,* vol. 1, ed. Boris Gasparov and Olga Raevsky-Hughes (Berkeley and Los Angeles, 1993), 179–214.

61. For an overview of such concepts, see Black, "The Individual and Society," and Jeannine Quillet, "Community, Counsel, and Representation," in Burns, *Cambridge,* 588–606, 520–72; Arthur O. Lovejoy, *The Great Chain of Being* (Cambridge, Mass., 1936).

62. Marshall T. Poe, "'Russian Despotism': The Origins and Dissemination of an Early Modern Commonplace" (Ph.D. diss., University of California, Berkeley, 1993).

63. An exemplar of this model is Charles Tilly, ed., *The Formation of National States in Western Europe* (Princeton, N.J., 1975).

64. For social theory on premodern states, see Anthony Giddens, *A Contemporary Critique of Historical Materialism,* vol. 1, *Power, Property, and the State* (Berkeley and Los Angeles, 1981) and vol. 2, *The National State and Violence* (Berkeley and Los Angeles, 1987); and Michael Mann, *The Sources of Social Power* (Cambridge, 1986). Michel Foucault's idea of power is also salient; see "The Subject and Power," in *Michel Foucault: Beyond Structuralism and Hermeneutics,* ed. Hubert L. Dreyfus and Paul Rabinow (Chicago, 1982), 208–26; and "Truth and Power," in *The Foucault Reader,* ed. Paul Rabinow (New York, 1984), 51–75.

65. In support of this point, see Antony Black's full comment on social terminology and social cohesion in the medieval West cited in note 31 above.

F R A N K E. S Y S Y N

UKRAINIAN SOCIAL TENSIONS BEFORE THE KHMEL'NYTS'KYI UPRISING

THE KHMEL'NYTS'KYI UPRISING stands out among seventeenth-century revolts for its success in overturning the social order. A new ruling elite, the Cossack officers, came to power. The structure of society was transformed as Cossacks became the most numerous corporate order. The populace threw off the control of landed elites and urban patriciates. Changes such as these inspired many East European historians to regard the Khmel'nyts'kyi uprising as revolutionary.

Revolts against the upper orders by peasants and the urban poor were common in early modern Europe, but emergence of new elites and transformations in the social structure were rare. During the Ukrainian revolt violence did bring about significant social change, although this change was far from total. Nineteenth-century Ukrainian populist historians often reacted with consternation, when their research showed their image of an egalitarian, classless Ukraine represented neither the reality after 1648 nor the goals of the rebel leadership. Subsequent research on early modern revolts has shifted the emphasis of inquiry from questioning why complete social reordering did not occur to examining how it was possible for an established elite to be overturned and for much of the populace to improve its social status. Such an examination requires attention to the social divisions and tensions of Ukraine before 1648, which engendered the great revolt and the crisis in Ukrainian society.[1] This social basis will be our topic here.

Three social systems shaped the social divisions and tensions in Ukraine. Corporate orders with their various privileges and obligations divided society into broad social categories (nobles, burghers, and clergy). Associations (religious brotherhoods, the army, confederations) and regional groups (villages, towns, districts) provided the institutions that guaranteed security, established economic mechanisms, and shaped social contacts. Centering on a relatively few great nobles, patronage-client relationships guaranteed rewards, protection, and support for people from the top to the bottom of the social order. Each of these social systems had its own tensions. All three intersected, at times supporting each other, at times creating situations of conflict. In the rapidly changing economic and demographic situation of the Dnieper Basin, the various social systems all had elements of newness and instability.[2]

FORMATION OF CORPORATE ORDERS

The corporate orders that existed in seventeenth-century Ukraine had been adapted from those in Poland and the West and then grafted onto the social institutions left over from the Rus' and Lithuanian periods. The results differed from the original models, since the society that emerged in the Latin Christian West could not be imported in toto into a Byzantine Orthodox culture.[3]

Like all societies of continental Europe, the Polish-Lithuanian Commonwealth was divided into legally defined, hereditary corporate orders. Common rights and obligations gave men in each order common status. Whereas most European societies had complex estate systems, with groups from aristocrats to free peasants maintaining their own institutions and corporate traditions as part of the body politic, the Polish-Lithuanian Commonwealth had an all-important social divide between two groups—nobles (or *szlachta*) who comprised from 5 to 10 percent of the population, and commoners.

Each nobleman enjoyed sweeping personal rights and property rights; and as a body the nobility controlled the institutions of political power, selecting all representatives to the House of Delegates of the Diet and electing those who would serve on the courts, drawing those people solely from its own ranks. All people in offices of the realm and senatorial posts were nobles. The nobles also elected the king. Even clerical ordination did not remove a noble's primary allegiance to his order, and all high ecclesiastical posts were reserved to the nobility. When the *szlachta* described itself as the totality of the nation, it was speaking a certain truth.[4]

The rest of the population were defined by their privileges and obligations, decreed by the king, or increasingly in later years, by the Diet. Burghers, Jews, Armenians, Scots, Tatars, and peasants lived as legally defined communities with no direct voice in the institutions of state. Catholic and

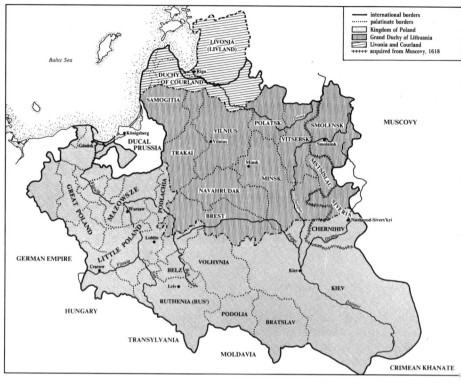

Fig. 1   From *Between Poland and the Ukraine: The Dilemma of Adam Kysil, 1600–1653* by Frank Sysyn (Cambridge, Mass., 1986). Used with permission of the Harvard Ukrainian Research Institute.

Orthodox clergymen observed their own laws, rights, and institutions, but only Catholic bishops sat in the Diet by virtue of their seats in the Senate.

The social structure in the Ukrainian territories had the same legal categories as that in the Polish lands but functioned quite differently. Regional differences were considerable between the lands that had been part of the Kingdom of Poland before 1569 (the Ruthenian, Podolian, and Belz palatinates and the Kholm land) and those lands that had until then been part of the Grand Duchy of Lithuania (the Volhynian, Bratslav, and Kiev palatinates, and the Chernihiv palatinate annexed from Muscovy after the Time of Troubles). In general, the western Ukrainian territories had taken part in the evolution of the Polish social system, although their religious, cultural, and economic differences made for considerable regional variations from many of the Polish territories. The other Ukrainian lands had only been influenced by the Polish model indirectly before 1569, since the Grand Duchy of Lithuania had come closer to Polish patterns in the sixteenth century. They shared many characteristics with the Belarusian lands of the Grand Duchy.

As the political nation of the Commonwealth, the noble order in Ukraine constituted the cement that held the vast territories together.[5] By the early seventeenth century the nobles of the western Ukrainian lands were well integrated into the noble order of the Kingdom. The boyars of the medieval Rus' kingdom-principality had been won over to the Polish political system in the fourteenth and fifteenth centuries by obtaining the political rights of the Polish nobility even though they adhered to the Orthodox faith. By the seventeenth century, only the petty nobles—numerous in certain regions of the Carpathian foothills—remained Orthodox. The middle and great nobles, frequently descendants of immigrants to the territory, were Catholic or Calvinist. Large holdings were common in the lowlands. Podolia had a less stable nobiliary society because it remained exposed to attacks from the steppe. In the western Ukraine, the Polish model of a juridically equal, allodial *szlachta* prevailed, although the *szlachta* rights of the petty nobles were sometimes challenged by their more powerful neighbors. Only Podlachia stood apart, with its Masovian model of a numerous small-holding nobility, primarily of Catholic immigrant origin.

The other Ukrainian lands, like the Grand Duchy of Lithuania, had not undergone the gradual evolution to a noble order that was, at least formally, equal. A small group of wealthy magnates controlled most of the land. Many, among them the Ostroz'kyi, Zaslavs'kyi, Vyshnevets'kyi, Ruzhyns'kyi, and Korets'kyi families, held the title of prince and were descendants of the Rurikids and the Gediminids, the ruling houses of Rus' and Lithuania. Not all the princes were at the top of the hierarchy, however, and some of those who were, such as the Radziwiłłs (Radvila) and Gasztolds, did not claim princely descent.

These great lords had servitors who either lived on lands they owned or resided on grand ducal lands surrounding castles to which they rendered military and other services. Until the sixteenth century, many groups owed service to the ruler or local lord; they ranged in occupation and status from distinguished land-owning families *(zemiane* and *pany)* and lesser military servitors *(boiare)* to couriers, beekeepers, hunters, carters, and tillers.

In the fifteenth and sixteenth centuries, the elite groups of the Grand Duchy were transformed. Large tracts of grand ducal lands passed into the possession of the elite as allodial landholdings, eventually diminishing the power of the ruler and the state. The upper orders of the military service groups secured the privileges of the Polish nobility—including, in the 1560s, the full importation of the nobiliary social and political system. Every family of boyars and military servitors wanted to be accepted as members of the *szlachta*. If they did not succeed, their right to land ownership could be questioned by castle administrators and recognized nobles greedy for the boyars' land.

Importing the Polish model produced elements of friction. The great lords ostensibly accepted the concept of an equal noble elite; they soon found, however, that they could continue to dominate social and political affairs because of their wealth and power. Although the dominant magnate stratum was not a closed group and admitted ambitious nobles and immigrants from other areas of the Commonwealth, a few families did aggregate great powers to the detriment of both the nobility as a whole and the institutions of state. At the other end of the social scale were the boyars and military servitors who did not obtain recognition as nobles. Fearful that their claims to land and privileges would be challenged, the boyars constituted an endangered but volatile element in areas such as the northern Ukraine and the Bar region where they were thickly settled. In the end, these Ukrainian lands had a much lower percentage of nobles than did the Polish territories or the western Ukraine. Except for Volhynia, with its relatively stable nobiliary society, the pre-1569 Lithuanian territories were an area in which new settlement and land acquisitions made for a rapidly changing group of nobles. Given that the nobles made up a smaller part of the total population and, in addition, were an elite in flux, especially since petty nobles from the Polish territories and the western Ukraine flocked to these lands, the position of the noble order was more precarious here than it was in territories such as Mazowsze (Masovia) or in western Ukraine.[6]

As the new nobility formed, so did a new peasantry. The peasantry of the western Ukrainian territories had been subjected to the same process of homogenization and enserfment as that of the Polish territories. By the early seventeenth century, most of the village population had been transformed into an enserfed peasantry performing onerous labor services on manorial estates, which increased in size at the expense of lands cultivated by the peasants. Peasant enserfment was least advanced in the Carpathians where pastoral Moldavian law prevailed and peasant resistance was strongest. In the Podolian palatinate, the spread of manorial economies and serf obligations was hindered by the Tatar attacks. In order to attract settlers, landlords in the early seventeenth century frequently founded *slobody*, that is, settlements free of obligations for between ten and twelve years.

In the lands of the Grand Duchy, the rural population (excluding the nobility) was transformed legally into an enserfed peasantry in the sixteenth century, as the remnants of slavery disappeared and the right of most rural dwellers to migrate from one place to another was restricted. The alienation of state lands to nobles hastened this process by undermining the numerous groups of villagers who paid dues to the ducal treasury. Both grand duke and nobles were interested in modifying their relations with the populace on their lands in order to increase revenues. The *voloka* reform of 1557, on the lands of Queen Bona and other state lands, resulted in resurveying territories and fixing higher taxes for units held by peasants. At first, taxes, produce, and serf labor were exacted principally to sustain the landlord and his servitors, but as the price of agricultural goods rose, peasants were expected also to produce grain for sale. Labor obligations were increased and lands were taken away from peasants, first in Volhynia and then further east. Poor soil and swampland kept the process from spreading to the north; the possibility that the peasants could flee east to free settlements, or *slobody*, for which landlords sought settlers, or even further, beyond the nobles' control, slowed its development in Ukraine. Peasants beyond the Dnieper and in the steppe had ample land, no manors nearby, and few corvée obligations. Legally they were in the same position as any serf; in practice they lived like boyars and Cossacks, although their status was tenuous.[7]

Finally, adding to the nobility and peasantry were the burghers, who in Poland reached their height in both proportion of the total population and economic and cultural significance in the sixteenth century. In the Ukrainian territories, however, this high point came later; new towns were founded and old towns grew in size in the Ruthenian and Volhynian palatinates well into the seventeenth century; further east, particularly in the forest-steppe zone, new settlements multiplied rapidly, and older centers grew larger. Some were royal towns but most were in private hands. Although burghers in private towns had only limited privileges and although the burghers of small settlements were often farmers, they were a rapidly expanding group in the palatinates of Kiev, Chernihiv, and Bratslav.

The burghers formed a corporate order modeled upon that of the Polish burghers, but they never succeeded in becoming a unified group. As in the Polish cities, the patricians, citizens *(pospólstwo)*, and lower groups *(plebs)* did not live in harmony. In the Ukrainian lands, national and religious tensions heightened these social divides. Native Ruthenians were frequently excluded from city councils, courts, and some guilds on religious grounds; they were not Roman Catholics. In the late sixteenth century, in large cities such as Lviv the Ruthenians frequently protested discrimination. Further east the relative strength of the Ruthenians grew, but this merely made any privileges for the Catholics all the more irritating, particularly because the burghers knew that Catholics would attempt to recreate western city law in the east.[8]

Divisions were deepened by the existence of prosperous Armenian communities in Lviv, Kamianets'-Podil's'kyi, and a number of other towns. Administered under their own laws and privileges, the Armenian communities dealt directly with the city magistrate, and as a result Armenians did not fully unite with the people among whom they lived but instead strove to protect their communal rights.[9]

The Jews constituted virtually a separate order. The relatively small Jewish population of the late fifteenth century in the entire Kingdom of Poland (estimated at ten thousand) increased many times in the sixteenth century because of immigration and a high birth rate.[10] In the western Ukrainian lands, old communities such as Lviv expanded rapidly; and new settlements were formed in the Ruthenian and Belz palatinates where the Jewish population was over fifty thousand by the mid-seventeenth century. The Jewish population increased most rapidly in the private cities, where the magnate dictated relations between the Jews and others. The Jews were forbidden to practice certain professions (such as tax farming), as stipulated by royal decrees or by the Catholic church, but these restrictions were now frequently disregarded. The easing of restrictions and the involvement of Jews in new activities were both more marked in the lands annexed to Poland at the Union of Lublin, where Jews increased most rapidly in number. In 1569 an estimated fifteen localities had a Jewish population of three thousand; by 1648 ninety-seven localities had at least forty-five thousand Jews. Positions as leaseholders, estate agents, and toll collectors attracted Jews to the countryside. The attainment of positions of authority as well as conditions on the frontier led to the obligation to bear arms. Consequently, the Jews in this area were far removed from traditional Jewish life and institutions and had closer relations with their neighbors than did the Jews further west.

In the Commonwealth, all men who were not part of the nobility or peasantry, who were not subject to a town magistrate or bound by Jewish privileges and obligations, or who were not members of the clergy, were regarded as a threat to the social order. No area contained as many men whose social status was in question as the Ukrainian frontier. How could one be sure that a new neighbor was the noble he claimed to be? Had a peasant been carried off by the Tatars? Or had he simply taken up residence in a new town? Whence came the hunters, fishers, and herdsmen who dwelled on the edge of the steppe or in the forest? Status, privileges, and obligations were impossible to determine or enforce in towns such as Bila Tserkva or Pereiaslav where officials simply described much of the population as "insubordinate." The frontiersmen, however, frequently looked on social order in a different manner. In addition to rejecting the restraints imposed on the traditional orders, many asserted that they belonged to the free estate of Cossacks.

The Cossacks constituted a free, armed population, which existed nowhere in the Commonwealth except Ukraine, on the border of the Slavic and Tatar worlds. In the mid-sixteenth century Cossacks had emerged as a military organization, based at a stronghold beyond the rapids of the Dnieper. Between 1560 and 1648, the Cossacks evolved from a military organization into a de facto corporate order. Their recruitment by Polish officials into a Cossack register in the late sixteenth century had given some of their numbers status as free warriors, with the right to maintain their families on royal lands. Although the government sought to limit their numbers and to prevent the Cossacks from developing into a hereditary corporate order, wars forced the government to permit the expansion of the Host. The inhabitants of the Dnieper Basin who viewed themselves as Cossacks, whether a male of the family was included in the register or not, continued to multiply. In essence, a corporate order of a new warrior class was *in statu nascendi,* but strong opposition existed among the nobility to any attempt to recognize the Cossacks as an order rather than just a military unit.[11]

A society of orders was in the process of being established, along lines already drawn in Poland and most of the western Ukraine, but the social reality of the Dnieper Basin was very different. According to the imported model, peasants were to be enserfed provisioners of labor and dues, not inhabitants of free settlements who recognized no overlords. All land was to be owned by nobles, not the Cossacks and boyars who had long farmed it. Commercial rights and privileges were to be the domain of townsmen and their guilds or of Jews and other privileged groups, not of frontier settlers who distilled their own alcohol and sold hides, horses, and furs. Eventually, the full vigor of city law would come to royal and private towns of the Dnieper Basin as it had to western Ukraine. Non-Catholics would be excluded from guilds and the government of towns. With the implementation of city law would come the more structured division of the towns' inhabitants that caused so much resentment among the plebs in Polish and western Ukrainian towns. In sum, if the Polish system of corporate orders provided substantial privileges that allowed certain segments of the population to conduct a more complex economy, it also excluded other segments of the population from activities they had long carried on. It froze men into social categories.

ASSOCIATIONAL AND REGIONAL TIES: SOURCES OF SOCIAL COHESION AND TENSION

Although people primarily thought of themselves in terms of their place in the corporate order, they also grouped themselves in professional or economic, religious (clerical orders, devotional societies), and political associations. Bonds were also formed on the basis of common residence. A village that contained peasants, priests, petty nobles, Jews, and even a manorial lord faced a common difficulty during a natural disaster or assault. Towns that otherwise had contending burghers, Jews, clergymen, and nobles buried differences in times of danger or economic crisis. An entire region was united when mutual interests were threatened or when foreign attack was imminent. Ties of collegiality or geography did, then, occasionally override distinctions of corporate order, although separation by social order was still inherent in the very structure of organizational and residence patterns. Guilds confined to burghers that excluded Jews and Armenians, or villages in Mazowsze and Podlachia inhabited entirely by nobles, did nothing to strengthen inter-order contacts.

Between the sixteenth and seventeenth centuries, the Ukrainian lands underwent changes in social relations that dissolved some bonds of community solidarity. In the mid-sixteenth century, the overriding concern of the inhabitants of the Kiev, Bratslav, and Podolian palatinates had been defense against Tatar raids. Led by the great princes and the keepers of royal castles and lands, the entire community was organized for mutual protection. Able-bodied men such as Cossacks were enlisted. Even burghers and Jews were required to bear arms so they could help defend the community should the need arise. Volhynia, although better protected, still shared many of the characteristics of the frontier lands. Gradually, social relations changed because of continuing economic development (above all the rising value of land) and population increase. This increase was accompanied by a growing divergence in social patterns of the population, a breaking of social ties, and the introduction of a system of rigidly defined corporate orders that did not correspond to the activities and division of power of the population.

As the frontier was pushed ever further south and east, militarization of the general population was not so vital. With the formation of the Quarter Army *(Wojsko Kwarciane)* in 1562, the primary responsibility for defense had passed to this standing army. The rise of great magnate estates with paid military troops also reduced the need to involve the whole population. Specialization in military affairs made for a more efficient defense, but it also shifted military power in Ukraine from the population at large to the hetmans, who led the standing army, and to the magnates with private troops. This most directly affected the Cossacks, who could no longer exercise the privileges they had won when they were needed for defense of the frontiers. For the same reason, specialization in military affairs reduced the independence of boyars, peasants, and burghers. The army that wintered on royal lands in Ukraine seemed to many inhabitants a greater pestilence than the Tatars. The private armies of the magnates lived off their great estates.

As the economy of the Dnieper Basin grew more complex, the social structure grew more rigid. Men were now more clearly divided into villagers and townsmen; agriculturalists, pastoralists, and hunter-gatherers; producers of agricultural goods, artisans, and traders. This process, virtually complete in the western Ukraine and Volhynia, had advanced far in the Right Bank and was reaching into the Left Bank and the Steppe.

Along with the new social patterns came a breaking of social ties. The frontier lords had led a society of boyars, Cossacks, townsmen, and rural settlers who had banded together in a harsh world. The new society was one in which Cossacks came to understand that government officials and magnates now considered them an unruly element of the population. Boyars no longer saw their lord as a benefactor to whom they owed military service but as an oppressor who questioned their rights to land and social status. Peasants who had once regarded the few towns as centers of defense and commerce now saw them as monopolizing artisanal and commercial activities once carried on by the entire population. Townsmen who had once welcomed the few Jews of the Ukraine as fellow defenders came to see them as a threat; burghers and Jews were pitted against each other to the magnate's own advantage.

At the same time that society in the Ukrainian lands saw the breakdown of an earlier cohesion, social formations existed that united people, at times across the lines of corporate order. Such groups served both as nuclei for maintaining the social order and for mobilizing forces of social discontent.

Although small, the most important of all associations was the standing army. Approximately four thousand troops were maintained in the 1640s. They could be augmented, however, by private armies, the royal guard (about twelve hundred strong), urban and palatinate troops, the Cossacks, and the levy of the nobility. The army, composed of both domestic and foreign units, included nobles, peasants, and some burghers. Social divisions still remained, however, as the nobles, always less than one-fifth of the total, tended to join the heavy cavalry units. However much the nobles in the army stressed their theoretical ties to the entire nobility who appropriated funds, they still faced the same problems as the common soldiers when it came to obtaining quarters and pay. They then provided the leadership for soldiers' confederations and for delegations sent to the authorities to demand remedial action. The standing army often functioned as a political entity just as the Cossacks did, and like the Cossacks, it was centered in the Ukrainian territories and often quartered on royal lands. Unlike the Cossacks, it did not evolve into a separate social order. Military service was not an end in itself: it was seen as a way of improving social status; bravery in battle could bring ennoblement. The *Wojsko Kwarciane* constituted the major support of the existing social and political system. Its destruction at the outset of the revolt removed this support.[12]

The other important military association was the Zaporozhian Host, which comprised men from noble, burgher, peasant, and old Cossack background. It could not be assimilated into the new system of orders or of security, which had no place for such a group. During the 1620s and 1630s, the Host had led a number of revolts in Ukraine. After the standing army put down the revolt of 1637–1638, the government assumed the right to appoint officers. A military unit of six thousand men in the 1630s, it was not part of the standing army but a poorly recompensed local militia. The Cossacks of the register of six thousand had more in common with the thousands of other "Cossacks" living on government lands who, without official recognition as Cossacks, melded with their families among the frontier settlers. Although the autonomy of the Host was much diminished after 1638, it remained an association of military men who smarted from their humiliation. It was the Zaporozhian Host that provided the structure to carry on the revolt of 1648.

The Orthodox bishoprics, monasteries, and parishes provided another unifying force, which could be used by the disaffected. The clearest example of an organization uniting men of various social strata, albeit based on the burghers, was the Orthodox brotherhood. Founded to promote religious and cultural renewal, to defend the interests of the church, to promote the economic welfare of its members, and to struggle against Catholic patricians, the brotherhoods enrolled not only Ruthenian burghers but also nobles, priests, and Cossacks into their ranks. In a way they resembled the communal institutions of the Jews and the Armenians, but without their juridical powers. The brotherhoods' willingness to enroll people regardless of order or rank laid the groundwork for the Orthodox unity of purpose after 1648. While all Orthodox might not support the revolt, the institutions of the church were effectively utilized by the rebels.[13]

In the Commonwealth most people lived in villages, which varied greatly in size, economic function, and social composition. Some villages (in Podlachia and Mazowsze) were almost exclusively inhabited by nobles; others (in Polish territories or western Ukraine and Volhynia) were divided up among several nobles. The most common pattern, however, was ownership by a noble. In the fifteenth and sixteenth centuries, the autonomy of the Polish village was undermined as the nobles who owned them established manorial domains and replaced community officials with their own bailiffs. In such villages, the manor controlled the parish priest and the revenues from taverns and mills.

A large number of settlements in the Dnieper Basin remained relatively free from these new trends. In the basin's northern reaches, the old settlements that exploited the forest and rendered dues to their owner retained their internal autonomy. In the Left Bank and the Steppe, new *slobody* settlements were frequently founded, on the promise of freedom from rents or before claims to ownership had been clearly established. These villages were often composed of large households *(dvoryshcha)* and related families who frequently cooperated in working the land and sharing the income *(siabry)*. Churches were few in this region, but the population had considerable choice in selecting clergy and could turn to neighboring monasteries to provide religious services. In the forests the villages were small with numerous isolated homesteads of beekeepers and hunters, but in the Steppe they were large for reasons of security and the inhabitants traveled far to fields and flocks.

Villages under the domain of royal castles or on territories where landlords had long-established claims were subject to regular dues and obligations and to greater outside influence: churches subject to patrons; collections of taxes and duties on measured lands; regulation of milling and distilling. These villages came to resemble settlements common in the Right Bank where the landlord had full control over the villages—exacting duties and labor according to his needs and inserting his bailiffs and collectors, at times Jews, into village life. In Volhynia and western Ukraine, the manorial economy was fully established and the village was divided between a subject peasantry and a manor and its staff. Social tension was thus greatest in the manorial domains in the west, yet the independent villages of the east proved to be the vital force when it came to overturning the established authorities and rebuilding the social order after 1648.

The towns (that is, settlements governed by urban law) were increasing rapidly in number throughout the Dnieper Basin in the early seventeenth century. A few great royal towns such as Kiev maintained relative autonomy, although they were under the influence of the palatine of the Kiev palatinate. The towns on royal lands were more directly controlled by administrators. Most numerous were the private towns, which had limited autonomy. In the steppe zone and Left Bank, magnates granted municipal rights to many settlements so they could collect revenue from their trade and artisan production. Otherwise, these towns differed little from the surrounding villages. The distinction between town and village was chiefly one of how the economy was regulated. In addition, towns were often founded with the sole aim of attracting settlers to a lord's lands.

Further north and west, the towns were older and the division between city and village was more marked. The Volhynian palatinate had numerous royal cities, such as Luts'k and Volodymyr, though no great metropolis; the private town of Ostrih was the largest. The Ruthenian palatinate had its great city of Lviv and many old royal cities that had the most developed urban traditions and maintained the clearest distinctions from the village.

The urban guilds, with their elaborate procedures and internal divisions, provided the major economic organizations for urban dwellers. In the frontier zones they were predominantly Orthodox; where they included Jews across traditional divisions of orders, they served as an integrating force. Further to the west, the guilds were more likely to reflect communal—Catholic, Orthodox, Armenian, Jewish—divisions, and therefore to serve as institutional structures of communal hostility.

Towns in the south and east were natural centers for rebellion. Although traditions of urban autonomy were new there and the degree of real autonomy severely limited, a large proportion of the population lived in the numerous urban settlements. Towns that still faced frequent Tatar raids were accustomed to common action; the common resentments of burghers, Cossacks, and undefined inhabitants outweighed internal social tensions. In the north above Kiev and in the Right Bank, towns were proportionately fewer, less dynamic, and had an older urban tradition. They were more likely to be populated by nobles, Catholics, and Jews than Cossacks. As one moved westward into Volhynia, towns were even more likely to be divided into contending factions of Catholics, Orthodox, Jews, nobles, and clergymen. In the Ruthenian palatinate, this pattern was more marked still, the institutions of urban life were more elaborate, and towns were less likely to be under the control of a single lord.

In general, in the south and east, towns were likely to be relatively homogeneous and easily united in revolt; in the north and west they were divided into hostile groups—patriciates, *pospólstwo,* and plebs—and conflicting communities. Since the urban underclasses were often Ukrainians and Orthodox, the support for revolt came from internal urban tensions. The differences between the west and the east can be seen in a comparison of Lviv and Kiev in the early seventeenth century.

Lviv had expanded rapidly in the sixteenth century, reaching its high point of over thirty thousand inhabitants just at midcentury. Ruled by a council of forty members, the city was dominated by a Roman Catholic patriciate of forty or fifty families. The Armenians and Orthodox were allowed two council members for each community, although the poorer Ukrainians were rarely permitted to avail themselves of this right. Catholics also dominated the approximately thirty guilds, with Ukrainians confined to the lower positions of journeymen or non-guild artisans. The numerous Jewish inhabitants, with their 150 guild masters (compared to 600 in the burgher guilds), constituted a major economic force in the city. With its fifteen Catholic and three Orthodox monasteries, thirty Catholic, fifteen Orthodox, and three Armenian churches, and its three synagogues, Lviv had large numbers of clergymen, religious, and retainers living under their own legal systems. The nobles within the city, the noble landowners in its periphery, and the villages dependent on the city all added to the heterogeneity of the town's population. Lviv had a deeply engrained urban tradition and rule, a population divided into numerous contending factions, and considerable social tension. The smaller towns in Galicia and Volhynia were more or less the same; they differed chiefly in their weaker urban traditions and in the structures that integrated the various groups in each city.[14]

Despite its ancient origin, Kiev reemerged as an urban society (as opposed to a center of administration and defense) only in the early seventeenth century. It consisted of three settlements—the upper city, the Podil, and the Pechers'k—but was beginning to take on the look of a single city. Poles, Armenians, and Jews numbered among the population, but in 1620 the overwhelming majority of its ten or fifteen thousand inhabitants were Orthodox

Ukrainians. There were also nobles and Cossacks. The Caves Monastery and other Orthodox institutions had considerable holdings, as did the Catholic bishop, the Dominican monastery, and the four Catholic churches. The leading burgher families were Ukrainians, with the Balyka and Khodyka families vying for power. The mayor of Kiev, Fedir Khodyka, created great tension by siding with the Uniates and Catholics in the 1620s, but other burgher patricians espoused the Orthodox cause.[15]

Municipal institutions and traditions were weaker in Kiev than in Lviv, but economic expansion in Kiev allowed the establishment of an ever more assertive urban stratum. The urban population that earned a living through handicrafts and trade was more homogeneous in Kiev than in Lviv. In the smaller and newer towns of the Kiev region, urban autonomy was weaker, but homogeneity was greater. Tensions certainly existed among the burghers, but they were not great enough to outweigh common resentment against the administrator or landlord who interfered in urban affairs.

Towns and villages were components in two of three types of regional groupings—the political and the economic. Regional political societies were formed by the counties and palatinates that provided for public order, raised local militias, and assessed taxes. Since the offices and institutions in these units were held exclusively by the nobility, they primarily served as regional units of noble society. Jews, burghers, and clergy merely regarded them as the source of the authority to which they collectively turned. In the Dnieper Basin, the counties were so vast that they could not easily serve as administrative units for noble society, to say nothing of general administration. More vital were the social ties formed by economic units. They included *starostwa* (royal lands), magnate *ordynacje* (entailed domains), *włości* or *kluczy* (large tracts belonging to one owner), and manorial units comprising more than one village. The first two also functioned as the administrative units for the state to collect taxes and military obligations. The third and fourth were limited to economic activities controlled by a single lord.[16]

Associations and regional groups provided structures that either furthered or hindered the revolt and social change. Ultimately the small standing army and the regional administrative associations drawn from the nobility proved unable to control the social groups arrayed against the old order. Those who rose in revolt had the advantage of the Cossack military structure, the Orthodox church institutions, and relatively intact village and urban communal institutions in the Dnieper Basin.

PATRON-CLIENT NETWORKS

The third major social division, the chain of patron-client relationships, cut across the social orders and associational-regional groups. These relationships frequently involved multiple and changing ties. The king often served as a patron for certain groups (Jews, Cossacks), royal cities, individuals (courtiers, magnates), but the same groups might have other patrons (particularly magnates) as well. Magnates could decide to withdraw from royal patronage. The Commonwealth and the eastern lands in particular contained numerous patronage networks as magnates assembled their own group of noble clients whose careers they fostered. Although allodial landholdings and royal lands under a magnate's administration constituted the core of a patronage system, those who could exert influence to obtain offices and land grants from the king and Diet, to resolve judicial disputes or to secure legislation, could also build networks of clients. In this way a magnate could assemble a clientele far beyond his own holdings.[17]

In the Polish lands, the magnate patronage system was a new phenomenon in the late sixteenth century, but in the east it was merely another form of the old system of princes and vassals. Innovation lay in the spread of the great holdings into new areas and the rise of new families (including immigrants to Ukraine) to magnate status. There were, however, more significant differences in the relation of the magnate elite to the rest of the population and to the institutions of the Commonwealth. No longer was the relationship one of a distant overlord to military servitors, such as the Ostroz'kyi princes had been in the Volhynian and Kiev palatinates in the sixteenth century.

By the early seventeenth century, the magnates' role had changed in a number of ways. First, they were drawn into the sphere of Polish society. Many converted to Catholicism and this, in addition to the arrival of Polish magnates who gained landholding in Ukraine (Stanisław Lubomirski, Tomasz Zamoyski), alienated the magnate stratum from the population at large. Second, they responded to the new economic opportunities to increase their revenues by constituting a new efficiency, demanding the replacement of imprecise obligations of military services and produce with contractual relations overseen and enforced by military men, leaseholders, and Jews who would provide the services of protection and provision of funds that the magnate's court required. Just as the demands increased and new groups (Jews, Polish nobles) were introduced to realize these demands, the magnates limited their contacts with much of the population; the holders of royal castles and lands rarely visited the territories that they were required to defend.

Jeremi Wiśniowiecki, who built an empire in the Left Bank, did reside in his vast domain, but he was something of an exception. Jakub Sobieski or Tomasz Zamoyski, for example, did not. In 1640 in the Kiev palatine, a mere 7 percent of all landholders (twenty-seven individuals) controlled 68 percent of the households (47,698). In 1629 in the Bratslav palatinate, the respective figures were 9 percent of landholders (eighteen individuals) controlling 80 percent of all households (51,918).[18] In other words a very few families controlled the economic and political affairs of the Ukrainian lands. Large numbers of servitors, agents, leaseholders, tax farmers, soldiers, clergymen, all depended on the magnate's benevolence; in particular, leaseholders and toll collectors who purchased their rights to lands and revenue collection depended on the magnate's favor. It was for this reason that they exacted the maximum from the people; they could not be sure their contract with the lord would last more than a short time.

The network each magnate built up was meant to regularize economic life, to control his subjects and their associations, and to establish the trappings of a society of orders similar to that in Polish territories. Nobles from the local population were allowed little economic and political autonomy. Although many middle and even petty nobles felt some class solidarity with the magnates as leaders of the noble order, they resented their power. City dwellers might benefit from a magnate's grant of municipal law, but they found magnates' interference in their affairs irksome. The boyars and peasants realized that the magnates' system attacked their economic activities and legal rights. Instead of integrating the Cossacks into their patronage/client system, as the magnate leaders of the mid-sixteenth century had done, the magnates of the seventeenth century challenged the Cossacks' social and economic status, especially after the revolts of the 1620s and 1630s. All groups resented the depredation of the magnates' troops.

The creation of the magnates' patron/client networks proved a major source of social tension in Ukraine. In the Dnieper Basin, the population became divided sharply into those who were integrated into these networks and those who were not. Ultimately those who were excluded struck out against the entire chain of the magnates' networks, which stretched from grand palaces to rickety Jewish taverns.

CONCLUSION

The Ukrainian territories had various interlocking social systems, and each system had its own tensions. The social system was least well entrenched in the Steppe and on the Left Bank. The system of social orders defining the population's activities and privileges had not been well established. Rural communities were little affected by outside forces, and the towns, although limited in privileges, were cohesive and growing. The Cossacks who lived below Kiev formed a group that did not have a place in the social order but that wielded considerable power. Although even there the magnates controlled the population with their military forces and agents, they could not depend on a dense network of noble landowners to police their domains and maintain order. In these regions a dynamic and growing population did not wish to be fit into a straitjacket of corporate orders that would limit their economic activities and freedom. The Cossack regiments, village communities, towns, and Orthodox religious brotherhoods were institutions that were all potential centers of resistance. Finally, the groups that did not benefit from the client/patronage system of the magnates were both numerous and active. They included boyars and vassal nobles whose right to land was questioned as well as the Cossacks, burghers, and peasants, whose prognosis for the future was one of increasing social oppression.

As one moved northward and westward social control increased, along with the division into stable corporate orders, with the exception of the sparsely populated forest zone. Here peasants performed labor services, and manorial domains and allodial landholding were the rule. Leaseholders were more numerous than military servitors. Cities and villages were more sharply differentiated. Townsmen were divided among Catholics, Orthodox, and Jews, making towns less united and therefore less able to act as a unit. Villages were firmly controlled by the landlord's administrators and bailiffs. Peasants had heavy obligations and neither the effective leadership nor the necessary weapons to express their discontent actively. Social tensions were rife in this area but were more complex than in the south and east, where it was mainly the population at large against the magnates and their followers.

In western Volhynia and the Ruthenian and Belz palatinates, landowners were more numerous and magnates possessed a lesser percentage of the land. Nobles were numerous and the petty nobles, who often could not match the wealth of boyars further east, were fully recognized members of the noble brotherhood. Here the density of nobles represented a stable influence—aside from petty Orthodox nobles in the Carpathians who were a source of religious discontent, and after 1648, for Cossack recruits. Manorial domains were worked by serfs. The cities were controlled by Catholic patriciates, and well-established Jewish communities engaged in trade and manufacture. Here, however, just as the Orthodox petty nobles—though not the leaders in their order—brought their status and experience to such causes as the struggle for Orthodoxy, so the Ukrainian burghers, particularly in Lviv, expressed grievances against discrimination and formed the brotherhoods that served as catalysts for religious and cultural activity. In general, however, the social order had considerable stability in these territories (except for the Carpathian zone and the Polissian marshes), and the forces supporting the social order had the area firmly under control. The revolt of 1648 would permit peasants and the urban plebs to rebel, but only the Cossack army's actual presence prevented the dominant social strata from restoring the pre-1648 order.

The social contradictions of the Ukrainian lands were great. A small magnate group had concentrated wealth and power, even though it was not a legally defined stratum and its members were officially merely nobles. However, in contrast to the Polish territories where the social weight of the *szlachta* order was great, Volhynia and the Dnieper Basin had only a thin *szlachta* stratum. These areas had instead vigorous groups of boyars, Cossacks, burghers, and peasants who were excluded from *szlachta* status. These groups felt threatened by the encroachment of the magnates. Opportunities within the magnates' empires were often taken by "interloper" petty nobles not native to the territory. But even small noble landowners, native or immigrant, feared expropriation by the magnates. The new social order corresponded neither to the espoused Polish social model nor to the social realities of Ukraine. It alienated the most assertive elements of Ukraine's population. It attempted to reduce peasants, burghers, boyars, and Cossacks to subject status. It was portrayed as bringing order and security to Ukraine, but it could not guarantee internal peace or external security. Thus it was a social system based on too small a segment of the population trying to impose a new social order on too large and restive a population. Although the circles of social discontent reached far into the western Ukrainian and Belarusian lands, the weakest point of the new social order was the lower Dnieper

Basin, the very region where it came into conflict with a restive military force, the Zaporozhian army.

As a consequence of the revolt, in the Dnieper Basin of Ukraine a social system of magnate power, noble privilege, and peasant subjugation—taking shape since the sixteenth century—collapsed. Where the system was not yet established and the population had not yet accepted its norms (it cannot be assumed, for example, that the peasants of the Left Bank provided any labor services), the revolt served to maintain the social order of frontiersmen against the new social system. Where the social system had become more entrenched, it was overthrown. In replacing the magnate networks by a society organized largely by the institutions of the Cossack army, a new social structure emerged in the lands where the revolt succeeded.

NOTES

1. Mykhailo Hrushevs'kyi, *Istoriia Ukrainy-Rusy,* 10 vols. (reprint, New York, 1954–1957), discusses Ukrainian society from the fifteenth to the seventeenth centuries (vols. 5–7) and the social aspects of the revolt (vols. 8–10). The most comprehensive discussion of social change is Vasyl Hryshko, "Do suspil'noi struktury Khmel'nychchyny," *Zapysky Naukovoho Tovarystva im Shevchenka* 156 (1948), 7–60. See also Veniamin Miakotin, *Ocherki sotsial'noi istorii Ukrainy v XVII–XVIII stol.* (Prague, 1925), 88

2. The most comprehensive discussion of Ukrainian society in the seventeenth century is A. I. Baranovich, *Ukraina nakanune osvoboditel'noi voiny serediny XVII v.* (Moscow, 1959). Other discussions of Ukrainian society can be found in V. I. Borysenko, *Sotsial'no-ekonomichnyi rozvytok Livoberezhnoi Ukrainy v druhii polovyni XVII st.* (Kiev, 1976); V. A. Diadychenko, *Narysy suspil'no-politychnoho ustroiu Livoberezhnoi Ukrainy kintsia XVII–pochatku XVIII st.* (Kiev, 1959); I. P. Kryp"iakevych, *Bohdan Khmel'nyts'kyi* (Kiev, 1954); M. V. Dovnar-Zapol'skii, "Sotsial'no-ekonomichnaia struktura litovsko-belaruskae dziarzhavy v XVI–XVIII vt.," *Historychno-Arkheolichichnyi Zbornik* 1 (1927), 3–66; Horst Jablonowski, *Westrussland zwischen Wilna und Moskau* (Leiden, 1955); and Rudolf Bächtold, *Südwestrussland im Spätmittelalter, Basler Beiträge zur Geschichtswissenschaft* 38 (Basel, 1951).

3. For general discussions of Polish society, see Ireneusz Ihnatowicz, Antoni Mączak, and Benedykt Zientara, *Społeczeństwo polskie od X do XX wieku* (Warsaw, 1979); Józef Andrzej Gierowski, *Historia Polski, 1505–1764* (Warsaw, 1979); Jarema Maciszewski, "Społeczeństwo," in *Polska XVII wieku: Państwo, społeczeństwo, kultura,* ed. Janusz Tazbir (Warsaw, 1969); and Andrzej Wyczański, *Polska-Rzeczpospolitą szlachecką, 1454–1764* (Warsaw, 1965).

4. For general discussions of the Polish nobility, see Jarema Maciszewski, *Szlachta polska i jej państwo* (Warsaw, 1969); Henryk Wisner, *Najjaśniejsza Rzeczpospolita: Szkice z dziejów Polski szlacheckiej, XVI–XVII wieku* (Warsaw, 1978); Andrzej Kamiński, "The *Szlachta* of the Polish-Lithuanian Commonwealth and Their Government," in *The Nobility in Russia and Eastern Europe,* ed. Ivo Banac and Paul Bushkovitch (New Haven, 1983), 17–46.

5. On the nobles of the Ukrainian lands, see Nataliia Iakovenko, *Ukrains'ka shliakhta z XIV st. do seredyny XVII st.* (Kiev, 1993); Frank Sysyn, "The Problem of Nobilities in the Ukrainian Past: The Polish Period, 1569–1648," in *Rethinking*

Ukrainian History, ed. Ivan L. Rudnytsky (Edmonton, 1981), 29–102; Viacheslav Lypyns'kyi (Wacław Lipiński), *Szlachta na Ukrainie: Udział jej w życiu na tle jego dziejów* (Cracow, 1909); Z. L. Radzimiński and W. Rulikowski, *Kniaziowie i szlachta między Sanem, Wieprzem, Bugiem, Prypecią, Siniucha, Dniestrem i północnymi stokami Karpat osiedleni* (Cracow, 1880), and for western Ukraine, Władysław Łoziński, *Prawem i lewem: Obyczaje na Czerwonej Rusi w pierwszej połowie XVII wieku,* 2 vols., 5th ed. (Cracow, 1957).

6. See F. Rawita-Gawroński, "Losy wielkiej fortuny na kresach ukrainnych," *Studja i szkice historyczne,* ser. 2 (Lviv, 1903); Oleksandr Baranovych, *Zaliudnennia Volyns'koho voevodstva v pershii polovyni XVII st.* (Kiev, 1930); and Zbigniew Anusik, "Struktura społeczna szlachty bracławskiej w świetle taryfy podymnego z 1629 roku," *Przegląd Historyczny* 76 (1985): 233–53.

7. On the peasantry in the Ukraine, see M. V. Dovnar-Zapol'skii, *Ocherki po organizatsii zapadno-russkogo krest'ianstva vo vtoroi polovine XVI v.* (Kiev, 1905); I. D. Boiko, *Selianstvo Ukrainy v druhii polovyni XVI–pershii polovyni XVII st.* (Kiev, 1963); V. O. Diadychenko, ed., *Istoriia selianstva URSR* (Kiev, 1967); O. M. Lazarevs'kyi, *Malorossiiskie pospolitie krest'iane, 1648–1783* (Kiev, 1908); Mykola Tkachenko, "Narysy z istorii selian na Livoberezhnyi Ukraini v XVII–XVIII vv.," *Zapysky Istorychno-Filolohychnoho Viddilu Vse-Ukrains'koi Akademii Nauk* 26 (1931): 33–179; Veniamin Miakotin, *Prikreplenie krestianstva levoberezhnoi Ukrainy v XVII–XVIII vv.* (Sofiia, 1932).

8. On towns in Poland, the basic work is J. Ptaśnik, *Miasta i mieszczaństwo w dawnej Polsce* (Warsaw, 1949). See also Tomasz Opas, "Miasta prywatne a Rzeczpospolita," *Kwartalnik Historyczny* 78 (1971): 28–48; A. Wyrobisz, "Small Towns in Sixteenth and Seventeenth Century Poland," *Acta Poloniae Historia* 34 (1976): 153–63; A. Wyrobisz, "Rola miast prywatnych w Polsce w XVI i XVII wieku," *Przegląd Historyczny* 65 (1974): 19–46; and Bohdan Baranowski, *Życie codzienne małego miasteczka w XVII i XVIII w.* (Warsaw, 1975). On Ukrainian towns, a useful starting point is the twenty-six-volume series *Istoriia mist i sil Ukrains'koi RSR* (Kiev, 1973). See also O. S. Kompan, *Mista Ukrainy v druhii polovyni XVII st.* (Kiev, 1963); P. V. Mykhailyna, *Mista Ukrainy v period feodalizmu* (Chernivtsi, 1971); S. Alexandrowicz, "Geneza i rozwój sieci miast Białorusi i Ukrainy do połowy XVII w.," *Acta Baltica-Slavica* 7 (1970): 47–100; Maurycy Horn, *Walka klasowa i konflikty społeczne w miastach Rusi Czerwonej w latach 1600–1647 na tle stosunków gospodarczych* (Wrocław, Cracow, Warsaw, 1972); and Eliżbieta Hornowa, *Stosunki ekonomiczno-społeczne w miastach ziemi halickiej w latach 1590–1648* (Opole, 1963). On urban participation in the Khmel'nyts'kyi revolt, see P. W. Mykhailyna, *Vyzvol'na borot'ba trudovoho naselennia mist Ukrainy, 1569–1654* (Kiev, 1975); O. S. Kompan, *Uchast' mis'koho naselennia u vyzvol'nii viini ukrains'koho narodu 1648–1654 rr.* (Kiev, 1954); and G. Karpov, "Malorossiiskie goroda v epokhu prisoedineniia Malorossii k Veliko-Rossii," *Letopis' Zaniatii Arkheograficheskoi Kommissii* 6 (1872–1875): 1–43.

9. Ia. Dashkevych, *Armianskie kolonii na Ukraine v istochnikakh i literature, XV–XIX vekov: Istoriograficheskii ocherk* (Erevan, 1962), and his "The Armenians in the Time of Bohdan Xmel'nyc'kyj," *Harvard Ukrainian Studies* 3–4 (1979–1980): 166–88.

10. On Jews in the Commonwealth and in Ukraine, see Bernard Weinryb, *The Jews of Poland: A Social and Economic History of the Jewish Community of Poland from 1160 to 1800* (Philadelphia, 1972); Simon Dubnow, *History of the Jews in Russia and Poland* (Philadelphia, 1916), vol. 1; Frank Sysyn, "The Jewish Factor in the Khmelnytsky Uprising," in *Ukrainian-Jewish Relations in Historical Perspective,* ed. Howard Aster and Peter Potichnyj, 2d ed. (Edmonton, 1990), 43–51; Salo Baron, *A Social and Religious History of the Jews,* vol. 16, *Poland-Lithuania, 1500–1650,* 2d ed. (New London,

1976); Shmuel Ettinger, "Jewish Participation in the Settlement of Ukraine in the Sixteenth and Seventeenth Centuries," in Aster and Potichnyj, *Ukrainian-Jewish Relations,* 22–30; and Maurycy Horn, *Żydzi na Rusi Czerwonej w XVI i pierwszej połowie XVII w działalność gospodarcza na tle rozwoju demograficznego* (Warsaw, 1975).

11. On the Cossacks, see V. Golobutskii, *Zaporozhskoe kazachestvo* (Kiev, 1957), and Zbigniew Wójcik, *Dzikie pola w ogniu: O Kozaczyźnie w Rzeczypospolitej,* 3d rev. ed. (Warsaw, 1968).

12. On the military, see Jan Wimmer, *Zarys dziejów wojskowości polskiej do roku 1864,* 2 vols. (Warsaw, 1965–1966); and Bohdan Baranowski, *Organizacja wojska polskiego w latach trzydziestych i czterdziestych XVII wieku,* Prace Komisji Wojskowo-Historycznej Ministerstwa Obrony Narodowej, ser. A, v. 10 (Warsaw, 1957).

13. On the church, see Kazimierz Chodynicki, *Kościół Prawosławny a Rzeczpospolita Polska, 1370–1632* (Warsaw, 1934). For the 1632–1648 period, see the monumental work of S. T. Golubev, *Kievskii Mitropolit Petr Mogila i ego spodvizhniki: Opyt tserkovno-istoricheskogo issledovaniia,* 2 vols. (Kiev, 1883–1898). Of more recent works, see Ludomir Bieńkowski, "Organizacja Kościoła Wschodniego w Polsce," in *Kościół w Polsce,* 2 vols. to date (Cracow, 1968–), 2: 733–1050 (on the Orthodox and Uniate churches); and Ivan Vlasovs'kyi, *Narys istorii ukrainskoi pravoslavnoi tserkvy,* 4 vols. in 5 books (New York, 1955–1966).

14. There is a great deal of material on Lviv. See Władysław Loziński, *Patrycyat i mieszczaństwo lwowskie w XVI–XVII wieku* (Lviv, 1895); S. Bilets'kyi, "Sotsial'na struktura naselennia L'vova u seredyni XVII st.," *Z istorii zakhidnoukrains'kykh zemel'* 4 (1960): 3–14; Ia. P. Kis', *Promyslovist' L'vova u period feodalizmu* (Lviv, 1968); Julian Ptaśnik, "Walka o demokratyzację Lwowa od XVI w. do XVIII w.," *Kwartalnik Historyczny* 39, no. 2 (1925): 228–57; A. Prochaska, *Lwów i szlachta* (Lviv, 1919); *Narysy istorii L'vova* (Lviv, 1956); *Istoriia L'vova* (Lviv, 1956).

15. Volodymyr Antonovych (Vladimir Antonovich), "Kiev, ego sud'ba i znachenie s XIV do XVI st.," *Kievskaia Starina* 1 (1882), 1–48; and his "Predislovie," *Arkhiv Iugo-Zapadnoi Rossii,* pt. 5, v. 1 (Kiev, 1869), 1–94; O. K. Kasymenko, *Istoriia Kieva* (Kiev, 1959–1960).

16. On the nobility and the dietines in the Ukrainian territories, see Stanisław Śreniowski, *Organizacja sejmiku halickiego* (Lviv, 1938); Tadeusz Kostkiewicz, *Działalność kulturalna sejmiku ruskiego* (Lviv, 1939); N. Ivanishev, "Predislovie," *Arkhiv IuZR,* pt. 2, vol. 1 (Kiev, 1861), xv–lxiv; Antoni J. [Rolle], "Dzieje szlachty okolicznej w owruckim powiecie," *Biblioteka Warszawska* (1881) no. 2, 18–39, 183–200, 352–67.

17. On the magnates, see Teresa Zielińska, *Magnateria polska epoki saskiej* (Wrocław, 1977); Władysław Czapliński and Adam Kersten, eds., *Magnateria polska jako warstwa społeczna* (Torun, 1974); and Andrzej Pośpiech and Wojciech Tygielski, "Społeczna rola dworu magnackiego, XVII–XVIII wieku," *Przegląd Historyczny* 69 (1978): 215–37. On magnate families, see Aleksander Tarnawski, *Działalność gospodarcza Jana Zamoyskiego, Kanclerza i Hetmana Wielkiego Koronnego, 1572–1605* (Lviv, 1935); Wanda Dobrowolska, *Młodość Jerzego i Krzysztofa Zbaraskich (z wstępem o rodzie Zbaraskich i życiorysem Janusza Zbaraskiego wojewodzy bracławskiego)* (Warsaw, 1969); Adam Witusik, *Młodość Tomasza Zamoyskiego* (Lublin, 1977); Mieczysław Lepecki, *Pan Jakobus Sobieski* (Warsaw, 1970); Władysław Tomkiewicz, *Jeremi Wiśniowiecki, 1612–1651* (Warsaw, 1933); "Testament Jeremiego Wiśniowieckiego," *Miesięcznik Heraldyczny* 9, no. 4 (1930): 67–77; and Myron Korduba, "Jeremias Wisniowiecki im Lichte der neuen Forschung," *Zeitschrift für osteuropäische Geschichte* 8 (1934): 221–38.

18. Kryp"iakevych, *Bohdan Khmel'nyts'kyi,* 18–19.

Religion and
Belief

M I C H A E L   S .   F L I E R

COURT CEREMONY
IN AN AGE OF REFORM

PATRIARCH NIKON AND THE PALM SUNDAY RITUAL

PAUL MEYENDORFF marshals considerable textual evidence in his monograph on the Nikonian liturgical reforms of the seventeenth century to bolster the claims of nineteenth-century scholars such as Sergei Belokurov, Aleksei Dmitrievskii, Nikolai Kapterev, and Ivan Mansvetov, that the changes made were based primarily on Greek and Ukrainian texts from the early seventeenth century and not at all on ancient Rusian and Greek sources as claimed by the reformers. In his concluding statement Meyendorff underscores the idea that the reform was less about "correction" than about "change," the desire of the tsar and the patriarch to bring Russian practice into line with the contemporary Greek.[1] His assessment of Nikon underscores this view:

> Nikon's personal role in the reform was generally limited to externals, to such things as the manner of making the sign of the Cross, the number of prostrations at the Prayer of St Ephrem, and the style of vestments. He did not know or understand the work that his correctors were doing in the Printing Office, and apparently believed that the new books were being published on the basis of ancient sources. Nikon's own interest was

in making the ritual look Greek, and he cared little for the substance of the reform. His real passion lay elsewhere, as in the building of Greek-style monasteries, and in presiding over splendid ceremonies, and in increasing the wealth
and glory of the Moscow Patriarchate.

Meyendorff's surmise that Nikon "did not know or understand" the substance of the reform suggests that ignorance rather than subterfuge lay behind Nikon's assertions that ancient books were the basis of the reform.
Without a firm knowledge of Greek, the patriarch had no direct way of veri-
fying the details of the changes introduced, and thus discern whether the
books were collated with ancient or contemporary Greek texts.[2]

Nonetheless, we have evidence of reform carried out by Nikon in specific
ceremonies that have no Greek or Ukrainian prototypes.[3] Details of this reform reflect the exegetic impulse of the liturgical reforms themselves. They
testify to Nikon's apparent acquaintance with the "commemorative" orientation of contemporary Greek liturgical interpretation, one that viewed the
liturgy primarily in terms of the major events in the life of the historical
Christ, rather than in the predominantly eschatological perspective of the
earlier "theophanic" liturgy that emphasized the divinity of Christ and the
future kingdom.[4] It appears that Nikon understood the spirit—if not necessarily the letter—of the reforms and could even immerse himself in ritual details when his own image was at stake.

The reforms I have in mind concern the major court ceremonies that included representatives from all levels of the secular and ecclesiastical hierarchy, most notably the tsar and the patriarch. For all the apparent discontinu-
ities between the Muscovite sixteenth and seventeenth centuries (the dynastic
crisis being only the most obvious), these ceremonies survived but were then
also subject to the "corrective" impulses of the 1650s. The actual impact of
the idea of reform on these royal rituals has never been dealt with in any
depth in the vast literature concerning the Nikonian reforms. Yet it is obvious that we cannot fully appreciate the nature of the reform, its extent and
its limits, until we go beyond its effect on the ritual witnessed by all the Orthodox—the liturgy itself—to examine its effect on the ritual intended primarily for the Orthodox elite at the royal court.

By the mid-sixteenth century, two court ceremonies—the Epiphany ritual
on January 6 and the Palm Sunday ritual a week before Easter—had become
the most important of the coordinated recurrent public appearances of the
heads of church and state in Moscow. A century later in 1655, these two rituals
were still characterized by Archdeacon Paul of Aleppo in much the same terms:
"We were told that in all the Muscovite Land only two holidays a year were
celebrated with particular solemnity, namely, Epiphany and Palm Sunday."[5]

Superficially the two rituals shared a number of features. Both referred to
specific historical events in the earthly ministry of Christ, the one to his baptism at the beginning and the other to his triumphant entry into Jerusalem
at the end. Both began in the main Cathedral of the Dormition *(Uspenskii
sobor)* inside the Kremlin and both prescribed processions beyond the walls

of the old fortress, well within public view. The sites involved had conventional associations with the Holy Land—the River Jordan in the case of Epiphany, Jerusalem in the case of Palm Sunday. Both processions returned to the Dormition for completion of the service and dismissal. Yet these congruences hardly explain why these two rituals alone were accorded such popularity over the last two centuries of Muscovite Rus'.

In previous studies I have analyzed the evolution of the Epiphany and Palm Sunday rituals, primarily in sixteenth-century Muscovy, in an attempt to elucidate their common function.[6] More than any other official actions, these annual rituals were shown to validate, in a politically and religiously charged space, the myth of Muscovite authority anointed by God and ready to lead Orthodox Christianity to redemption in the face of an Apocalypse that might come at any time. Responding as well to pivotal events in the history of Christian Rus' (the baptism of Volodimer in 988 and the defeat of the Kazan' Tatars in 1552, respectively), these rituals conveyed their message through the medium of Orthodox iconography. Both were informed by images of the Baptism and of the Entry into Jerusalem that had been inherited from the Byzantine Greeks.

The demise of the Rurikid dynasty in 1598—and the onset of the Time of Troubles with its succession of native and foreign rulers, famine, civil war, and invasion—determined that even after a reunited Muscovy emerged under Romanov rule a fundamental reevaluation of all Muscovite institutions was inevitable. Through all this the Epiphany and Palm Sunday rituals survived. It was only in the middle of the seventeenth century that the Palm Sunday ritual underwent a major change, and by century's end it was eliminated from the Muscovite repertoire. My task here is limited to determining the circumstances behind that change. The wholesale elimination of a number of important religious rites, including the Palm Sunday ritual, is the subject of a related but independent study.

On the face of it, ritual and change appear incompatible. A ritual is, after all, a sequence of gestures, movements, utterances, whose very replication is at the heart of the mystery that sustains a community of believers. The familiar in this case breeds comfort rather than contempt. It generates fervor, promotes stability, maintains faith. It is the known quantity in ritual that is all-important, not the novel. The repetitive or cyclical nature of its performance ensures its universality, imparting a continuing significance that the ephemeral or accidental cannot.

In Kievan Rus', for example, an oath was sealed with a kissing of the cross *(krestnoe tselovanie)*. Touching the cross, kissing the prince's ring, offering money, or performing any other gesture designed to convince those present of one's sincerity was inadequate. Without the status of a ritual act, such signs lacked the necessary social value.[7]

It is all the more remarkable that in a society filled with rituals both large and small it was possible to introduce major new ones and change them once they were established. Such is the nature of ritual that its various components may, over a period of time, cease to be motivated within the ritual

structure. Signs that carry specific weight, that indicate definite social or political relationships, can become opaque, ambiguous, even contradictory.
Under such circumstances it becomes possible, and at times even mandatory,
to clarify the motivation for ritual signs. The same sign may be accorded a
new significance or the original motivation may elicit a new sign. Whatever
the outcome, the unifying principle behind change in ritual is conceptual;
the function of the ritual or its parts has changed, in a part of or all of the society that practices it, and this different perspective, emphasis, or interpretation serves to stimulate teleological evolution.

THE EPIPHANY AND PALM SUNDAY RITUALS IN MOSCOW

Our knowledge of the court rituals performed on Epiphany and Palm
Sunday in Moscow in the sixteenth century is gleaned exclusively from foreign sources.[8] Visiting merchant delegations, royalty, and mercenaries have
given us descriptions ranging from a few lines to several pages, all bearing
witness to magnificent spectacles that impressed the foreign eye in their
solemnity as well as in their presenting the tsar as humble shepherd of the
people. With allowances for minor errors of fact and interpretation, these accounts are reasonably accurate representations. They are corroborated by
many foreign and domestic seventeenth-century sources, the latter including
church ceremonials *(chinovniki)* and official records of court appearances
(vykhody tsaria, patriarshie vykhody, dvortsovye razriady).

In midmorning of January 6, the Epiphany (Theophany) service was conducted in the major cathedral church of the Kremlin, the Dormition, in the
presence of the patriarch and the tsar. Following the litany *(ekteniia)*, both
participated in a cross procession that made its way south through the gates
of the Tainitsky Tower out onto the frozen ice of the Moscow River to a
raised wooden platform built around a large hole cut in the ice called the
Jordan' *(Iordan')*. After the Blessing of the Waters, the patriarch sprinkled
holy water on the bare head of the tsar, then on himself, then on the rest of
the nobility, and the clergy—a symbolic renewal of the tsar and, by extension, all Muscovy. The tsar's horses were brought to the Jordan' as well, to
drink of the sanctified water. The principals returned to the Kremlin; the tsar
on horseback to a service at the chapel of the Trinity Monastery Hostel, the
patriarch and the rest of the clergy on foot in a cross procession to the Dormition. Thereupon the people observing the ceremony from a distance hastened to the Jordan' with vessels of all kinds to take the holy water back to
their homes.[9]

The Palm Sunday ritual in Moscow was an even more elaborate and dramatic ceremony. After the litany in the Dormition, a cross procession made
its way outside the Kremlin to the Chapel of the Entry into Jerusalem, located in the Church of the Intercession on the Moat (now Saint Basil's
Cathedral), dominating Red Square.[10] Leading the procession were one or
two pairs of horses pulling a low-slung wagon on which a large "tree" had

been constructed out of willow branches with all manner of fruit hanging from its branches. Four or six young boys dressed in white vestments stood in the branches of the tree singing Palm Sunday hymns. A large group of young acolytes followed, carrying banners, crosses, icons, and other ecclesiastical paraphernalia. The centerpiece of the procession was the representation of Christ's triumphant entry into Jerusalem. In imitation of the Savior, the head of the Russian church (the metropolitan of Moscow, later the patriarch) sat sidesaddle on the back of a horse that was covered with white linen and disguised as an ass with long white ears. The patriarch held a Gospelbook in his left hand and a gold crucifix in his right with which he blessed those in attendance as he rode past. The tsar walked on foot pulling the "ass" at the end of a long rein. From one to four of the tsar's courtiers held up the rein in the middle, whereas a patriarchal boyar held the ass by the bridle. Young boys, numbering in the tens or even hundreds in the second half of the seventeenth century, laid down robes *(kaftany)* and large pieces of cloth in many colors before the approaching tsar and patriarch, picked them up as soon as the ass had passed over them, and then ran ahead to lay them down again. They covered the entire path of the Procession on the Ass in this way in both directions. The Procession on the Ass was followed by the higher clergy, patriarchal boyars, and the highest-ranking members of the tsar's regiments, the *strel'tsy*. Once inside the Jerusalem Chapel of the Intercession, the choir sang the *polychronia* ("May you live many years, O master!"), first to the tsar, then to the patriarch. The reading of the Gospel narrative of the Entry by the patriarch was performed between the Small and Great Litanies. The participants then left the Jerusalem Chapel, the patriarch mounted the ass once more, and with the thundering of the city bells as accompaniment, the entire entourage processed back into the Kremlin through the Savior Gate and on to the Dormition for a continuation of the service. The tsar left the service for a private mass in the Jerusalem Chapel of the palace church, the Annunciation. The patriarch blessed the palms and willows and distributed them to those in attendance before dismissal.

It was this second version of the Palm Sunday ritual that was performed through the year 1655, the year for which we have a detailed and lengthy description by Paul of Aleppo during the visit of his father, Patriarch Makarios of Antioch, to East Slavic lands in 1655–1656. Paul provided interesting and informed insight into many mid-seventeenth-century Russian religious practices and was clearly moved by the spirit expressed in the Muscovite ceremony for Palm Sunday. The third version was introduced in 1656 and is described in some detail in the book of patriarchal appearances under that year.[11] The differences between the 1655 and 1656 ceremonies are significant (see fig. 1).

After the litany in the Kremlin's Dormition, a simple cross procession made its way on foot beyond the walls to the Jerusalem Chapel on Red Square. The tree was not pulled ahead on the cart and the tsar and the patriarch did not perform the Procession on the Ass *(shestvie na osliati)*. The litany was chanted inside the Jerusalem Chapel, but there was no reading of

Fig. 1   Comparison of Second and Third Versions of Palm Sunday Ritual

1655 Ritual	1656 Ritual
Procession **on Ass** to Jerusalem Chapel with tree	Cross procession **on foot** to Jerusalem Chapel
Service in Jerusalem Chapel	Service in Jerusalem Chapel
Little litany	Little litany
Reading of Gospel	
Great litany	
	Cross Procession to Lobnoe Mesto
	Little litany
	Reading of Gospel
	Ass brought to Lobnoe Mesto
	Tree brought to Lobnoe Mesto
Procession on Ass to Dormition with tree	Procession on Ass to Dormition with tree
Concluding service	Concluding service
Distribution of willow tree branches	Distribution of willow tree branches

the Gospel text. The wording of the book of patriarchal appearances is quite explicit in indicating the differences:

> And after the litany came the concluding prayer *[vozglas]*; and the Sovereign Patriarch said the prayers in the Cyprian prayerbook before the altar and then joined in a cross procession to the chapel of the feast, to the Entry into Jerusalem, *and the Holy Sovereign Patriarch went on foot, and not on the ass.* And the choir and subdeacons, all the ranks *[vse stanitsy]*, walked in the procession ahead of him, the Sovereign, and they sang various hymns until reaching the chapel and did not proceed towards Golgotha *[Lobnoe mesto]*. And the Sovereign Patriarch and Sovereign Tsar arrived at the chapel of the church; and the litany and the final prayer with the cross were performed in accordance with the office *[po chinu]*, but the Holy Patriarch did not read the Gospel.[12] (Emphasis added)

From this and later accounts, we know that the participants moved to Lobnoe Mesto, a semicircular raised dais to the north of the church, where the archdeacon and the patriarch each said a litany. The patriarch then had the archdeacon read the narrative of the Entry into Jerusalem from the Gospel of Mark. When the words "he sendeth forth two of his disciples" were spoken, the patriarch blessed an archpriest and archdeacon (sacristan) and sent them after a colt tied to a nearby post "in a place where two ways met" as described in the Gospel account (Mark 11:4). The patriarch spoke the words of Christ; the archpriest and the archdeacon spoke the words of the disciples seeking the colt. A patriarchal boyar spoke the words of a townsperson asking what the disciples were doing, untying the colt. The "disciples" responded and brought the colt of the ass up to Lobnoe Mesto. The patriarch blessed and distributed palm fronds, willow branches, and a candle to the tsar, then ordered that the previously prepared willow tree, decorated abundantly with fruit, be brought before the crosses in procession. When the archdeacon read the verse in the Gospel account describing how Christ sat on the ass, the patriarch mounted the ass sidesaddle, and with the tsar on foot pulling the reins, the procession moved from Lobnoe Mesto back inside the Kremlin to the Dormition where the service was concluded and the tree broken apart and distributed as before.

"Radical" is hardly too strong a word to characterize the change that took effect in the Palm Sunday ritual in midcentury. In a society in which ritual was dogmatic theology, in which the spelling of the words for "Jesus" and "amen" and the number of fingers used to cross oneself were major points of contention, the emendations and additions noted above were by no means minor.[13] Yet the sources are virtually silent. There is no explanation of the function of the change, who was responsible for it, or why it was implemented in 1656. There is no record of protest against it, even though the Zealots of Piety were not reluctant on other occasions to criticize in the harshest of terms the ritual reforms introduced by the patriarch and supported by the tsar. This is probably due to the fairly restricted, elite nature of the ritual—an annual ceremony without the universal effect of the Liturgy, which touches every Orthodox worshiper. It is perhaps because of its restricted performance that the vast literature on seventeenth-century religious reform and its critics scarcely mentions the change in the Palm Sunday ritual in Moscow. Nonetheless once we begin to search for answers to some of the questions posed, we discover that the change in ritual reveals much more than previously thought about the reform of Russian religious practices in general and the reform practiced by Patriarch Nikon in particular.

THE 1656 PALM SUNDAY RITUAL AND THE IDEA OF REFORM

Several questions about the changed Palm Sunday ritual can be answered to a high degree of probability. There can be no doubt that Patriarch Nikon himself approved the changes and introduced the revised ritual in the year after Patriarch Makarios witnessed the older version. The patriarch was, after all, the central figure in the procession on the ass; it is inconceivable that his role in imitation of Christ could be altered without his full consent and support.

The timing of the change is also explicable. It falls precisely within the period that the earliest editions of the *Sluzhebnik* (1655–1658) and the *Skrizhal'* (1656) were introduced in Moscow, when the concern for appropriate ritual decorum and the symbolic value of Orthodox material and spiritual culture were especially keen. The new *Sluzhebnik* represents the tangible result of the Nikonian reform movement, ostensibly based on ancient Rusian and Greek texts, but in fact adhering more strictly to Greek liturgical practice from the late sixteenth or early seventeenth centuries. The *Skrizhal'* was written by the Greek hieromonk Ioannis Nathanail and published in Venice in 1574. It was sent to Nikon by Paisios, patriarch of Constantinople, in 1653 and translated into Church Slavonic by Arsenios the Greek.[14]

In his monograph on Russian Orthodox ritual, Nikol'skii characterizes the third and last version of the Palm Sunday ritual as a "corrected" *(ispravlennyi)* version of the old second version.[15] But corrected on the basis of what model? The earlier Greek practice in Constantinople is out of the question as a source, since the ceremony in the capital bore little resemblance to the Muscovite third version and had not been performed there for more than two centuries. The patriarch rode on a horse from Hagia Sophia to the Church of the Forty Martyrs. Following a brief service there, he proceeded on foot to the Column of Constantine, where he, and not the archdeacon, read from the Gospel. He then returned on foot to Hagia Sophia. Unlike the tsar, the Byzantine emperor did not participate at all in the Palm Sunday ritual involving the patriarch, preferring to hold his own special rites in the palace.[16] Nikol'skii pointed to the Greek practice in Jerusalem as the probable source.[17] According to the early seventeenth-century description of the Franciscan Franciscus Quaresmius (1583–1656):

> In order to preserve the memory of the Savior's solemn procession every year on the feast of the Entry the archpriest of Mt. Zion [the patriarch of Jerusalem] and the brethren, pilgrims, and residents of Jerusalem, in accordance with the example of Christ and his disciples, go to Bethphage and there, having kissed the holy ground, say a prayer. Then the archpriest delivers a homily to his tiny flock, appropriate for the time and place. After finishing the sacred speech, the deacon dressed in his vestments reads from the Gospel of Matthew, which is normally arranged for reading in church that day and with the words: "then Jesus sent two disciples and said to them . . ." the archpriest speaks to two brethren, who approach and bow before him: "Go to the village over against you" [Matt. 21:2]. Then the deacon finishes the Gospel. Meanwhile the two brethren go to the town where the village of the ass was located and finding the ass ready there bring it to the archpriest. The archpriest, after mounting the ass, rides over the Mount of Olives to Jerusalem accompanied by the clergy and others of the faithful who strew his path with grasses, flowers, and their clothes, and like the Jewish children sing "Hosanna!" After arriving at the spot where Christ saw the city and wept for it, the nineteenth chapter of Luke is read in which the lament of Jesus is described. Then the procession continues in the presence of an enormous confluence of people. Inasmuch as one cannot now enter through the Golden Gate, the procession enters through the Zion Gate and from there makes its way to the Church of the Savior [Holy Sepulcher]. The archpriest dismounts from the ass there and in accordance with the *typikon* completes the service in the church, ending with a blessing of the people.[18]

There are several possible sources from which Nikon might have learned about the Greek rites practiced in Jerusalem. In early 1649 Nikon, then the archimandrite of the Novospasskii Monastery in Moscow, met Paisios, the visiting patriarch of Jerusalem, and made a great impression on him. Paisios heartily approved of Nikon's selection as metropolitan of Novgorod in March 1649 and helped officiate at his ordination. In the preface to the new Slavonic translation of the *Skrizhal'*, Nikon included Paisios among those Eastern prelates who made him aware of textual errors and mistaken practices in the Russian church.[19]

Another potential source was the archdeacon Arsenii Sukhanov, who traveled a circuitous route to Jerusalem, mostly with Patriarch Paisios, from 1649 to 1652. After returning to Moscow in 1653, Arsenii produced his *Proskinitarii,* a detailed description of places and customs he found in the Holy Land with special note taken of Greek rituals practiced there.[20] Yet another source might have been Patriarch Makarios of Antioch, who visited Moscow in 1655 and spent considerable time with Nikon discussing matters of ritual.

Although we cannot know for sure where Nikon received his information on the Greek rites in Jerusalem on Palm Sunday, the description of the geographic setting provided by Arsenii Sukhanov seems to emphasize the very features that distinguish the new 1656 version from the older version of the previous year:

> From Bethany there is a road straight to Jerusalem, beneath the Mount of Olives, and another road toward the Mount of Olives leading to the village of Bethphage. It is this road that Christ our God took from Bethany to Jerusalem; *to Bethphage on foot, and in Bethphage he sat on the colt of an ass, and rode on to Jerusalem;* it is written in the Gospel of John, heading 41. It is about a verst or so from Bethany to Bethphage; and now the village is empty, not even the barest foundation is left. They just point out the spot where Christ our God sat on the colt, and they kiss it.[21] (Emphasis added)

Arsenii's specific reference to the distinct modes of travel in Christ's journey to Jerusalem suggests a historical motivation for the change in the Muscovite ritual. Instead of the patriarch riding on the ass from the Kremlin to the Jerusalem Chapel and back, a historically more accurate sequence is followed. The trip from the Kremlin to Red Square is accomplished on foot. Following the brief service in the Jerusalem Chapel, the Muscovites, like Christ, walk on foot from "Bethany" (Church of the Intercession)[22] to "Bethphage" near the "Mount of Olives" (Lobnoe Mesto). It is only from here that the patriarch in imitation of Christ mounts the ass and rides through the main gates of "Jerusalem" (Moscow) to the "Holy Sepulcher" (Cathedral of the Dormition). The emphasis on historical accuracy explains why the reading of the Gospel is postponed until the procession reaches the Mount of Olives. To do otherwise would violate the sequence of historical events connected with Christ's humanity.

Nikon's decision to alter the ritual was probably influenced by his reading of the new translation of the *Skrizhal'*, actually prepared by October 1655 but not published until April 1656, following approval by the synod. As an interpretive liturgy, the *Skrizhal'* represented a synthesis of several late Byzantine strains of liturgical development. The Greek hieromonk Ioannis Nathanail published the *Skrizhal'* in Venice in 1574, based on the liturgical exegesis of Patriarch Germanos of Constantinople (seventh and eighth centuries), Nikolaos Kabasilas (fourteenth century), and Symeon of Thessalonike (fifteenth century). Nathanail underscored the sacramental character of the liturgy over the strictly symbolic, an approach representative of the Antiochene strain of Orthodoxy as against the Alexandrian noted earlier. In the former, the liturgy is viewed as a symbolic representation of the history of the Incarnation, Christ's life on earth. The commemoration of Christ's life in ritual sanctifies the participants through the celebration of the Eucharist. It is this commemorative basis rather than the more abstract theophanic one that marks the primary difference in the character of the Russian liturgy in the seventeenth century as compared to the period preceding.[23] This commemorative view, so clearly expressed in the *Skrizhal'*, finds its primary source in Kabasilas's *Commentary on the Divine Liturgy:*

> As far as the ceremonies performed in the eucharistic liturgy are concerned, they all have some connection with the scheme of the work of redemption. Their purpose is to set before us the Divine plan, that by looking upon it our souls may be sanctified, and thus we may be made fit to receive these sacred gifts. . . . That is why it was necessary that actions of this sort, capable of inspiring such feelings in us, should find a place in the ordering of the liturgy. It was necessary, not only that we should think about it, but also that to some extent we should see the utter poverty of him who possesses all, the coming on earth of him who dwells everywhere, the shame of the most blessed God, the sufferings of the impassible; that we should see how much he was hated and how much he loved; how he, the Most High, humbled himself; what torments he endured, what deeds he accomplished in order to prepare for us this holy table. . . . This is why the symbolism of which I have spoken was conceived. It does not confine itself to the indication of all this by words alone, but it places it before our eyes in its entirety throughout the liturgy. The aim of setting all this before us is to influence our souls the more easily thereby; not merely to offer us a simple picture but to create in us a feeling; for the very good reason that an idea is more deeply impressed upon us if we can see it depicted. This goes on throughout the liturgy, in order that it may not be forgotten, and our thoughts be not distracted by anything else before it has led us to the holy table. Filled with these ideas, and with their memory fresh within us, we receive Communion.[24]

It is in considering Kabasilas's interpretation of particular parts of the liturgy that we come to appreciate the larger purpose of the new Palm Sunday ritual in Red Square. The dramatic highpoints of the Liturgy of the Catechumens and the Liturgy of the Faithful are the Little and Great Entrances, the processions that accompany the Gospel and Eucharistic offerings, respectively, to the altar:

For example, we have the bringing of the Gospel to the altar, then the bringing of the offerings. Each is done for a practical reason—the one that the
Gospel may be read, the other that the sacrifice may be performed; besides
this, however, one represents the appearance, the other the manifestation of
the Saviour. The first, obscure and imperfect, at the beginning of his life, the
second the perfect and supreme manifestation.[25]

Later he returns to a more detailed accounting of the Great Entrance preceding the celebration of the Eucharist:

The priest . . . takes the offerings, and reverently holding them head-high, de-
parts. Carrying them thus, he goes to the altar, after walking in slow and
solemn procession through the nave of the church. The faithful chant during
this procession, kneeling down reverently and devoutly, and praying that they
may be remembered when the offering is made. The priest goes on, sur-
rounded by candles and incense, until he comes to the altar. This is done, no
doubt, for practical reasons; it was necessary to bring the offerings which are
to be sacrificed to the altar and set them down there, and to do all this with
reverence and devotion. This is the way in which kings of old brought their
gifts to God; they did not allow others to do it for them, but brought their offerings themselves, wearing their crowns. Also, this ceremony signifies the last
manifestation of Christ, which aroused the hatred of the Jews, when he em-
barked on the journey from his native country to Jerusalem, where he was to
be sacrificed; then he rode into the Holy City on the back of an ass, escorted
by a cheering crowd.[26]

When Nikon introduced greater historical accuracy into the Palm Sunday
ritual on March 30, 1656, he was motivated not simply by a desire to reproduce the Greek rites in Jerusalem (if, indeed, they were still performed), but
to enhance the macro-liturgy in the "nave" that was Red Square, to engage
more deeply the hearts and minds of those participating in this cyclical mass
communion that ended with the distribution of the sanctified branches of
the willow tree.

Nikon may have given up one leg of the Procession on the Ass for historical accuracy, but he also placed himself in the position of further assimilating
Christ by participating more directly in the events that preceded the Entry
and by uttering the very words of Christ before all present in Red Square.
His previously mute, iconographic Christ, invoking the theophanic presence
of God, was turned into a commemorative likeness of the Savior, which was
seen and heard before the gates of the New Jerusalem.

The same quest by Nikon for a historically more accurate assimilation to
Christ is marked elsewhere in the spring of 1656. On April 23 he presided
over a synod that officially approved the clearly influential *Skrizhal'*, and on
June 3 he formally purchased the land near Istra for his New Jerusalem
Monastery. It was on this site that he began building a precise replica of the
Church of the Holy Sepulcher, based on a model probably given to him ear-
lier by Patriarch Paisios of Jerusalem; on the detailed descriptions of Arsenii
Sukhanov, including precise physical measurements; and on a copy of

Bernardino Amico's precise plans, published in Florence in 1620.[27] He built a replica of the Church of the Ascension on the Mount of Olives close by. For Nikon, the emphasis on historical accuracy was apparently an act of piety, a *podvig*, in Nikon's own striving toward a more profound Orthodoxy and a more prominent role for its sovereign patriarch. In his reform Nikon did not necessarily slavishly imitate Greek practice, either ancient or modern, despite the rhetoric of his accusers. This becomes clear when we examine particular details of the new ritual.

The seventeenth-century Greek rite described by Franciscus Quaresmius above is by no means identical to the 1656 Muscovite Palm Sunday ritual. First, there is no mention there of anyone leading the ass mounted by the patriarch of Jerusalem into the city, nor in the Gospel accounts of Christ's Entry; nonetheless Nikon chose to preserve the traditional role for the tsar. Here historical accuracy yielded to specifically Muscovite considerations. The tsar was, after all, God's chosen representative on earth, a holy figure in his own right. No more appropriate person might present the offering of the sacrifice of Christ in the person of the patriarch at this cosmic liturgical service. Additionally, the relative performatory position of patriarch and tsar in the ceremony, riding versus walking, exalted versus humbled, would certainly not have been lost on Nikon, who believed his own authority to be superior to that of the tsar.[28]

Second, in the Jerusalem rite there is no symbolic tree pulled ahead of Christ on the ass. The constructed willow tree was a holdover from the earlier Muscovite ritual, an element that had become so central to the Muscovite celebration, in its symbolic connection to the Palm Sunday icon, to the Eucharist, and its likely allusion to fertility and to the Tree of Life at the End of Time, it could not be removed.[29] The tree, laden with various kinds of fruits, underscored the eschatological significance of the Entry into Moscow, the New Jerusalem:

> And he shewed me a pure river of water of life, clear as crystal, proceeding out of the throne of God and of the Lamb. In the midst of the street of it, and on either side of the river, was there the tree of life, which bare twelve manner of fruits, and yielded her fruit every month: and the leaves of the trees were for the healing of nations. . . . I am Alpha and Omega, the beginning and the end, the first and the last. Blessed are they that do his commandments, that they may have the right to the tree of life, and may enter in through the gates into the city.[30]

The preservation in the ritual of specifically Russian elements associated with the destiny of Moscow or its authority figures is paralleled in the publication of the *Sluzhebnik* (1655) by the retention of petitions in the litany for the tsar, his family, and the army, and by the addition of commemorative petitions for deceased Orthodox patriarchs and tsars.[31]

Third, in bringing the words of the Gospel to life, the Muscovite ritual—unlike the Greek—leaves out Christ's lament as he approached the city (from Luke 19:41–44):

And when he was come near, he beheld the city and wept over it, saying, If thou hadst known, even thou, at least in this thy day, the things which belong unto thy peace! but now they are hid from thine eyes. For the days shall come upon thee, that thine enemies shall cast a trench about thee, and compass thee round, and keep thee in on every side, and they shall lay thee even with the ground, and thy children within thee; and they shall not leave within thee one stone upon another; because thou knewest not the time of thy visitation.

It is not difficult to see why Nikon would have eliminated this passage from the ritual, words that would have to be uttered from his own mouth as part of his *imitatio Christi*. This was to be a ceremony that affirmed Moscow's position in the Orthodox world as the New Jerusalem, not an occasion for an annual prophecy of its death and destruction through a lack of faith and vision among its people. Once again strictly local religious and political concerns overrode the principle of historical accuracy in diverging from the Greek practice at Jerusalem.

Fourth, and perhaps most suprising of all, Nikon chose the Gospel reading for Red Square from the Book of Mark rather than Matthew, as prescribed in the ceremonial and as performed in Jerusalem by the Greeks.[32] This is an extraordinary substitution that requires comment. Every Slavonic Gospelbook is unequivocal about which Gospel selections are assigned for specific days. In the case of Palm Sunday, the Orthodox matins service prescribes Matthew 21:1–17, whereas the liturgy prescribes John 12:1–18. The individual selection from Mark is indeed extraordinary, the sort of alteration in the rigid scheme of things that might be ventured only by a very high-ranking prelate, and rarely at that. Available evidence suggests that among the Russian dioceses in which the Palm Sunday ritual was performed, the substitution of Mark for Matthew was limited to Red Square in Moscow.[33] Once the procession returned to the Dormition for the remainder of the service, the Gospel reading picked up the narrative from Matthew 21:10. In order to understand Nikon's actions here we need to compare both Gospel readings (see fig. 2).

The differences between the two Gospels stand out vividly in their descriptions of the participants and the sequence of events in the dramatic action of the Entry. Mark permits the retention of a single colt or an ass, as in the earlier Muscovite ritual and the Palm Sunday icon, rather than an ass and a colt. In terms of dramatic impact within the scriptural tradition (which is certainly a measure of success for liturgists like Kabasilas), Mark is narrowly focused on the details of the historical event as it unfolds; his version lacks the digression about the prophets in the narrative of Matthew.[34] Mark has more dialogue, or indirect speech convertible to dialogue, and a greater cast of characters. In the interest of commemorating the life of Christ in a historically more vivid way, then, Mark is undoubtedly the better choice, albeit a noncanonical one.

In the last analysis, the words used above to describe the elements of the Gospel reading—narrative, dialogue, cast of characters—refer, as it were, to a liturgical drama. The head priest, in this case the patriarch, relinquishes his

Fig. 2 Comparison of Entry into Jerusalem from Gospels of Matthew and Mark
(the dialogue of Christ is underscored, other dialogue is in italics).

Gospel Reading for Palm Sunday, 1656
Red Square

MATTHEW 21	MARK 11
1 And when they drew nigh unto Jerusalem, and were come to Beth-phage, unto the mount of Olives, then sent Jesus two disciples	1 And when they came nigh to Jerusalem, unto Bethphage and Bethany, at the mount of Olives, he sendeth two of his disciples,
2 Saying unto them, <u>Go into the village over against you, and straight-way ye shall find an ass tied, and a colt with her: loose them, and bring them unto me.</u>	2 And saith unto them, <u>Go your way into the village over against you: and as soon as ye be entered into it, ye shall find a colt tied, whereon never man sat; loose him and bring him.</u>
3 <u>And if any man say ought unto you, ye shall say,</u> *The Lord hath need of them; and straightway he will send them.*	3 <u>And if any man say unto you</u> *Why do ye this?* <u>say ye that the Lord hath need of him and straightway he will send him hither.</u>
4 All this was done, that it might be fulfilled which was spoken by the prophet, saying,	
5 Tell ye the daughter of Sion, Be-hold, thy King cometh unto thee, meek, and sitting upon an ass, and a colt the foal of an ass.	
6 And the disciples went, and did as Jesus commanded them,	4 And they went their way and found the colt tied by the door without in a place where two ways met; and they loose him.
	5 And certain of them that stood there said unto them, *What do ye, loosing the colt?*
	6 And they said unto them even as Je-sus had commanded: and they let them go.
7 And brought the ass, and the colt, and put on them their clothes, and they set him thereon.	7 And they brought the colt to Jesus and cast their garments on him; and he sat upon him
8 And a very great multitude spread their garments in the way; others cut down branches from the trees, and strawed them in the way.	8 And many spread their garments in the way: and others cut down branches off the trees and strawed them in the way.

9 And the multitudes that went before, and that followed, cried, saying, *Hosanna to the Son of David: Blessed is he that cometh in the name of the Lord; Hosanna in the highest*

9 And they that went before, and they that followed, cried, saying, *Hosanna; Blessed is he that cometh in the name of the Lord:*

10 *Blessed be the kingdom of our father David that cometh in the name of the Lord: Hosanna in the highest.*

Gospel Reading for Palm Sunday, 1656
Cathedral of the Dormition

MATTHEW 21

10 And when he was come into Jerusalem, all the city was moved, saying, *Who is this?*

11 And the multitude said, This is Jesus the prophet of Nazareth of Galilee.

12 And Jesus went into the temple of God, and cast out all them that sold and bought in the temple, and overthrew the tables of the moneychangers, and the seats of them that sold doves,

13 And said unto them, *It is written, My house shall be called the house of prayer; but ye have made it a den of thieves.*

14 And the blind and the lame came to him in the temple; and he healed them.

15 And when the chief priests and scribes saw the wonderful things that he did, and the children crying in the temple, and saying, *Hosanna to the Son of David*; they were sore displeased.

16 And said unto him, *Hearest thou what these say?* And Jesus saith unto them, *Yea; have ye never read, Out of the mouths of babes and sucklings thou hast perfected praise?*

17 And he left them, and went out of the city into Bethany; and he lodged there.

MARK 11

11 And Jesus entered into Jerusalem, and into the temple: and when he had looked round about upon all things, and now the eventide was come, he went out unto Bethany with the twelve.

normal duty of reading the Gospel text to the deacon, reserving for himself only the spoken words of Christ.[35] The function of imitating Christ was central to Nikon's conception of the office of patriarch, as seen in his self-referential language (for example, *bogopodrazhatel'ne vsikh*, "most imitative of God")[36] and, after his withdrawal from Moscow in 1658, in his critical reaction to Metropolitan Pitirim for daring to replace him in the Palm Sunday ritual of 1659. He claimed that it was terrifying for the patriarch to represent the person of Christ in the ceremony, but it was an honor worthy of that rank alone in Moscow.

In his "Refutation" *(Vozrazhenie),* Nikon criticizes Pitirim, a mere metropolitan from a small town (Krutitsy), for daring to perform liturgical responsibilities reserved for a patriarch: "Since it is revealed in writ that a patriarch bears upon himself the representation of Christ *[Khristov obraz],* and city bishops symbolize *[po obrazu sut']* the Twelve Apostles, and small-town bishops *[selstii]* are the 70 Disciples." Nikon's fears on this score are expressed in a slightly earlier section, which takes Pitirim to task for overreaching his station:

> And I do not know where the patriarchs took such a ritual from in Rus', and I do not know whether its performance is appropriate *[blagougodno].* I myself felt unsure performing it, and it was terrifying, since it [the Entry into Jerusalem] is said of Christ by the prophet, as the Holy Writ interprets it: "He who has Heaven as a throne mounts a colt and enters Jerusalem."[37]

In retrospect, it must be said that such fear and trembling articulated by Nikon in exile rings somewhat hollow in light of his decision in 1656 not only to continue performing the ritual in Red Square, but to embellish it through reform and in so doing, to permit himself to utter the very words of Christ during his performance as the representation of Christ. In fact, Nikon's perceived hubris in identifying himself with Christ drew criticism for his decision to name his monastery in Istra after the New Jerusalem and for his precise duplication of the Church of the Holy Sepulcher within its walls.[38]

In the new Palm Sunday ritual each dialogue or dialogized segment of indirect speech (as noted earlier) was assigned to a member of the patriarchal court. With this compact cast of characters and a narrator, the events of the Gospel were brought to life in the vast expanse of Red Square. During the actual performance of the new ritual, the dialogue was pronounced only a single time, in accordance with history, while many of the narrative lines were repeated again and again to cover the long stretches of time in which the corresponding action was being carried out.[39] Once the "Entry" was completed and the major participants had entered the "Church of the Holy Sepulcher" (Dormition), the reading of the Gospel was continued from Matthew, as prescribed. It is at this point that Matthew provides the description of Christ in the temple that is lacking in the Gospel of Mark. The end of the service is followed by the distribution of the "Eucharist," the sanctified willow branches.

Tikhonravov, in his introduction to the theater in Russia, was highly critical of the clumsy dramatic element in such early liturgical ceremonies as the Palm Sunday ritual and the Fiery Furnace Play.

> The Procession on the Ass and the Fiery Furnace Play in their poverty of dialogue and action might better be called episodes from the puppet theater than religious dramas. In the first instance, they were limited to some dialogue between the patriarch and the archpriest and sacristan impersonating Christ's disciples, while the rest of the time was taken up by the solemn procession of the patriarch and the decorated willow tree. It was not the dramatic conversation of the dramatis personae but the "procession" that constituted the primary content of this ritual.[40]

Nikol'skii was offended by Tikhonravov's projection of notions from the theater onto a liturgical service, faulting him for failing to recognize the meaning and purpose of religious ritual and admonishing him for thinking that a theatrical performance and a religious service were even comparable. The former only seeks to entertain, to distract, to stimulate an aesthetic sensibility, whereas the latter intends to stimulate greater faith, to educate, to correct sinful behavior.[41] From our temporal vantage point, it is not difficult to see how limited both writers were by their own narrow perspectives on what constitutes the form and content of drama. If "drama" implies serious subject matter presented in a sequence of events with a conscious manipulation of motion, gestures, discourse, and staging for expressive effect, then there is no question about the dramatic impact of church ritual. It is precisely this function, underscored and elaborated by the late Byzantine liturgists, that informed Nikon's impulse in introducing "corrective" change into a major court ceremony like the Palm Sunday ritual in Moscow. Yet this impulse did not lead Nikon toward the greater "reality" witnessed in the West in the form of various mystery plays and passion cycles with their more highly developed dramatic action, dialogue, costumes, stage effects, and even introduction of the vernacular.[42]

Felmy is surely correct in juxtaposing the theophanic character of Russian liturgy in the fifteenth and sixteenth centuries to its commemorative (rememorative) character in the seventeenth century, but these are contrary rather than contradictory notions.[43] The one does not necessarily exclude the presence of the other, or at least its effect. The development of the Palm Sunday ritual provides testimony to the accuracy of this view, demonstrating the shift in emphasis from one perspective to the other while maintaining constraints of the former over the latter.

In my earlier analysis of the Palm Sunday ritual in the sixteenth century, I indicated its essentially iconographical conception, its greater reliance on the depiction of the Entry into Jerusalem in Orthodox iconography rather than on Gospel text.[44] As an icon, with its holy figures and the tree with boys singing in the branches, the procession was activated by the tsar, who led it from the "altar" of the cathedral church through the "iconostasis" of the Kremlin walls, to the "analogion" of the Jerusalem chapel, and back, in the function of a humble head priest consecrating the Eucharist. The actual presence of Christ was invoked by the presentation of the image or *obraz,* thus the ritual's theophanic character. In the middle of the seventeenth century, text complements image. It is the reenactment of the historical event as part of the immediacy of liturgical commemoration that dominates the ritual function, in word as well as in deed. Through the discourse of Mark the Evangelist, the participants in the "nave" of Red Square not only bear witness to the image of the Entry, they become spectators at its unfolding, its verbal and visual likeness or *podobie.* The lessening of the theophanic character of the ritual might diminish the eschatological dimension of the ritual,[45] but in compensation, each beholder is all the more directly inspired by the sacramental spectacle of Christ's Entry into Jerusalem, a greater likeness prefiguring his own sacrifice and resurrection and the redemptive promise of the New Jerusalem.

"Likeness" in this case is not to be confused with "naturalism." The theophanic character of the ritual was not erased by attention to the word. To Tikhonravov's obvious dismay, Nikon's Orthodoxy was not willing to embellish the words of the New Testament to make the commemoration even more striking, more vivid, more *aktuell,* as was clearly possible in the West. For the Orthodox, the images of things holy are purposely distorted. Their prototypes cannot be fully comprehended or understood by man until his deification (theosis) in the divine light at the General Resurrection. It is this Hesychast strain in Orthodox thought that affects the image in all senses, in ritual as well as in painting, architecture, and sculpture:

> Consequently, it is quite understandable that after the victory of hesychasm, the Church put an end to the development of those elements in its sacred art which undermined its doctrine in one way or another. It was due precisely to hesychasm that "the last Byzantines—in contrast to the Italians—made room for the natural, but without developing a naturalism; made use of depth without imprisoning it in the laws of perspective; and explored the human, without isolating it from the divine." . . . Art retained its link with revelation and preserved its synergistic character between man and God.[46]

As evidenced by the evolution of the Palm Sunday ritual in Moscow, Nikon's restraint in reform was motivated by a number of concerns. A close reading of relevant texts has shown that rather than slavishly following the practice of the Greeks (Byzantine or post-Byzantine) or the Ukrainians, as was largely the case with the reform of the liturgy proper, Nikon was governed by a desire to bring royal ritual into line with current commemorative thinking—without sacrificing those peculiarly Muscovite elements that presented in the same message his own vision of Moscow's destiny as the New Jerusalem, with himself as the dominant authority. It is ironic that Nikon's new Palm Sunday ritual outlasted its author as head of the Russian church by some three decades. But in 1678 it was confined to Moscow alone.[47] And by the end of the century, both the ritual and the patriarchate were eliminated in the first stirrings of a new and more far-reaching reformer.

NOTES

1. Paul Meyendorff, *Russia, Ritual, and Reform* (Crestwood, N.Y, 1991), 219–27, also the selected bibliography, 15–23. The focus of Meyendorff's analysis is the liturgy itself (especially that of John Chrysostom), but he assumes that his claims are valid for other services as well, including matins and vespers.

2. Ibid., 222. In his meetings with the Greek-speaking Makarios, patriarch of Antioch, Nikon spoke through an interpreter. See Paul of Aleppo, *Puteshestvie antiokhiiskogo Patriarkha Makariia v Rossiiu v polovine XVII veka, opisannoe ego synom, arkhidiakonom Pavlom Aleppskim*, trans. F. Murkos, 5 pts. (Moscow, 1896–1900), pt. 3, *Moskva* (1898), 23; and N. F. Kapterev, "Ispravlenie tserkovno-bogosluzhebnykh knig pri patriarkhe Nikone," in *Bogoslovskii vestnik*, no. 1 (1909), 34.

3. I use the name "Nikon" here and in other contexts relevant to reform to refer to the patriarch and his circle of liturgical advisers, since we have no direct knowledge of individual responsibility for specific liturgical changes and innnovations. I assume that Nikon tacitly, if not explicitly, approved all such reform activity conducted during his tenure as patriarch.

4. The term "theophanic" refers to a transcendent interpretation of the liturgy according to which the service helps eliminate the boundaries between heaven and earth, thus permitting the faithful to experience the divine. See Fairy von Lilienfeld, "Russisch-orthodoxe Kirche," in *Konfessionskunde,* ed. Friedrich Heyer (Berlin, 1977), 44–66, esp. 44, cited in Karl Christian Felmy, *Die Deutung der göttlichen Liturgie in der russischen Theologie: Wege und Wandlungen russischer Liturgie-Auslegung* (Berlin, 1984), 16. The emphasis on the transcendent is characteristic of the Alexandrian liturgical tradition as expressed by Pseudo-Dionysius the Areopagite and Maximus the Confessor. The mere symbolism of the material world is only a means that allows the soul to partake of divine communion; see Paul Meyendorff, *St Germanus of Constantinople on the Divine Liturgy* (Crestwood, N.Y., 1984), 26–28. The commemorative orientation is typical of the allegorical exegesis practiced in Antioch and later associated with exegetes like Germanos of Constantinople, Nikolaos Kabasilas, and Symeon of Thessalonike. The history of the fully human Christ is linked in the words and actions of the liturgy to the history of salvation; see Meyendorff, *St Germanus,* 48; and Hugh Wybrew, *The Orthodox Liturgy: The Development of the Eucharistic Liturgy in the Byzantine Rite* (Crestwood, N.Y., 1990), 123–71.

5. Paul of Aleppo, *Puteshestvie,* pt. 2, *Ot Dnestra do Moskvy* (Moscow, 1897), 195.

6. Michael S. Flier, "The Iconology of Royal Ritual in Sixteenth-Century Muscovy," in *Byzantine Studies: Essays on the Slavic World and the Eleventh Century,* ed. Speros Vryonis Jr. (New York, 1992), 53–76; Flier, "The Iconography of Royal Procession: Ivan the Terrible and the Muscovite Palm Sunday Ritual," in *European Monarchy: Its Evolution and Practice from Roman Antiquity to Modern Times,* ed. Heinz Duchhardt, Richard A. Jackson, and David Sturdy (Stuttgart, 1992), 109–25; Flier, "Breaking the Code: The Image of the Tsar in the Muscovite Palm Sunday Ritual," in *Medieval Russian Culture,* vol. 2, ed. Michael S. Flier and Daniel Rowland (Berkeley and Los Angeles, 1994), 213–42; and Flier, "Tsar' kak mifotvorets: Ivan Groznyi i Obriad v Nedeliu Vaii," in *Rossika,* ed. C. Ingerflom and T. Kondrat'eva (Moscow, in press).

7. Cf. Clifford Geertz, "Religion as a Cultural System," reprinted in his *Interpretation of Cultures* (New York, 1973), 91–100; and David I. Kertzer, *Ritual, Politics, and Power* (New Haven, 1988), 8–14.

8. For a detailed listing, see Flier, "Breaking the Code." The evidence from sixteenth-century Muscovite sources pertains to a Palm Sunday ceremony performed in Novgorod: I. K. Kuprianov, "Otryvki iz Raskhodnykh knig Sofiiskogo doma za 1548–i god," *Izvestiia Imp. Arkheologicheskogo obshchestva* 3, no. 1 (1861), col. 48.

9. The Epiphany ritual retained its place in the church ceremonial when the capital was transferred to St. Petersburg in 1712. By midcentury the procession made its way down the "Jordan Steps" of the fourth Winter Palace to the Jordan' that was set up on the ice of the Neva River.

10. The extension of the procession beyond the walls of the Kremlin occurred sometime after 1561, when the Church of the Intercession on the Moat was officially consecrated. Previously the ceremony had been contained within the Kremlin, among the three major cathedrals surrounding Cathedral Square. This was the first version of the Palm Sunday ritual. See also the commentary of Anthony Jenkinson and his entourage from 1557–1558 in Richard Hakluyt, *The Principall Navigations Voiages and Discoveries of the English Nation* (1589; facsimile reprint, Cambridge, 1965), 341–42.

11. N. Dubrovskii, "Patriarshie vykhody," in *Chteniia Obshchestva istorii i drevnostei rossiiskikh* (1869), bk. 2, pt. 5, 13–17, 28–35. This text is reproduced with slight differences in A. P. Golubtsov, *Chinovniki Moskovskogo Uspenskogo sobora* in *ChOIDR* (1907), bk. 4, pt. 1, 250–52 (ceremonial notebook from 1656 with annotations in margins for 1657).

12. Ibid., 15.

13. Meyendorff, *Russia, Ritual, and Reform,* 28.

14. S. D. Muretov, *Grecheskii podlinnik Nikonovskoi Skrizhali* (Moscow, 1892). The *Sluzhebnik* is the Slavic Orthodox service book for the officiating priest and choir that contains the fixed parts or ordinary of three Orthodox masses (Saint Chrysostom, Saint Basil, Presanctified Gifts). Sacramental rites, other occasional offices, and various other public and private services are contained in a separate prayer book, the *Trebnik.* These are analogues of the Greek *hieratikon* and *hagiasmatarion,* respectively. The *Skrizhal'* (literally, "stone," "sacred tablet") is an explanatory ceremonial.

15. K. Nikol'skii, *O sluzhbakh russkoi tserkvi byvshikh v prezhnikh pechatnykh bogosluzhebnykh knigakh* (St. Petersburg, 1885), 73.

16. A. Dmitrievskii, "Khozhdenie patriarkha Konstantinopol'skogo na zhrebiati v nedeliu vaii v IX i X vekakh," in *Sbornik statei v chest' akademika Alekseia Ivanovicha Sobolevskogo* (Leningrad, 1928), 69–75; and Averil Cameron, "The Construction of Court Ritual: The Byzantine *Book of Ceremonies*," in *Rituals of Royalty: Power and Ceremonial in Traditional Societies,* ed. David Cannadine and Simon Price (Cambridge, 1987), 116.

17. Nikol'skii, *O sluzhbakh,* 75.

18. Johann Christian Wilhelm Augusti, *Die Feste der alten Christen für Religions-Lehrer und gebildete Leser aus allen christlichen Confessionen,* vol. 2 (Leipzig, 1818), 48–50. Quaresmius's description was published in his two-volume work *Elucidationes terrae sanctae* (Antwerp, 1634–1639), and republished in 1880–1881, vol. 2, lib. 4, c. 11, p. 256 (not p. 333 as cited by Augusti). Nikol'skii, in *O sluzhbakh,* 75–76, incorrectly ascribes Quaresmius's account to the thirteenth century.

19. For the meeting of Nikon and Paisios, see N. Kapterev, *Snosheniia ierusalimskikh patriarkhov s russkim pravitel'stvom s poloviny XVI do kontsa XVIII stoletiia* (St. Petersburg, 1895) [*Pravoslavnyi Palestinskii sbornik* 15, no. 1], 141. For Nikon's ordination, see *Sobranie gosudarstvennykh gramot i dogovorov khraniashchikhsia v go-*

sudarstvennoi kollegii inostrannykh del, vol. 3 (St. Petersburg, 1822), no. 135, 447–49. "Slovo otveshchatel'noe," in *Skrizhal'* (Moscow, 1656), lv.

20. Arsenii Sukhanov, *Proskinitarii,* ed. N. Ivanovskii (St. Petersburg, 1889) [*Pravoslavnyi Palestinskii sbornik* 7, no. 3].

21. Ibid., 81. It seems that Arsenii actually witnessed no procession on the ass on Palm Sunday in Jerusalem in 1652. He describes the patriarch only presiding over a matins service (Mount of Olives?) and then a liturgy in the Holy Sepulcher (ibid., 75–76). It is unlikely he would have omitted this important detail. Throughout his commentary he notes the difficult circumstances under which Christians of all confessions try to practice their faith in the Holy Land, competing for time at various Holy sites, bribing local authorities to use churches, and so on. The apparent absence of the Procession on the Ass conflicts with the earlier testimony by Quaresmius. In his "Debates with the Greeks about the Faith," Arsenii juxtaposes the other patriarchs to the Muscovite patriarch, who has taken over the primacy of position earlier accorded to the pope. He specifically notes: "Your patriarchs cannot process through the city with crosses, wear crosses on their heads, put crosses on their churches . . . or ring their bells and ride on the ass." Cited from "Preniia s grekami o vere," in S. Belokurov, ed. *Arsenii Sukhanov,* pt. 2, *Sochineniia Arseniia Sukhanova,* ChOIDR (1894), bk. 2, pt. 1, 94 (cf. 168). Nonetheless, his mentioning the ride on the ass to the Greeks presupposes their understanding of that reference. Whether or not the Greek ceremony was still practiced in Jerusalem in the 1650s, the knowledge of it was surely maintained.

22. Even in 1655 Paul of Aleppo noted this symbolism: "and [the patriarch] dismounted from the horse by the steps of the staircase and ascended to one of the chapels of this cathedral, named for the Entry into Jerusalem, for all these chapels are likened to Bethany and the Kremlin to Jerusalem" (Paul of Aleppo, *Puteshestvie,* pt. 3, 178).

23. Felmy, *Die Deutung,* 105–111. See also O. B. Hardison Jr., *Christian Rite and Christian Drama in the Middle Ages: Essays in the Origin and Early History of Modern Drama* (Baltimore, 1965), 44.

24. Nicholas Cabasilas, *A Commentary on the Divine Liturgy,* trans. J. M. Hussey and P. A. McNulty (London, 1960), 28–30.

25. Ibid., 53; cf. *Skrizhal',* 265–66.

26. Ibid., 65; cf. *Skrizhal',* 309–11.

27. M. A. Il'in, *Letopis' Moskovskoi Rusi: Svetskie osnovy kamennogo zodchestva, XV–XVII vv.* (Moscow, 1966), 176–204; Leonid (archimandrite), *Istoricheskoe opisanie stavropigial'nogo voskresenskogo Novyi Ierusalim imenuemogo monastyria,* ChOIDR (1874), bk. 3, 2–11; Sukhanov, *Proskinitarii,* 141–96. The new Palm Sunday ritual and the replication of the Holy Sepulcher belie Ivanovskii's statement (viii) that the *Proskinitarii* essentially had no impact during the period of reforms in the middle of the seventeenth century. On the Amico connection, see James Cracraft, *The Petrine Revolution in Russian Architecture* (Chicago, 1988), 71, 343 (n. 53).

28. It is worth noting in this context that in the 1655 Palm Sunday ritual, with the tsar out of Moscow and thus unavailable to lead the ass, Nikon apparently extended an offer to Patriarch Makarios to take his own place in the Procession on the Ass. The visiting prelate demurred, saying that he wished to witness the full ritual as a spectator (Paul of Aleppo, *Puteshestvie,* pt. 3, 176).

29. Flier, "Tsar' kak mifotvorets," in press.

30. Cf. Rev. 22:1–2, 13–14.

31. See Meyendorff, *Russia, Ritual, and Reform,* 161.

32. Meyerberg reports the reading from the book of Matthew, but a close reading of the text from the Russian ceremonials makes it clear the reading is from Mark: Matt. 21:1 has ". . . then sent Jesus two disciples" (два оученика) and Mark 11:1 has ". . . he sendeth forth two of his disciples" (два от оученикъ своихъ). Cf. Friedrich Adelung, ed., *Augustin Freiherr von Meyerberg und seine Reise nach Russland* (St. Petersburg, 1827), 202.

33. The Rostov office from the seventeenth century, which apparently reflects Novgorod practice, clearly contains the text from Matthew; cf. Nikol'skii, *O sluzhbakh*, 95–97.

34. An allusion to Zech. 9:9.

35. The same transfer of reading responsibilities occurs in the celebration of the liturgy; see Nikol'skii, *O sluzhbakh*, 74–75.

36. RGB 3670, *Chin osviashcheniia vody v Kreshchenie* (Moscow, ca. 1655), 2.

37. *Patriarch Nikon on Church and State: Nikon's "Refutation,"* ed. Valerie A. Tumins and George Vernadsky (Berlin, New York, Amsterdam, 1982), 237, 235.

38. Ibid., 149–50, 156–60. I am grateful to my colleague Edward L. Keenan for his discussion of this and related issues. He has suggested (personal communication) that the "Refutation" and not Nikon's letter to Aleksei Mikhailovich of 30 March 1659, was the likely source alluded to in V. M. Zhivov and B. A. Uspenskii, "Tsar' i Bog: Semioticheskie aspekty sakralizatsii monarkha v Rossii," in *Iazyki kul'tury i problemy perevodimosti,* ed. B. A. Uspenskii (Moscow, 1987), 110. My investigations have confirmed his conjecture and have determined a likely path of misattribution. The two authors provide no text, but simply a paraphrase: "Nikon govorit, chto kogda on sam sovershil ètot obriad v Nedeliu vaii (Verbnoe voskresenie), to emu—patriarkhu—bylo strashno izobrazhat' litso Khrista; rech', tem samym, idet imenno o patriarkhe kak zhivoi ikone Khrista, obraze Bozhiem" (110). This paraphrase is nearly identical with the account presented in M. V. Zyzykin, *Patriarkh Nikon: Ego gosudarstvennye i kanonicheskie idei,* pt. 2 (Warsaw, 1934), 213, a reference cited by Zhivov and Uspenskii (110). But nothing approaching a phrase similar to "it is terrifying for the patriarch to represent the person of Christ" is contained within Nikon's letter, at least as translated by William Palmer in his work, *The Patriarch and the Tsar,* vol. 4 (Oxford, 1876), 164–66 (the original Russian Church Slavonic text is not provided). Palmer prefaces his translation of Nikon's letter, however, with an account of the events that occasioned its writing. He ends the preface as follows: "The performance of [the Palm Sunday ritual] he regarded as belonging exclusively—if only it were right to perform it at all, of which he doubted—to the patriarch, who was appointed *to represent the person of Jesus Christ:* and in this act of Pitirim he saw a lawless assumption of the rights of the patriarch, and personally of his own, which had not as yet been taken from him by the election of a new patriarch" (164; emphasis added). Here Palmer relates the essence not of the letter so much as Nikon's "Refutation," an unnamed source whose inclusion resulted in the confusion found in the Zyzykin and the Zhivov and Uspenskii references.

39. For the ritual of 1656, see Dubrovskii, "Patriarshie vykhody," 15; for the ritual of 1668, see *Rossiiskaia vivliofika,* 2d ed., vol. 11 (1789), 66; for the ritual of 1675, see Makarii (archimandrite), "Chinovnik Patriarkha Ioakima za 1675 god," *Vremennik imperatorskogo Moskovskogo obshchestva istorii i drevnostei rossiiskikh* 24 (1856): 76–77.

40. "Nachalo russkogo teatra" (published 1861), reprinted in *Sochineniia N. S. Tikhonravova,* vol. 2, *Russkaia literatura, XVII i XVIII vv.* (Moscow, 1898), 65.

41. Nikol'skii, *O sluzhbakh*, 76–77.

42. E. K. Chambers, *The Medieval Stage,* vol. 2 (Oxford, 1903), 1–176; Hardison, *Christian Rite,* 178–292; V. A. Kolve, *The Play Called Corpus Christi* (Stanford, 1966), 1–32.

43. Felmy, *Die Deutung,* 105–111.

44. Flier, "The Iconology," 64–66, and "The Iconography," 119–20.

45. Felmy, *Die Deutung,* 105.

46. Leonid Ouspensky, *Theology of the Icon,* trans. Anthony Gythiel, vol. 2 (Crestwood, N.Y., 1992), 249 (a translation of Léonide Ouspensky, *La Théologie de l'icône dans l'église orthodoxe* [Paris, 1980]). Ouspensky cites from Olivier Clément, *Byzance et le christianisme* (Paris, 1964), 76–77.

47. *Akty, sobrannye v bibliotekakh i arkhivakh Rossiiskoi Imperii Arkheologicheskoiu ekspeditsieiu Imperatorskoi Akademii nauk,* vol. 4: *1645–1700* (St. Petersburg, 1836), no. 223, 308–9.

EVE LEVIN

SUPPLICATORY PRAYERS AS A
SOURCE FOR POPULAR RELIGIOUS CULTURE IN
MUSCOVITE RUSSIA

SCHOLARS RESEARCHING popular religion in the premodern period constantly run up against the problem of
limited sources. Most texts arise from the elite, who defined the Faith in its ideal form, turning their attention
to popular practices only when they diverged from established norms. The result is a distorted picture of popular devotion, focused on the most heterodox elements.
However, the prayers that the laity recited, or had recited for them, might serve as a less biased source of information on popular religious perspectives. I offer here
suggestions on approaches to prayers as a source, and
some preliminary and thus tentative observations.

I have in mind the prayers for special occasions that
occurred in the lives of ordinary lay men and lay
women: illnesses of body and mind, events in the agricultural calendar (planting, reaping), momentous personal interactions (departing on a journey, going to
court, making peace with neighbors).[1] Prayers of these
types were frequently included in parish service books
(trebniki), as well as in miscellanies *(sborniki)* and
herbals *(travniki, lechebniki, tselebniki,* or *vertogrady).*
Snippets appeared in the testimony of witchcraft trials.

Very similar prayers were found in manuscripts of different genres. In some prayers, the priest spoke on behalf of the people; in others, the petitioners spoke for themselves. (For convenience, I will term the former "ecclesiastical" and the latter "lay.") These prayers survive in large numbers, and hundreds of examples have been published.[2]

The origin of supplicatory prayers has not been well researched. Tracing the origin of prayers—even official, canonical ones—is a difficult enterprise.[3] Like official prayers, the prayers of the laity traveled across linguistic and ethnic boundaries, but because they were often transmitted orally, they left few traces along the way.[4] Certain of the prayers have analogues in Greek and early Slavic manuscripts; others seem to have been composed in Russia. Some appear to be the work of individuals well versed in liturgy and Scripture. Some incorporated material from Slavic, Finnic, and even ancient Greek mythology, although no similar, purely pagan texts have been found. Many prayers combined Orthodox and mythological motifs, leading some scholars to hypothesize that they were the work of ignorant or unscrupulous clerics who catered to popular superstition.[5] Perhaps. But lay authorship should not be ruled out, because lay people spoke some of the prayers for themselves. Ethnographic studies of *zagovory* (charms) suggest that the speakers do not so much recite *zagovory* as recreate them from poetic fonds of rhythmical patterns, alliterative phrases, and standard motifs. As Barbara Halpern and John Foley noted in fieldwork in Yugoslavia, one peasant informant produced eight different variants of a single *zagovor*.[6] If the same pattern held true in Muscovy, each speaker invented a new prayer, and the texts preserved in our manuscripts represent a calcification of but a few of the many varieties of oral prayers in circulation.

A study of the origin of supplicatory prayers is beyond the purview of this essay, which focuses not on the distant roots of popular beliefs but rather on their manifestation in Muscovite Russia. In many cases, the manuscripts from Muscovy give no clue about the compilers' identity or purpose. It is not certain that the mediators (to use Peter Burke's term) were clerics or government bureaucrats, because at least a few lay people were literate; however, the copyists certainly selected and emended their material.[7] The scholars who published "charms" and "apocryphal prayers" in the nineteenth and twentieth centuries similarly acted as mediators, selecting out the texts they regarded as significant, often because of their pagan content. All too often, they provided only the most superficial information about the manuscripts in which they found their texts.

Because most of these prayers never entered the official canon, scholars such as A. I. Almazov have tended to label them as "apochryphal," *zagovory,* or *zaklinaniia* (imprecations).[8] In Almazov's schematization, official prayers, in general, were marked by a spiritual rather than a ritualistic approach to supplication; they possessed an ancient pedigree and remained in use in official *trebniki* in the nineteenth-century Russian Orthodox church. Apocryphal prayers diverged from Orthodox ones by including non-canonical material, such as secret words, but they still addressed appropriate figures

(Jesus, the saints) and sought their help toward good ends. *Zagovory* did not appeal to the power of God or heavenly figures; instead speakers invoked their own strength to accomplish their ends. *Zaklinaniia* addressed the sources of evil in order to bring them under the speaker's power, whether for good ends or ill. Because of the dualistic view of the universe inherent in this approach, *zaklinaniia* could not be considered Orthodox.

This type of classification is unsatisfactory, however; even Almazov noted certain ambiguities and inconsistencies. For example, the rite for the casting out of demons, which enjoyed long-standing inclusion in Eastern Orthodox service books, resembled *zaklinaniia* because it addressed the Devil. "Apocryphal" prayers often did not differ significantly from official ones; rather, they shared many elements, both in language and philosophy, with Orthodox ecclesiastical texts.[9] Some lay prayers were composed entirely of Orthodox phrases and sentiments, whereas some prayers in officially published *trebniki* contained "magical" elements.[10]

Before the development of printing in Russia, and the enforced standardization of prayer books under Patriarch Nikon, each *trebnik* differed from others, often in significant ways. If hierarchs sometimes condemned "prayer books of village priests with false prayers for healing, quakes, *nezhit*, and ailments," most lay people and their priests did not know about it, and probably would not have thought that their prayers fell under those rubrics. When a prayer appeared in a *trebnik*, then it was—to the scribe who copied the book, the priest who read from it, and the believers who heard it—a canonical prayer. Certainly the laity regarded their prayers as legitimate; one text describes how "Christ ordered the old man to make charms *[zagovarivati]* with all proper words."[11] That clerics argued over the content of their prayer books demonstrates that there existed in Muscovite Russia a range of views on what constituted proper Orthodoxy. The distinction between superstition and religion often had more to do with who authorized the procedure than what was said or done.[12] The line between elite and popular culture was both nebulous and permeable, and the supplicatory prayers for the laity lay at the intersection between them.[13]

Muscovite prayers for the laity, for all their pagan elements, reflected a profoundly Christian identity. The speakers, whether they were priests or peasants, referred to themselves as Christians and named themselves *rab bozhii* or *raba/rabynia bozhiia*, "servant of God." For example, a lay prayer against temptation from a *trebnik* from the 1690s asked of God, "teach me how I ought to act and speak . . . so that the Orthodox Christian faith will not be shamed."[14] These prayers were liberally sprinkled with phrases from the liturgy: *"blagoslovi, otche"* (bless us, Father); *"vo imia ottsa i syna i sviatago dukha"* (in the name of the Father, Son, and Holy Spirit); *"nyne i prisno i vo veke vekom""* (now and forever, for ages upon ages). However, this Christian identity did not coincide with the cognitive Christianity that was developing among the Muscovite elite in the seventeenth century.[15] It did not emphasize moral virtue or a striving to understand and do God's will. Instead, the focus of popular Christianity was the framing of people's lives with rituals to protect them from the terrible things that were loose in the world: the Devil and his minions, capricious forces of nature, evil people who sought to do harm. The supplicatory prayers evoke a sense of threat, sometimes overt and sometimes merely potential, but always present.

The Muscovites' ally against the dangers of this world were the forces of an otherworld, where analogous problems were resolved. Modern scholars looking into Muscovite culture can identify two distinct otherworlds: one, a world of folkloric myth, derived from pre-Christian traditions imperfectly remembered; and second, a world of Christian myth, incompletely assimilated. For the Muscovite laity, however, the two otherworlds were indistinguishable. In both cases, lay prayers tended to use the analogy of the otherworld mechanistically, as though the correction of the problem there would automatically alleviate it in this world—a phenomenon usually termed "sympathetic magic."[16]

The invocations of the otherworld of Slavic myth typically read: "There is the ocean-sea, and in the ocean-sea is a golden island, and on the golden island is a golden man. . . ."[17] Parts of this narrative might be omitted, or more descriptors added. The sea might be blue or black; the man white, black, red, maybe a woman; the island might be a mountain or a tree or a stone.[18] Some lay prayers stopped with a description of this otherworld. Others continued the narrative, describing an action that had a salubrious effect in this world; for example, the beautiful maiden sewing in the otherworld mended the wounds of the patient in this one. An archer fired arrows against spells and other dangers.[19] Iron people and implements in the otherworld translated into strength and impenetrability in this world.[20] Another common setting sketched location: from east to west, south to north; earth, sea, sky; sun, moon, stars, clouds.[21] The "ocean-sea" model did not appear often in ecclesiastical prayers, but the directional and astronomical settings did, perhaps because they resonated better with biblical imagery of God's domain.

In addition to references to the mythic setting, lay prayers included references to folk beliefs and practices not of Christian origin. For example, the name given to the island, Alatyr, matched the name of the isle to which evil spirits were exiled in pagan Greek curses from Late Antiquity.[22] The special attention to rowan trees, and the imprecations against trees thrown by malevolent forces, reflected Finno-Ugric motifs. The use of the bathhouse as a setting for rituals of birth and purification also stemmed from Finno-Ugric tradition, although Russian hierarchs authorized it as early as the twelfth century.[23] In one of the few prayers designed especially for women, a new mother went to the bathhouse by herself, placed the infant between her legs, crossed her arms and legs, and asked that no force harm her child.[24] However, the names of pagan deities did not appear in folk prayers, even in those few that lacked any Christian references.

Other prayers, both ecclesiastical and lay, invoked an otherworld from Christian mythology, most often from Scripture rather than from the lives of the saints. The most Orthodox usage of scriptural allusions was illustrative: to demonstrate that God both had the power to remedy problems and used this power for the benefit of his people, as in this ecclesiastical prayer against grief:

> Most holy Master, who heard the prayer of St. Apostle Peter and sent an angel to him, and lifted from him all unhappiness, [cf. Acts 12:6–11] have mercy on your servant N. who prays to you and hear his prayer. Send your angel to him, and hear his sorrow, and turn it to joy. Father, Son, and Holy Spirit. Now.

Whereas this prayer involved an appeal for a change in the petitioner's emotion (something consonant with a cognitive understanding of prayer), to medieval Russians the model applied equally to physical needs: "You who came to Bethany and resurrected Lazarus from the dead [cf. John 11:1–40], now strengthen this your servant N., and heal him of all disease, spiritual and bodily." A prayer to bless milk, recited while the cow is eating, made allusion to the Old Testament promise to Abraham, Isaac, and Jacob to endow their descendants with "a promised land flowing with honey and milk." An ecclesiastical prayer for departure on a journey addressed "Our God, true and living path, who traveled with your servant Joseph; accompany, Master, also your servant N." In this prayer, a double analogy was drawn: between the biblical traveler and the later petitioner, and between God as the way to salvation and the physical journey.[25]

Biblical examples also functioned as a form of sympathetic magic, especially in lay prayers. A layman's prayer before a court suit asked, "As King David calmed and reconciled the Hebrew tsars and princes, so may the heart of this judge, servant of God N., be calmed toward me." Lay prayers sometimes used biblical material in untraditional or inaccurate ways. For example, prayers to stop bleeding invoked the dissimilar model of the biblical drought under King Ahab (1 Kings 18:1) or Judas's suicide. A prayer to cure headache addressed Jesus, "who walked on Mount Zion and found a grave and opened it. And he said to the maiden lying in it, 'Why are you lying there?' and she said, 'My head hurts.'" Another prayer, against spells and trees, included the phrase, "as the Jews crucified Jesus Christ their lord, king of heaven, on Mount Sinai." A later reader of the manuscript wrote in a correction, "Golgotha."[26]

Whereas stories from the Bible, especially the Old Testament, appeared frequently, references to the lives of the saints were much less common in supplicatory prayers. A few saints were clear choices for certain problems. The Archangel Michael, military defender of heaven, was commissioned for general guard duty. A lay prayer, apparently for a soldier, invoked (among others) Muscovite national saints: "Petr, Aleksei, Iona, and Filipp of Moscow, and Muscovite miracle-workers of all Russia." Sometimes the vitae or icons suggested a reason for the association of a particular saint with a particular need. For example, the life of Kozma and Damian identified them as physicians, which explains why they figured in some prayers for the healing of illness. These saints, as well as St. Vlasii, traditionally connected with the fostering of animals, were invoked to protect livestock. Martyrs in general could relieve the suffering of the sick because they themselves had suffered.[27]

Often the choice of saints seems arbitrary. A seventeenth-century miscellany recommended (among others) Saints Mina, Lavrentii, or Loggin for blindness; Catherine for childbirth; Konon for juvenile smallpox; Miron, Fetinia, and Vasilii the New for epilepsy; and Gurii, Samon, and Aviv for marital discord. Although these saints had no obvious connection to the problems they were said to solve, the same text recommended that for headaches a patient approach John the Baptist, on August 29, the day in the Orthodox calendar that commemorates his beheading. Perhaps in the interests of security in numbers, some prayers listed as many saints—important and otherwise—as the speaker could muster. One example included seventeen saints by name, as well as "all saints, prophets, apostles, martyrs, and priestly martyrs."[28]

In use, the invocations of the Christian otherworld resembled those of the otherworld of folk myth. Thus it is not surprising that lay prayers interchange the two. A prayer to protect horses placed Christian figures in the otherworld of folkloric myth.

> On a clear field stands George's oak, and under George's oak sits the most holy Mother of God with her 33 apostles and Archangel Michael and Archangel Gabriel and Peter and Paul and John the Baptist and John the Evangelist and John Chrysostom and all the angels and archangels and cherubim and seraphim and all the apostles.

In another prayer, Christ sewed heaven and earth together with a golden needle and silk thread, while the Mother of God protected the speaker with her robe and "three nines of expensive German locks." A prayer against sorcerers contained the usual mythic sequence of sea, island, and stone but then described a "church of God" containing "lock and key" and a "golden ladder to the heights of heaven." The locks, needle, and thread stemmed from the folkloric tradition, whereas the Virgin's robe was a Byzantine symbol of divine protection, and the ladder recalled the *Lestvitsa* (ladder), a guide to monastic spirituality.[29]

In addition to inserting Christian references into the settings of the folkloric otherworld, supplicatory prayers fitted folkloric motifs into the Christian otherworld. For example, a seventeenth-century *trebnik* contained a prayer against *nezhit,* a malevolent destructive force that caused illness and insanity:

> In the name of the Father, Son, and Holy Spirit. Just as Adam, the first created, did not become ill, neither in his head nor his eyes, nor his teeth, nor in any organ of his body, so may this servant of God N. not become ill with any ailment, but may he take himself from any ailment. Just as sea foam and smoke from the wind, and wax from fire, and rain from the sun, may *nezhit* take itself from the servant of God N. Chase it to the empty hills and lead it to the deer's head. Lord Jesus Christ, Father of all things, sends you there. Now and forever.[30]

In this passage, the speaker used mostly Christian motifs: the Trinity from the liturgy; Adam from Genesis; smoke, wax, and empty hills from the Psalms (68:3 and 75:7). However, the concept of *nezhit* comes from Slavic pagan tradition, and the deer's head probably from Finno-Ugric sources. The prayer relied for efficacy on sympathetic magic as much as divine intervention.

Other lay prayers, although similarly combining Christian and folkloric motifs, invoked heavenly power in an Orthodox manner. In a prayer for a safe journey, the traveler pleaded:

> A great heavenly force and goodness and strength and wisdom and force against all my enemies, seen and unseen, fighting with me, servant of God N. and at my side two hundred ninety hands. . . . Be with me, servant of God N., in every place on the path, on the road, at home, in sittings, on the water, on the ninth day of days, in the night of nights, in every day and in every hour.

The repetitions and cataloging of constituent items recall the style of *zagovory*, even though the speaker addressed the powers of heaven in terms reminiscent of the Psalms. A lay prayer against frostbite intertwined the nature images of Russian folk tradition with Christian conceptions of God as creator of the natural world:

> Our true Lord, Jesus Christ, you, Lord, created, You, lord, heaven and earth, and you established on earth all things, four winds, east, west, south, north, and the sea, and rivers, and evil frosts. By your order, the sea freezes, and rivers, and all the earth, and this your servant bitten by frost N. And you, Lord, established that the righteous sun in the heavens hide, and that it warm the sea, the rivers, the lakes, and all the earth. So may it be with your servant of God N. Warm the frostbite with the righteous sun.

This sort of skillful manipulation of Christian symbols suggests that some lay people possessed much more than a superficial acquaintance with the Orthodox faith. At the same time, they continued to accept a magical approach to healing: the further instructions in this prayer implored God to remove the curse *(shchepotu)* and illness from the speaker's injuries and lay them on a cloth.[31]

Some of the goals of lay prayers, even though couched in terms affirming a Christian identity, transgressed the ordinances of the hierarchy. For example, numerous articles of canon law forbade fortune-telling, but a lay ritual for that purpose was performed in front of an icon, with prayers to Jesus Christ and the Mother of God. Similarly, lay prayers included services for preparing holy water on the Epiphany. But the making of holy water was a rite reserved to the clergy, and the clerical author of a set of penitential questions asked of his peasant parishioners: "On the day of the holy Epiphany, in the morning, did you chop a cross in the ice, making holy water, although that is not permitted to you, and it is the evilest of evils?"[32]

Although sermons emphasized the need for humility and respect for the social order, lay people saw nothing wrong in asking for divine help in gaining the favor of social superiors. One prayer read

King Solomon ruled forty satans, and in their mouths fire burned. So may the heart of the ruler, the servant of God N. [male] or servant of God N. [female] be to me, servant of God. As King Solomon ruled those forty satans, may I rule this servant of God.

Another lay prayer invoked the "bright world, morning dawn, and red sun" to influence all persons in power, both secular and ecclesiastical.[33] The strictest Orthodox teachings regarded the pursuit of physical beauty as vain and potentially concupiscent, but Muscovite lay people regarded it as completely compatible with Christianity:

There is the Jordan river, and in the middle of the Jordan river is a white stone, and on that holy white stone I, servant of God N. And I wash from myself ugliness and I wash on myself beauty and prettiness. And as the world rejoiced at the baptism of Christ's Easter *[krshchnoi Khsvy paskhi]* and great day, so may it rejoice at me.[34]

The wording of this prayer for beauty suggests that it was accompanied by rituals. Similarly, the common opening of lay prayers, "I stand, blessing myself, I go, crossing myself, from the doors of the house, from the gates of the gateposts," may be taken not only as a verbal formula but also as a description of activity. Many of the prayers, both ecclesiastical and lay, were framed by specific instructions on accompanying actions. The prayer for a court case, cited above, was to be recited over water and soap, and then the litigant would wash his face. The peasant celebrations for St. George's Day, when the livestock were traditionally sent to pasture, included both ritual actions and ritual words. In one version, the peasant walked three times around the pasture, with an axe in one hand, a candle in the other, a sickle around his neck, an icon of St. George, and an egg. In another, the speaker invoked Christian figures such as Saints George, and Kozma and Damian, asking, in Orthodox manner, that they pray to God and the Mother of God *(Bogoroditsa)* for the speaker and his herd, protecting them from "pagan hands, . . . beasts black and gray, . . . thieves and brigands." He asked Jesus Christ, "who rules all heavenly spheres and worldly things," to place a fiery river around the herd. In a third version of the ritual, the speaker took a spear, walked a circle around the yard, and stated, "May there be this iron ring around my cattle . . . from this day and the whole summer to the white snow." Thus, just as the prayers themselves intertwined Christian and mythic motifs, so the actions of the rituals drew elements from Orthodox liturgy, pagan ceremony, and mundane activity.[35]

Lay rituals may strike the modern reader as odd and unchristian, and certain ecclesiastical rituals of the seventeenth century seem equally so. Take, for example, the ritual for repurifying a church, "after a dog has bounded in or an unbeliever has entered," included in printed *trebniki* of the mid-seventeenth century. After some initial prayers, the priest needed to take holy water sanctified on the first day of August, and sprinkle it in the shape of a cross over the entire church and altar, to the east, west, south, and north. He also censed the same way. If there was filth *(prokaza)* from the dog, the de-filed material had to be cleaned out, and the place singed with fire. Similar *prokazy* from drunks or young children required only cleaning and repurifi-cation with holy water.[36] A prayer for heart disease in a *trebnik* (completely canonical otherwise) included instructions to write six words of power and tie the paper on the patient.[37] A number of prayers were designed to be writ-ten down in tiny booklets to serve as talismans. One prayer to repel spells and demons included these instructions: "If someone wears this prayer on oneself and reads it each day and each hour so that neither person nor devil can draw near or tempt him." The prayer itself was addressed to the Mother of God and the Trinity.[38]

Both lay and ecclesiastical prayers sometimes addressed the source of trou-ble in the manner of a *zagovor*. Certain such prayers had an ancient pedigree: Orthodox tradition recognized the reality of demon possession, and official prayer books in both the Byzantine and Slavic recensions contained services of exorcism.[39] But in addition to services of exorcism, Muscovite *trebniki* of-ten contained prayers to prevent demons from entering persons and places in the first place:

> Go out, Satan, from the two doors of this house, and from the four corners of this house, and from the foundation of this home. And here are the Apostles Peter and Paul, and here the saintly Mother of God gave birth to Christ, and here, you, Devil, and all our enemies, have no portion. The Archangels Michael, Gabriel, Raphael, and Sichael, and Uriel are here, at the doors pro-tecting this house and the servant of God N. Now the archangelic forces con-voke the waters of the seas and the race of humanity, so that this servant of God N. not be entrapped. Now and forever and ages of ages.[40]

Although directed to the Devil instead of God or heavenly figures, in other ways this prayer conformed to Orthodox norms. It drew on the power of an-gels and Christian saints, completely rejecting the powers of evil. Another prayer for driving evil spirits out of a house, contained in printed *potrebniki*, was similar, except that it addressed God.[41]

Lay prayers, much more frequently than ecclesiastical ones, addressed forces in this world instead of Christian figures or even Satan. But although a few texts of this sort omitted any mention of Christian figures (suggesting that the speaker did not need the backup of any supernatural power), most either implicitly or explicitly recognized the power of the Christian pantheon. The speaker in one peasant prayer for planting fields, after unexceptionally calling upon the "true Christ," then turned to "Christ's birds," imploring them not to "think evil" about him and his property. Similarly, lay prayers to protect against storms might address clouds. A lay prayer for protection against enemies asked the help of an herb called *molchana*, the silent one.[42]

The presupposition for petitioning things in this world was that they had a will of their own and could be cajoled into behaving in a certain way. Cer-tain lay prayers, such as one against toothaches, invoked the dead, harking back to Slavic traditions of ancestor worship. A similar prayer to help the speaker avoid the temptation of alcohol addressed both Mother Earth and the dead body exhumed for the accompanying ritual:

> Mother Earth, you give me to drink and to eat . . . from you, Mother Earth, arise all fruits, good, bad, and intoxicating. May I, servant of God N., not drink, not see, not want, and not think of that intoxicating drink! Adam my father, I am your son. Rescue me, your son, the servant of God N., from this intoxicating drink. And you, dead person N., so much time you lie there, and you do not drink so much intoxicating [liquor], nor do you eat bread, so may I, servant of God N., not drink intoxicating drink, not eat, nor want, nor see, nor see [sic], nor hear, nor think about, until the cover of the grave. And to you, dead person, eternal remembrance forever.

This prayer reveals that the lay speaker shared the ecclesiastical view that overindulgence in alcohol was inappropriate. But whereas sermons focused on the sinfulness of drunkenness and its evil consequences, this prayer suggests no moral considerations. Sermons exhorted listeners to self-restraint; this prayer invoked external, but nondivine, powers.[43]

Just as the sources of trouble, whether natural or demonic, were sentient enough to respond to petitions, they were solid enough to be physically banished. Misused natural substances, such as iron in weapons, were remanded "to your mother earth." A prayer to ease the discomfort of a baby read, "And you, teething, do not bite this infant, child of God . . . leave this child and go to the dark forests, to the moss and swamps where no one goes." The sources of evil were exiled from the community of Christians to "impassible places," "the empty expanses of the sea [compare Psalms 8:9]," "the cold north," or "the pagan Germans."[44]

The prayers for the laity drew a sharp distinction between Russian Christians and strangers—frequently misidentified as "pagans"—who sought to do harm. Although modern scholars like to equate "witches" and "sorcerers" with the folk healers sought by the laity but condemned by the church, lay prayers unequivocally classed them as malevolent figures who used their powers for evil.[45] Lay prayers depicted all outsiders as suspicious and dangerous, warding off sorcerers along with tsars, kings, princes, boyars, pagans, Tatars, Turks, Muslims, Kalmyks, Cheremis, Germans, Kirgiz, and "all the believing and unbelieving seventy tribes."[46]

Some miscellanies recorded incantations to cause injury along with charms for good purposes; such incantations resemble those found in transcripts of witchcraft investigations. Christian references in these texts were few and fleeting; even so, they were not so much pagan as anti-Christian. A spell for victory in a fistfight replaced the usual ritual formula *"se iaz" rab" bozhii"* with *"se iaz" rab","* blatantly omitting the reference to God. Instead of invoking Christian powers, the speaker summoned help "from the woods, woody things, from the water, watery things." Similarly, a spell to incite sexual desire in a woman acknowledged that the end being sought contradicted Christian righteousness and altered the usual formula to omit reference to God. A speaker who desired power over others inverted the usual formula in his charm: "I stand, not blessing myself, I go, not crossing myself," demon-strating his rejection of Christian behavior. He then invoked the help of the marginalized dead: "you murdered ones . . . lost ones . . . you eaten by beasts, awake, unbaptized ones . . . awake, nameless ones!" As in this exam-ple, repudiating Christian conduct did not necessarily involve soliciting de-monic assistance. Agaf'itsa Savkina, accused of witchcraft in 1648, used a folkloric charm and invoked sympathetic magic: "as a dead man does not stand, so may he, Fedor not stand; as a dead man's body has fallen, so may Fedor fall entirely." Although uncommon, some texts included renunciation of God and declaration of faith in Satan.[47]

Ecclesiastical prayers and prosecution records suggest that the governmen-tal elite shared the popular distinction between the invocations of supernatu-ral power for good and those for ill and did not focus on the form or canon-icity of the prayers themselves. For all the official railing against "pagans" and "sorcerers," neither the state nor the church created an apparatus to ferret out offenders. Instead officials waited for private citizens to register com-plaints. Church magistrates directed their inquests against persons who caused harm to people's bodies and souls or who subverted clerical authority.[48] That authorities took complaints about hexes and curses seri-ously testifies to the widespread belief, even among the elite, that spells were efficacious.[49] Seventeenth-century courts not only ordered the prosecution of persons who bewitched someone but also ordered the burning of written ver-sions of their spells.[50]

It is significant that persons accused of witchcraft defended themselves by claiming that their incantations included appeals to the saints and the sign of the cross. When Simon Danilov was accused of sorcery in 1647, for exam-ple, he pleaded that he had used only roots, herbs, and water he blessed with the sign of the cross to heal and to cast out demons. However, he was con-victed anyway, perhaps because he had become involved with the politically prominent Streshnev boyar family. Evtiushka Markov, a former pharmacy student, was charged with sorcery under similar circumstances in 1699. He claimed that he used roots, herbs, and vodka, "all for good and not for crimi-nal purposes [vse dobroe i ne vorovskoe]," without incantantions, but using his cross in the presence of icons.[51] In this way, the invocation of Christian sym-bols testified to the speaker's benign intent.

Russell Zguta suggested that Muscovite folk healers lived a precarious ex-istence, always under suspicion of witchcraft should their treatments fail.[52] The prayers for healing themselves neither confirm nor refute his con-tention. They do demonstrate that some conceptions of illness and methods of treatment were shared by ecclesiastics and lay people alike, while others were peculiar to one group or the other.

Ecclesiastical prayers shared the premise of folk prayers that illness re-sulted from the invasion of the body by a force from outside. In both tradi-tions, the force could be demonic, or the disease itself in a personified form. A prayer in a monastic trebnik depicted demons as the cause of illness, in ac-cordance with the Gospel (Matt. 10:1), and granted the priest with power to heal: "I give you power over all unclean spirits so as to drive them out and to heal every disease and every ailment."[53] In a prayer found in an herbal manual, the lay speaker removed blood from a wound by ordering the "accursed Devil," to depart "from my white body, be it dead to you!" Some ecclesiastical prayers personified diseases in the manner of popular charms, as in the one that invoked examples of Jesus' forgiveness and mercy, and then pleaded, "chase away from him [the patient] this headache!" Because the illness was a sentient force, it had to be warned away from all parts of the body, lest it hide in one not mentioned in the prayer.[54]

Whether ecclesiastical prayers addressed divine figures or the malevolent sources of disease, they invoked the power of God. God was identified as "physician of souls and bodies [vrach' dusham" i tielom"]; who took on our ailments without labor, and who cured us with his wounds." Ecclesiastical texts frequently associated illness with the wages of sin. In one prayer, the patient was equated with biblical figures, such as the thief crucified with Christ or the Prodigal Son, who still managed to gain God's mercy. Thus the healing of the patient involved not only correcting the illness, but also asking God to "purify him from all fleshly and spiritual defilement."[55]

Lay prayers also acknowledged God's power to heal. According to lechebniki, physicians were able to cure their patients because "God has permitted them to know the things created by God."[56] However, lay compositions, whether for healing or other purposes, rarely referred to human sinfulness or the need for God's mercy. The phrase "Gospodi pomilui" (Lord, have mercy), so common in liturgical prayers, was not a normal part of lay prayers; lay speakers usually did not refer to themselves or their patients as "sinful" (greshnye).[57] Either lay people did not accept the notion that they were sinners, or they thought it best not to remind God of it when they were asking for something.

The emphasis on the spiritual element in healing did not rule out physical means; many of the surviving prayers from both the ecclesiastical and lay traditions were accompanied by rituals of treatment and herbal remedies. Although ecclesiastical prayers attributed healing to the power of God, monastic healers also used herbal remedies, which worked according to God's will.[58] One prayer in a trebnik was intended for recitation while the patient bathed in warm springs. The priest speaks the words of the Mother of God's appeal to her Son:

> Generous Lord, listen to me on behalf of your servant, and grant him the blessing of this place and his stay in it with faith. May this spring of warm waters flow and may all who bathe in it be worthy of healing from all ailments and sores, and receive life in heaven.[59]

Religious practitioners might be expected to use prayers and physical treatments together, and the same was also true of Muscovite medical professionals. One "medical" cure for headache from a lechebnik differed little from "religious" ones: "If your head hurts, take your head with your hand and say this:

'Christ is crucified and buried and risen.' By this word you will be healed."[60]

Some recipes for medicines in herbals made explicit the supernatural component in healing. For example, the pharmacist preparing a remedy for toothache was directed to recite the "psalm, 'God have mercy upon me'" repeatedly while boiling the wine for the medicine. To prepare another herb, popularly called Adam's head, the practitioner should "tear that herb with the cross of the Lord, and say, 'Our Father, have mercy on me, God.' And whoever does not know how to read should recite the Jesus prayer 300 times." (Adam's head not only cured physical illnesses and pain in childbirth but also provided clairvoyance: "Whoever wants to see a devil or heretic, take that root and put it in sanctified water, and lay it on the altar and do not move it for 40 days. On that day come and take it with you, and you will see demons of water and air.") In addition to the direct influence from God, Muscovite medicine accepted the notion that medicines prepared at specific times, such as St. John's Day or St. Peter's Day, would be more effective. In short, Muscovites regarded herbal and spiritual healing to be mutually compatible.[61]

SUPPLICATORY PRAYERS provide a considerable amount of information about popular religious conceptions in Muscovite Russia. Elements of high culture filtered down even to peasants in isolated localities; members of the elite, including the highest clergy, participated in rituals of popular origin. Boyars consulted folk healers, with their herbs and incantations; peasants reported incidences of sorcery to the authorities. Lay people had no doubt of their Christian identity, but their level of knowledge varied. Some prayers reflected considerable knowledge of Scripture and ecclesiastical literature; others reflected barely a passing acquaintance with a handful of stories and figures. But lay people felt comfortable enough with their Christianity to invent their own prayers and to coin meaningful similes and images. Their prayers intermixed elements from Christian sources and pagan mythologies; they also reflected a basically magical conception of supernatural power. Lay people believed that the problems of this world—whether physical, mental, or social—might be resolved by invoking the analogy of an otherworld where the problem had already occurred and been corrected. The power of natural substances could be awakened through proper rituals of preparation and the recitation of phrases, usually drawn from Christian liturgy.

Although lay prayers tended to be mechanistic and laced with heterodox references and rituals, they shared with ecclesiastical prayers their basic approach to the role of the supernatural in daily life. Both clergy and laity distinguished between the invocations of supernatural power for benign and evil purposes, and to a great extent their understandings of good and evil coincided. Ecclesiastical prayers, like their lay equivalents, invoked the model of an otherworld populated by biblical figures and saints. Clerics also acknowledged the efficacy of rituals and holy objects, apart from the moral virtue and worthiness of persons who sought their aid. The laity did not distinguish magic from religion, but neither did many of their clergy. Instead of a Christian cosmos in which power arose from God for good purposes but could be perverted for evil, most lay people—and many clergy, too—conceived of a universe in which powerful natural forces were neither good nor evil but arbitrary and willful. Despite attempts on the part of certain members of the ecclesiastical elite to enforce conformity, Muscovite Orthodoxy encompassed a wide diversity of beliefs and practices.

The religious ferment in the ecclesiastical and secular elite in the mid-seventeenth century altered official attitudes toward the religion of the laity. As official Orthodoxy, under the influence of Jesuit-inspired intellectualism, became more cognitive and less tolerant of magic, a gap grew between ecclesiastical and lay traditions of prayer. The correction of prayer books under Patriarch Nikon and his successors effectively pushed traditional folk prayers out of the canon—or perhaps into the ranks of the Old Believers. The elite, including the seminary-trained parish priests of later generations, came to deride as ignorant, pagan, and superstitious the uneducated lay people who clung to an older understanding of what constituted the Christian faith. Modern scholars should not make the same mistake.

NOTES

I would like to acknowledge research support from the International Research and Exchanges Board, the Fulbright-Hays program of the Department of Education, the Summer Research Laboratory of the University of Illinois, and the Hilandar Research Library at Ohio State University. In addition, Dr. Mary MacRobert provided invaluable assistance in identifying biblical references and early Slavic antecedents in Muscovite prayers.

1. On the range of purposes in Russian charms, see Elena Eleonskaia, *K izucheniiu zagovora i koldovstva v Rossii* (Moscow, 1917). She makes some distinctions between Muscovite and twentieth-century *zagovory.* See also Sergei V. Maksimov's classic monograph, recently reissued, *Nechistaia, nevedomaia, i krestnaia sila* (Moscow, 1989); Linda J. Ivanits, *Russian Folk Belief* (Armonk, N.Y., 1989); and Joseph L. Conrad, "Russian Ritual Incantations: Tradition, Diversity, and Continuity," *Slavic and East European Journal,* 33, no. 3 (fall, 1989): 422–37.

2. I base my survey on the prayers in the following publications: A. I. Almazov, *Apokrificheskie molitvy, zaklinaniia, i zagovory* (Odessa, 1901); A. I. Almazov, *K istorii molitv na raznye sluchai* (Odessa, 1896); A. I. Almazov, *Vracheval'nye molitvy* (Odessa, 1900); S. A. Blokhin, "Zagovory," *Trudy Orlovskoi uchenoi arkhivnoi komissii* 5 (Orel, 1889): 12–20; Iu. A. Iavorskii, "Zagovory i apokroficheskie molitvy po karpato-russkim rukopisiam XVIII-go i nach. XIX-go v.," *Russkii filologicheskii vestnik* no. 2 (1915): 193–223; I. Karatygin, "Obzor nekotorykh osobennostei v chinoposledovaniiakh rukopisnykh trebnikov, prinadlezhashchikh biblioteke S.-Peterburgskoi Dukhovnoi Akademii," *Khristianskoe chtenie* 3–4 (1877): 423–48; L. N. Maikov, *Velikorusskie zaklinaniia* (St. Petersburg, 1869); I. Ia. Porfir'ev, "Apokroficheskie molitvy po rukopisiam Solovetskoi biblioteki," *Trudy chetvertogo arkheologicheskogo s"ezda v Rossii, byvshogo v Kazani, s 31 iiulia po 18 avgusta 1877 goda* 2 (Kazan', 1891): 1–24; V. Sokolov, "Materialy dlia istorii starinnoi russkoi lechebnoi

literatury (Lechebnik No. 480 Moskovskoi patriarshei—nyne Sinodal'noi biblioteki)," *Varshavskie universitetskie izvestiia* no. 6 (1872): 65–115; V. I. Sreznevskii,
*Opisanie rukopisei i knig sobrannykh dlia Imperatorskoi Akademii nauk v Olonetskom
krae* (St. Petersburg, 1913), 196–205, 481–513; P. A. Syrku, "Otryvok mal-
orusskogo prostonarodnogo lechebnogo travnika i dva zagovora," *Filologicheskie zapiski* 1 (1883): 1–12; Nikolai Tikhonravov, *Pamiatniki otrechennoi russkoi literatury*
(Moscow, 1863; reprint, London, 1973), vol. 2: 351–60; P. Zenbitskii, "Zagovory,"
Zhivaia starina 1 (1907): sect. 2, 1–6. I also consulted the following early printed
books: *Trebnik* (Kiev 1606; Ohio State University, Hilandar Research Library [here-
after, HRL], Kiev Slavic Collection [hereafter, KSC]), 49; *Trebnik* (Moscow 1637;
KSC 127); *Potrebnik mirskoi* (Moscow, 1639; KSC 136); *Potrebnik* (Moscow 1651;
KSC 191); and these unpublished manuscripts: HRL, Uppsala 44 (Prayer book,
169–); Russian State Library, Manuscript Division (hereafter RGB), f. 199, Sobranie
Nikiforova, no. 30 (*Trebnik s nomokanonom,* 15th c.) probably from a monastery;
RGB, f. 310, no. 58 (*Sluzhebnik,* 17th c.); RGB, f. 412, Sobranie G. M. Zaklinda,
no. 110 (*Sbornik dukhovnikh stikhov,* 17th c.); Russian State Archive of Ancient Acts
(hereafter RGADA), f. 196, Sobranie Mazurina, no. 312 (*Trebnik,* 15–16th c.):
RGADA, f. 196, no. 1447 (*Sbornik,* 16th c.). Although *zagovory* and apocryphal
prayers exist among the Russian peasantry to this day, I use here only materials from
the Muscovite period, because, although later peasant culture can provide hints on
how to read seventeenth-century culture, peasant materials recorded later may not be
of medieval provenance.

    3. See, for example, John H. Lind's analysis of a list of Danish saints in a Rus-
sian prayer: "The Martyria of Odense and a Twelfth-Century Russian Prayer: The
Question of Bohemian Influence on Russian Religious Literature," *Slavonic and East
European Review* 68, no. 1 (January 1990): 1–21.

    4. Cf. T. M. Smallwood, "'God Was Born in Bethlehem': The Tradition of a
Middle English Charm," *Medium Aevum* 58, no. 2 (1989): 206–23.

    5. Almazov, *Apokrificheskie molitvy,* 23–25, 80–82, and *Vracheval'nye molitvy,*
4–21; Profir'ev, "Apokrificheskie molitvy," 1–2.

    6. Barbara Kerewsky Halpern and John Miles Foley, "The Power of the
Word: Healing Charms as an Oral Genre," *Journal of American Folklore* 91, no. 362
(October–December 1978): 903–24. The classicist Milman Parry made use of research on Serbo-Croatian epics to develop his theories concerning the development
and preservation of Homeric poetry. He argued that a large number of rhythmic and
alliterative half-lines of poetry, developed over many generations, formed a reservoir
of text readily available to the singer of an epic. Although Parry's theory is still dis-
puted by Homeric experts, it has attracted the interest of scholars of Slavic *zagovory*
and Anglo-Saxon charms. See J. M. Foley, "Epic and Charm in Old English and
Serbo-Croatian Oral Tradition," *Comparative Criticism* (1981): 71–79. I am grateful
to my father, Professor Saul Levin, for providing me with a summary of the status of
the debate on Parry's theory.

    7. Peter Burke, *Popular Culture in Early Modern Europe* (London, 1978), 73.
Gary Marker demonstrates that huge print runs of primers were produced in Muscovy but still concludes that literacy was exceptional among the laity. See "Primers
and Literacy in Muscovy: A Taxonomic Investigation," *Russian Review* 48, no. 1
(January 1989): 1–20.

    8. Almazov, *Vracheval'nye molitvy,* 39–40, and *Apokrificheskie molitvy,* 11–27,
31–33; see also Karatygin, "Obzor," 441.

    9. Karen Louise Jolly observed a similar situation in her study of Anglo-Saxon

popular prayers; I am much indebted to her insights. See her articles "Anglo-Saxon Charms in the Context of a Christian World View," *Journal of Medieval History* 11, no. 4 (December 1985): 279–93; and her "Magic, Miracle, and Popular Practice in the Early Medieval West: Anglo-Saxon England," in *Religion, Science, and Magic,* ed. Jacob Neusner, Ernest S. Frerichs, and Paul Virgil McCracken Flesher (New York, 1989), 166–82. Jolly's conceptualization is particularly attractive because of the rough similarity in conditions between eleventh-century England and seventeenth-century Russia. Both countries, at those times, had been formally Christian for several centuries. Both had recently experienced the strains of unification, civil war, and foreign invasion. Both states were undergoing centralization of governmental authority. Finally (and most pertinent for this study), the staffing of rural parishes had finally been achieved, although the priests shared their peasant parishioners' background, needs, and perspectives. On the clear parallels between Anglo-Saxon and Slavic charms, see Foley, "Epic and Charm," 71–92.

10. I use the term "magical" in the sense defined by Keith Thomas, *Religion and the Decline of Magic* (New York, 1971).

11. Quotations are from Almazov, *Apokrificheskie molitvy,* 11 (*nezhit* discussed later in this essay); and Sreznevskii, *Opisanie,* 486.

12. Ronald C. Finucane notes a similar ambiguity in magical and religious healing in medieval England in *Miracles and Pilgrims: Popular Beliefs in Medieval England* (London, 1977), 62–64.

13. On the intersection between high and low religious cultures, see T. A. Bernshtam, "Russian Folk Culture and Folk Religion," in *Russian Traditional Culture,* ed. Marjorie Mandelstam Balzer (Armonk, N.Y., 1992), 34–47. Scholars of western Europe face similar issues. Cf. Burke, *Popular Culture,* esp. 23–64; A. Ia. Gurevich, *Srednevekovyi mir: Kul'tura bezmolvstvuiushchego bol'shinstva* (Moscow, 1990); Natalie Zemon Davis, "From 'Popular Religion' to Religious Cultures," in *Reformation Europe: A Guide to Research,* ed. Steven Ozment (St. Louis, 1982), 321–41. On the problems with the concept of *dvoeverie* as a characterization of popular religion in medieval Russia, see Eve Levin, "*Dvoeverie* and Popular Religion," *Seeking God: The Recovery of Religious Identity in Orthodox Russia, Ukraine, and Georgia,* ed. Stephen K. Batalden (DeKalb, 1993), 31–52.

14. HRL, Uppsala 44, fols. 19–20v.

15. Paul Bushkovitch, *Religion and Society in Russia: The Sixteenth and Seventeenth Centuries* (New York, 1992).

16. Ethnographers have identified this characteristic as the essence of the *zagovor.* See Conrad, "Russian Ritual Incantations," 425–26, 434; Russell Zguta, "Witchcraft and Medicine in Pre-Petrine Russia," *Russian Review* 37, no. 4 (October 1978): 444–48; Harold L. Klagstad Jr., "Great Russian Charm Structure," *Indiana Slavic Studies* 2 (1958): 135–44; V. J. Mansikka, *Über russische Zauberformeln, Annales Academiae Acientiarum Fennicae,* ser. B, vol. 1 (Helsinki, 1909); and Almazov, *Apokificheskie molitvy,* 30. For comparison, see Joseph L. Conrad, "Bulgarian Magic Charms: Ritual, Form, and Content," *Slavic and East European Journal* 31, no. 4 (winter, 1987): 548–62; Louis Petroff, "Magical Beliefs and Practices in Old Bulgaria," *Midwest Folklore* 7, no. 4 (winter, 1957): 214–20; Anisava Miltenova and Anni Kirilova, eds., *Srednovekovni lekovitsi i amuleti* (Sofia, 1994); and Edina Bozoky, "Mythic Mediation in Healing Incantations," in *Health, Disease, and Healing in Medieval Culture,* ed. Sheila Campbell, Bert Hall, and David Klausner (New York, 1992), pp. 84–92.

17. Sreznevskii, *Opisanie,* 506.

18. Cf. ibid., 486 (white sea, white rock, bloody crow; sea, oak, moist mother), 499–500 (black river, black man, black bow), 503 (ocean, white stone, maiden; ocean, white island, white man; ocean, bronze man, bronze horse); Zenbitskii, "Zagovory," 3–4 (ocean, oak, old woman Solomeia).

19. Sreznevskii, *Opisanie,* 482, 485, 503.

20. For example, protection against danger; cf. Blokhin, "Zagovory," 14.

21. Sreznevskii, *Opisanie,* 511–12.

22. Professor Sarah Iles Johnston pointed out the similarity to me.

23. For rowan trees, see Sreznevskii, *Opisanie,* 493, 494, 500. For the bathhouse, see Eve Levin, "Childbirth in Medieval Russia," in *Russia's Women: Accommodation, Resistance, Transformation,* ed. Barbara Evans Clements, Barbara Alpern Engel, and Christine D. Worobec (Berkeley and Los Angeles, 1991), 51.

24. Sreznevskii, *Opisanie,* 495. See also the prayer for healing wounds, pp. 484–85. The collection of prayers that Sreznevskii published came from North Russia and particularly reflects motifs of the indigenous non-Slavic population. A few prayers even include words in the Ves' language, for example on p. 497.

25. For grief, see Almazov, *Vracheval'nye molitvy,* 126 (also Karatygin, "Obzor," 443). For physical disease, see Porfir'ev, "Apokrificheskie molitvy," 8 (also p. 10); and Tikhonravov, *Pamiatniki,* 359. For milk, see Karatygin, "Obzor," 443. For the journey, see *Trebnik,* HRL, KSC 127, fol. 674–75; also *Potrebnik* HRL, KSC 136, fol. 392; *Potrebnik,* HRL, KSC 191, fol. 541v; RGB, f. 412, Sobranie G. M. Zaklinda, no. 110, fols. 272–72v. RGADA, f. 196, Sobranie Mazurina, no. 1447, fols. 7–7v, cites Mary and Joseph's departure to Egypt.

26. For the court suit, see Sreznevskii, *Opisanie,* 491 (also 492). For bleeding, see M. Iu. Lakhtin, *Starinnye pamiatniki meditsinskoi pis'mennosti* (Moscow, 1911), 32; and Sreznevskii, *Opisanie,* 564 (also 486, 500). A version in Zenbitskii, "Zagovory," 4–5, changes Ahab to Agaf. For headache, see Porfir'ev, "Apokrificheskie molitvy," 12. For spells and trees, see Sreznevskii, *Opisanie,* 510–11.

27. For Michael, see Blokhin, "Zagovory," 18; Zenbitskii, "Zagovory," 2–3; Maikov, *Velikorusskie zaklinaniia,* 155. For the soldier's prayer, see Zenbitskii, "Zagovory," 1. For illness, see Almazov, *Vracheval'nye molitvy,* 31–32, 118; and Tikhonravov, *Pamiatniki,* 356. For livestock, see Sreznevskii, *Opisanie,* 495–96; and Zenbitskii, "Zagovory," 5. For suffering, see Alamazov, *Vracheval'nye molitvy,* 120–21, a prayer addressed to the nine martyrs.

28. For headache, see RGB, f. 412, Sobranie G. M. Zaklinda, no. 110, fols. 299–305. For all saints, see Almazov, *Vracheval'nye molitvy,* 118–19; also Blokhin, "Zagovory," 18; and RGB, f. 199, Sobranie Mazurina, no. 30, fols. 17v–18v. For another odd grouping of saints, see Eleonskaia, *K izucheniiu,* 9–10.

29. For the Mother of God and the oak, see Sreznevskii, *Opisanie,* 494. For Christ's sewing, see Zenbitskii, "Zagovory," 4; also Sreznevskii, *Opisanie,* 498, 512. For the church of God, see Sreznevskii, *Opisanie,* 486–87 (also 507).

30. Almazov, *Vracheval'nye molitvy,* 114 (also 48–49); Porfir'ev, "Apokrificheskie molitvy," 4, 5, 11. RGADA, f. 196, Sobranie Mazurina, no. 312, f. 271v, omits the passage about sea foam, smoke, and wax, which is based on Psalm 67:3. Some prayers against *nezhit* address it instead of God; cf. Porfir'ev, "Apokrificheskie molitvy," 11–12.

31. For safe journey, see Blokhin, "Zagovory," 14. For frostbite, see Sreznevskii, *Opisanie,* 504.

32. For fortune-telling, see Sreznevskii, *Opisanie,* 482. For making holy water, see A. I. Almazov, *Tainaia ispoved' v pravoslavnoi vostochnoi tserkvi* (Odessa, 1894),

vol. 3, 170. An eighteenth-century Carpatho-Russian version calls for the lay speaker to begin by taking holy water from the church "if you can," and then to gather people together, calling upon God, "all heavenly forces," and St. Zosima for help; see Iavorskii, "Zagovory," 210–11.

33. For King Solomon, see Sreznevskii, *Opisanie*, 492. See also the text in Zenbitskii, "Zagovory," 4: "as Orthodox Christians reverence *[pokloniaiutsia]* the true Christ, so may princes and boyars and great powers reverence me, servant of God." For the bright world, see Sreznevskii, *Opisanie*, 491 (also 501).

34. For beauty, see Sreznevskii, *Opisanie*, 500–501. The phrase "servant of God" is in the masculine form.

35. For the prayer opening, see ibid., 500, 498. The latter example continues, "from my father with permission, from my mother with blessing," which reinforces the expression of propriety. For water and soap, see ibid., 491 (also 492). For livestock, see ibid., 487, 495–96; also Zenbitskii, "Zagovory," 5.

36. *Potrebnik,* HRL, KSC 136, fols. 57–57v; also *Potrebnik,* HRL, KSC 191, fol. 51. RGB, f. 310, Sobranie Mazurina, no. 58, fols. 326–27, omits the section concerning *prokaza.*

37. The six words of power are *"Elam".Selam".Vargotha.Tothathi.Thivva.Rasis","* Almazov, *Vracheval'nye molitvy,* 119. The writing of the words of a prayer in itself formed a ritual. Both lay and ecclesiastical prayers sometimes contain indecipherable words of power; see Syrku, "Otryvok," 11–12.

38. For talismans, see Eleonskaia, *K izucheniiu,* 13. On amulets in general, see Almazov, *Apokrificheskie molitvy,* 27–29. For spells and demons, see Almazov, *Vracheval'nye molitvy,* 128; also Zenbitskii, "Zagovory," 4.

39. A. I. Almazov, *Chin nad besnovatym* (Odessa, 1901); Alzamov, *Vracheval'nye molitvy,* 131–48; Porfir'ev, "Apokrificheskie molitvy," 6–7, 14–20; *Trebnik,* HRL, KSC 137, fols. 677–78; *Potrebnik,* HRL, KSC 136, fols. 386–89v.

40. Almazov, *Vracheval'nye molitvy,* 130 (also 127, 129); Porfir'ev, "Apokrificheskie molitvy," 13; Karatygin, "Obzor," 446.

41. *Potrebnik,* HRL, KSC 136, fol. 390v; *Potrebnik,* HRL, KSC 191, fol. 541.

42. For Christ's birds, see Zenbitskii, "Zagovory," 5. For storms, see Iavorskii, "Zagovory," 197–202. For protection against enemies, see Sreznevskii, *Opisanie,* 481.

43. For toothaches, see Sreznevskii, *Opisanie,* 500 (also 493). For alcohol, see ibid., 497–98. See also Eve Levin, *Sex and Society in the World of the Orthodox Slavs, 900–1700* (Ithaca, N.Y., 1989), 55–57, 235–36, 270, 280.

44. For natural substances, see Zenbitskii, "Zagovory," 2. For teething, see Sreznevskii, *Opisanie,* 502. For banishing the sources of evil, see Almazov, *Vracheval'nye molitvy,* 127; Porfir'ev, "Apokrificheskie molitvy," 5, 11; and Sreznevskii, *Opisanie,* 493, 485.

45. This view is accepted uncritically nearly everywhere. See, for example, N. P. Zagoskin, *Vrachi i vrachebnoe delo v starinnoi Rossii* (Kazan, 1891), 4–10; A. P. Levitskii, "Ocherki po istorii meditsiny v Rossii: Osnovy iazycheskogo vrachevaniia na Rusi," *Meditsinskoe obozrenie* 68, no. 13 (1907): 143–46; V. D. Otomanovskii, *Bor'ba meditsiny s religiei v drevnei Rusi* (Moscow, 1965), 15–66; Zguta, "Witchcraft," 440, 448.

46. Blokhin, "Zagovory," 15. See also similar lists on p. 13 and especially on p. 17, where clerics were included as well.

47. For woods and woody things, see Sreznevskii, *Opisanie,* 505. For sexual desire, see ibid., 509–10. For power over others, see ibid., 508–9. For Agaf'itsa Savkina, see N. I. Novombergskii, *Koldovstvo v Moskovskoi Rusi XVII–go stoletiia* (St.

Petersburg, 1906), 66–67. For faith in Satan, see Valerie A. Kivelson, "Through the Prism of Witchcraft: Gender and Social Change in Seventeenth-Century Muscovy," in *Russia's Women,* 82; and Zguta, "Witchcraft," 446.

48. For a selection of the most commonly cited clerical condemnations of witches, see Levitskii, "Ocherki," 144–45. For a fuller discussion of conceptions of witchcraft in Muscovy, see Kivelson, "Through the Prism," as well as her forthcoming articles, "Patrolling the Boundaries: Witchcraft Accusations and Household Strife in Seventeenth-Century Muscovy," *Harvard Ukrainian Studies,* and "Political Sorcery in Sixteenth-Century Muscovy," in *Cultural Identity in Muscovite Rus',* *1359–1584,* ed. Gail Lenhoff and Ann M. Kleimola.

49. Kivelson, "Through the Prism," 74–94. In western Europe in the same period, by comparison, the Roman Catholic church sought to stamp out good magic as well as evil. See Mary O'Neil, "Magical Healing, Love Magic, and the Inquisition in Late Sixteenth-Century Modena," in *Inquisition and Society in Early Modern Europe,* ed. Stephen Haliczer (London, 1987), 88–114.

50. Eleonskaia, *K izucheniiu,* 15–16. Eleonskaia does not distinguish between spells to cause harm and other *zagovory.*

51. G. Esipov, "Koldovstvo v XVII i XVIII stoletiiakh," *Drevniaia i novaia Rossiia* 3, no. 9 (1878): 68–69; for further discussion of these cases, see N. I. Novombergskii, *Vrachebnoe stroenie v do-Petrovskoi Rusi* (Tomsk, 1907), 9. Prayers drawn from the transcripts of witchcraft trials are likely to be "deviant," because the prosecutors (and presumably their scribes) were most interested in evidence to prove the charge. Peter Burke notes this phenomenon in inquisitional proceedings in *Popular Culture,* 74–75.

52. Zguta, "Witchcraft," 448.

53. RGB, f. 199, Sobranie Nikiforova, no. 30, fol. 18v. The scribe forgot the phrase "so as to drive them out" and inserted it later in the margin.

54. For blood from a wound, see Lakhtin, *Starinnye pamiatniki,* 33 (also Almazov, *Vracheval'nye molitvy,* 109, 110, 117). For the headache, see Almazov, 107. For covering all parts of the body, see ibid., 109–10; Porfir'ev, "Apokrificheskie molitvy," 8, 21–22, 23; Tikhonravov, *Pamiatniki,* 357–60; and Maikov, *Velikorusskie zaklinaniia,* 96–97.

55. For God as physician of souls and bodies, see Almazov, *Vracheval'nye molitvy,* 111 (also 23, 27, 33, 106, 107; Porfir'ev, "Apokrificheskie molitvy," 9, 12; RGB, f. 199, Sobranie Nikiforova, no. 30, fols. 19v–20; RGADA, f. 196, Sobranie Mazurina, no. 312, fols. 262, 263–63v.). For the wages of sin, see Almazov, *Vracheval'nye molitvy,* 109. For asking God to purify, see Almazov, 112.

56. Sokolov, "Materialy," 92.

57. Eleonskaia, *K izucheniiu,* 33–34, cites 125 examples of opening formulae of *zagovory,* none containing these phrases.

58. Russell Zguta, "Monastic Medicine in Kievan Rus' and Early Muscovy," in *Medieval Russian Culture,* ed. Henrik Birnbaum and Michael S. Flier (Berkeley and Los Angeles, 1984), 60.

59. HRL, Uppsala 44, fol. 46v.

60. Sokolov, "Materialy," 81.

61. For toothache, see ibid., 67. For Adam's head, see V. I. Florinskii, *Russkie prostonarodnye travniki i lechebniki: Sobranie meditsinskikh ruskopisei, XVI i XVII stoletiia* (Kazan', 1879), 4. For preparing medicines at specific times, see Levitskii, "Ocherki," 150; also Sokolov, "Materialy," 81.

I S O L D E   T H Y R Ê T

MUSCOVITE MIRACLE STORIES AS SOURCES FOR GENDER-SPECIFIC RELIGIOUS EXPERIENCE

ALTHOUGH NUMEROUS, the miracle stories of Muscovite saints have generally been ignored by scholars of medieval Russian culture. Their stereotypical style and seemingly fantastic content traditionally aroused the distrust of Russian and Soviet historians, who were accustomed to probing with a critical eye into the historical truth of all medieval Russian sources. Only V. O. Kliuchevskii—out of all the scholars who examined the hagiographical literature of medieval Russia with a source-critical attitude—considered the miracle stories as valuable sources for the history of medieval Russian monasteries and for cultural and ethnographic features of the local population.[1] Standing outside the mainstream of medieval scholarship, Russian historians have not encountered the form-critical method their European and American colleagues have used to explore patterns of popular piety in hagiographic writings. If we are to use the miracle stories of Muscovite saints, we must first show how they represent reliable historical sources that respond to the form-critical method of analysis. Having established the validity of the medieval Russian miracle material, we shall then explore how this approach can yield important insights into the differing religious experience of medieval Russian men and women.

MIRACLE STORIES AS HISTORICAL SOURCES

The notion that the miracle stories of medieval saints could serve as a basis for the exploration of social and religious conventions in the Middle Ages gained popularity after Gerd Theissen's ground-breaking form-critical analysis of the miracle stories in the synoptic Gospels.[2] The form-critical method, which consists of a synchronic, diachronic, and functional approach to the respective texts, considers both their form and content. The synchronic approach identifies the similarities in the texts that stem from the same time period and cultural environment. A diachronic analysis explores the origin of a text and its changes through time. The functionalist approach sees stories as an expression of a specific social situation, the so-called *Sitz im Leben,* which is responsible for the transmission of the genre.[3] The application of the synchronic approach in particular provided new insights into the social conditions that shaped the worship of holy men and women in the Middle Ages. In their form-critical analysis of the popular cults of English and French saints, R. C. Finucane and Pierre-André Sigal classified the posthumous miracles at the sacred shrines. Benedicta Ward arrived at a sophisticated explanation of the dynamics of miraculous cures and elucidated the role the miraculous played in society and in the personal lives of medieval men and women.[4]

Although these studies successfully demonstrate that the miracle cycles of Western medieval saints can be treated as historical source material in spite of their stereotypical form, the studies' exclusive reliance on the synchronic approach may skew their findings. Their strictly statistical approach is not sensitive to possible regional variations in miraculous healings. Medieval saints, for example, often specialized in curing certain illnesses or showed a preference for healing a certain social group.[5] It is therefore necessary to balance the search for underlying uniform structures in the medieval miracle stories with a sensitivity for the unique features of individual cults.[6]

This balance can be achieved if we apply the synchronic approach to each miracle cycle separately. As a second step, the *Sitz im Leben* of each cycle must be compared with that of other cycles. By grouping cycles according to shared parameters (such as a common regional or chronological background) or a specific social or cultural environment, it is then possible to investigate the dynamics of the cult of holy figures in a larger area without losing sight of changes in the saints' appeal. Such an approach can also help reconstruct the social conditions of the human actors in each of the miracle cycles and to establish their interaction with their environment.

A study of the miracle cycles of Muscovite saints must also take into account the source-critical problems associated with the medieval Russian hagiographic tradition.[7] Very little is known about the circumstances in which the miracle stories of medieval Russian saints were written down. In most cases the author of a Russian miracle cycle, either a priest or a monk, remains anonymous. The date of composition is only seldom mentioned in the text of the miracle cycle, and outside references to the origin of a miracle cult are equally rare. At the most general level, the chronological boundaries of a miracle cycle are determined by the year of a saint's death and by the date of the manuscript, which can be established by watermark and handwriting analysis. However, in many instances, the date of the discovery or translation of the miracle-working relics identifies more clearly the time span during which the miracles occurred.

Since the medieval Russian miracle cycles survive in copies of the original accounts, scholars are well advised to consider changes that might have occurred during the transmission of texts. Fortunately the miracle cycles of the Muscovite period were not subject to frequent rewriting, as was the case with the medieval Russian *vitae*. Out of approximately forty miracle cycles, which form the basis of this study, only the miracles of Saints Nikita of Novgorod, Makarii of Zheltye Vody and Unzha, and Ioann and Loggin of Iarenga seem to have been redacted. The first miracle cycle of Saint Nikita of Novgorod was composed by a hegumen named Ioasaf after the discovery of Nikita's relics in 1558.[8] A second version of these events was produced by the Pskov priest Vasilii (Varlaam).[9] The first miracle cycle of Makarii of Zheltye Vody and Unzha contains eight miracles, which cover the period from approximately 1522 to 1552. A second redaction includes all miracles, except the first, and an additional six new ones. It was composed after 1615 (the date provided in miracle 8 of the second redaction) and before 1633 (the redaction is included in Tulupov's *cheti minei* of 1633).[10] The miracles of Ioann and Loggin of Iarenga survive in four redactions, only two of which belong to the medieval period. The first redaction by the priest Varlaam—later appended by the monk Martinian from the Solovki Monastery—covers events from 1544 to 1623. The second redaction, composed by Sergii Shelonskii after the saints' canonization in 1638, reworks a number of miracles of the earlier account (notably miracles 2, 5, 3, 13). It also includes an elaborate version of several cures reported in the official inquests of 1625 and 1627 concerning the saints' miraculous power.[11]

The rewriting of the miracle cycles in all three cases was prompted by ecclesiastical considerations that reached beyond the establishment of the cults in question. The author of the second redaction of Saint Nikita's miracles felt compelled to rewrite Nikita's life and miracles to combat the heretical view held by men (such as Fedor Kosoi) in Novgorod that relics and icons should not be worshiped. In his intentions Varlaam followed Zinovii Otenskii, who composed a eulogy on the discovery of Saint Nikita's relics.[12] Makarii of Zheltye Vody and Unzha's *vita* and miracles were reworked in connection with Patriarch Filaret's and Tsar Mikhail Romanov's efforts in 1619 to centralize the saint's cult. Sergii Shelonskii updated the miracles of Ioann and Loggin of Iarenga in a similar way, after their relics in 1638 were translated to the Church of Saints Zosima and Savvatii in Iarenga, at the order of Patriarch Ioasaf and tsar Mikhail Fedorovich.[13]

Although redactions of Muscovite miracle cycles are rare, the number of stories in a particular cycle may vary from manuscript to manuscript.[14] In general, the more active a cult was, the more miracle stories it produced. In view of the open-endedness of miracle cycles, the approach of Soviet scholars such as L. A. Dmitriev—who have used the variable number of stories in a cycle as a criterion in establishing different redactions—makes little sense.[15] We had better speak of a redaction only when the original text has been altered.

The evidence for the origin of the popular veneration of medieval Russian holy figures is derived almost exclusively from literary sources, that is, eulogies of the saints, tales of the translations of their relics, and the miracle stories themselves. The hagiographers relied on eye witnesses who claimed to have seen the miracles or their effects. They worked this material into edifying tales in Old Church Slavonic according to the standard Early Christian/Byzantine stylistic and structural conventions. The manner of gathering and processing the original information is often described in a segment interspersed among the individual episodes of a miracle cycle.

Muscovite hagiographers—like their counterparts in the medieval West—made little or no effort to question what the witnesses had actually seen or experienced. As Benedicta Ward points out, medieval people did not oppose the miraculous to nature. A critical approach toward miracles limited itself to the question as to whether a miracle was the result of divine action or illusive magic (that is, the work of the Devil).[16] In the case of miraculous cures, the recovery of the patient automatically proved the involvement of a saint.

Since the reporting of miracles to monastic or ecclesiastical authorities occurred orally, and was at best validated by character witnesses, one cannot readily distinguish the actual miracle witnessed by a believer and the interpretation of the event by the Russian hagiographer. However, the experience of the miraculous emerges in more detail in inquest records concerning the saints' cults that were budding at the periphery of the Russian realm in the later sixteenth century.[17] The inquest documents—sent back to the church authorities in Moscow by envoys investigating the deeds of Russian miracle workers—contain information about the time of origin and the place of the reported miracles, the persons who experienced them, and the sequence of events that led up to the actual miraculous intervention of the saints. In the case of Saints Ioann and Loggin of Iarenga, we actually possess the evidence gathered at two of such inquests, conducted in 1625 and 1627 at the order of Patriarch Filaret—in addition to the miracle cycle later produced by Sergii Shelonskii.[18] A comparison of the testimony of Ivan, son of Pavl Panov, at the inquest of 1625 and Sergii's version of it shows that the literary rendition closely follows the oral testimony of the believers.[19]

The differences between the two versions of the story are primarily stylistic. Whereas the inquest report narrates the peasant's statement in simple language, Sergii tries to elevate the style of the story by including Church Slavonicisms such as dative absolutes and participial constructions. Contrary to the persons conducting the inquest, Sergii is less concerned with giving exact dates to establish the credibility of the miracle. He prefers to proclaim the already established miraculous powers of Ioann and Loggin of Iarenga. In spite of Sergii's literary license, his story reproduces the oral version of the miraculous cure accurately, with regard to both the facts and the sequence of events. We may therefore conclude that, in some cases at least, the medieval Russian miracle story corresponds fairly reliably to an underlying historical reality.

Even in cases where more than one redaction of a Russian miracle cycle exists, the texts can still be mined for historical material. In the case of Saint Nikita of Novgorod, the saint's first miracle cycle—recorded by the hegumen Ioasaf of the Danilov Monastery—closely resembles the composition of another cycle by Vasilii/Varlaam, the author of a second redaction of the *vita*.[20] Although Varlaam distinguishes his own miracle stories from the previously recorded ones ("More . . . miraculous deeds have been recorded elsewhere"), he merely reproduced Ioasaf's cycle in abbreviated form.[21] Whereas Ioasaf paid much attention to the identity of the persons who reported cures by supernatural means, Varlaam was primarily interested in proclaiming that a miracle happened at all. Compare Varlaam's terse summary of the healing of the blind Fevroniia with the original story, for example. Varlaam wrote, "The same day another woman was brought to the shrine of the bishop Nikita. She had been blind one year. She stood and prayed, and suddenly she started to see and praised God and the saint." In contrast, Ioasaf's original story reads:

> Another woman by the name of Fevroniia from the same Novgorod the Great, who had been blind for one year and did not see anything, not even a little, was taken by relatives and friends [to the shrine] . . . Fevroniia started to see through the prayers of Saint Nikita. She shed many tears and sent many prayers to God. Those who are kindled by the faith like a fire are not disgraced by hopeful faith. What she asked she received. And she left the tomb of the saint with great joy and heard with the ears of her heart the words: You will receive what you wish according to your faith.[22]

The fact that Varlaam's version merely reproduces Ioasaf's stories in abbreviated form without altering their content or structure suggests that redactions of miracle stories also represent valid historical sources.

The readiness of medieval Russian hagiographers to copy miracle cycles and claim them as independent works raises the question of how Russian miracle stories can be distinguished from literary borrowings. The textual affinity of a large number of Russian miracle tales does not necessarily mean that these miracles were invented, as Ivan Iakhontov implied in his study of northern Russian miracle stories.[23] The repetition of standard phrases makes it difficult to uncover the reality underlying a miracle story. But we can reconstruct its historical core if we separate the fixed phrases and structural elements from the variable ones, using the method of form criticism. Whereas the fixed themes reflect the author's indebtedness to earlier models, the choice and arrangement of the variable themes express the *Sitz im Leben* underlying the miracle story. Commonly repeated phrases include references to a person's finding out about a saint's healing power (the traditional phrase is,

"After hearing about the miracles that the saint was working . . ."), and his profuse thanksgiving to the saint after receiving the miraculous cure ("and he went home . . . praising God and his servant"). Variable expressions are used to describe the person's illness, the manner in which he or she arrives at the shrine, and the events that lead up to the supernatural healing.

In spite of the limitations the genre imposed on the Russian hagiographer, he was able to manipulate the content of a tale. A typical miracle story falls into four distinct parts: an introduction, which identifies the person who is about to experience the saint's grace and describes his problem; a description of the person's preparation for the miraculous event; the climax, which focuses on the saint's miraculous intervention; and an afterword, which describes the general reaction to the miracle and the thanksgiving of the recipient of the miraculous cure. The order of these segments and the information in the introduction and the afterword are usually fixed. However, segments two and three vary greatly in the choice and arrangement of themes, which are influenced by the social background and the gender of the afflicted person, the nature of his or her experience of the supernatural, and the type of institution that controlled the saint's cult. Thus, when a medieval Russian author wrote down a miraculous experience, he selected, from a general literary pattern, a particular variant that best suited the circumstances described by his oral source. He then inserted the variable information into the appropriate spots. As a result, miracles with different contents often appear similar with regard to their formal structure.

The visibility of the peculiarities of individual saints' cults and of witnesses' testimony in medieval Russian miracle stories reflects the attitudes of the communities that fostered these cults, as Ian Wood points out for the Western medieval situation.[24] The communal nature of the saints' cults presupposed the existence of certain rules that regulated believers' access to the holy shrines. These socioreligious conventions not only were expressed in the eye-witness accounts but also influenced the authors' choice of *topoi* and ultimately defined a miracle cycle. So, for example, if the shrine of a specific saint was controlled by a monastery in a remote rural area, the *topoi* of each story of the corresponding miracle cycle reflect the rural and monastic quality of the saint's cult. Although the possibility of literary fiction cannot be ruled out when a miracle cycle contains an erratic distribution of *topoi,* in practice Muscovite miracle stories display a remarkable consistency in this respect and thus can be used to explore the socioreligious aspects of medieval Russian culture.

THE ROLE OF GENDER IN THE SPIRITUAL EXPERIENCE OF MUSCOVITE MEN AND WOMEN

Since the Russian miracle cycles from the sixteenth and seventeenth centuries give evidence of the pattern of patronage of the saints' clientele, they represent a particularly valuable source for the gender-specific religious life of medieval Russian men and women. To demonstrate the usefulness of the form-critical method with regard to this topic we shall examine the religious experience of Muscovite men and women in three different types of cults: (1) cults arising in a still pagan environment, (2) monastic cults, and (3) cults that are controlled by ecclesiastics.

All known medieval miracle workers from the Russian north are male. It is tempting to attribute this phenomenon to a general Russian Orthodox gender bias, but other factors, such as local patriarchal norms or harsh frontier conditions, may well have played a more important role. A few central Russian female miracle workers of the period tend to be of noble background, such as Evdokiia Donskaia and Solomoniia Saburova. The miracles of Evfrosiniia of Suzdal' occurred mostly after the discovery of her relics in 1699. The limited number of women miracle workers impedes a useful comparison of their healing pattern with that of their male counterparts.[25]

The miracle cycles of saints from the Russian north, especially from the Vologda region, suggest that the initial encounter with the new cults was made primarily by men. In the miracle tales considered here, on average only about 25 percent of the people experiencing the miraculous power of saints were women.[26] It is interesting, however, that a comparative study of men's and women's relations to the saints during the time of intensive contact suggests that women, not men, were more inclined to engage the help of the new miracle workers and to develop an affective spiritual relationship with them. The most violent perpetrations against the saints or their shrines in the miracle stories were exclusively committed by men. The bribery of an abbot with a bearskin, for example, which eventually led to the destruction of the resting place of Saints Grigorii and Kassian of Avnega, has no equivalent among the female clientele at the holy shrines:

> This [man] Gavriil summoned the hegumen of the Glushitskii Monastery, Iakim, and an elder named Ilinarkh from the same monastery, who had the rank of priest, and he received them with great hospitality. He took council with them about his situation and honored them with gifts. He gave the hegumen a bearskin and the priest one hundred silver coins. He took them with him to the place where the saints lay. In a frenzy from drunkenness, or rather envy and insatiability, both destroyed the tomb over the relics of the saints and hurled the holy icons in it on the ground. And with this they left.[27]

Women of the Russian north seem to have been just as deeply steeped in the pagan traditions as the men but did not represent a threat to the saints. For example, when household members tried to take a possessed woman to the shrine of Saint Sergii of Obnora, the woman was afraid she was being taken to a bear. Although she entertained decisively pagan notions of the supernatural, the saint healed her immediately on her arrival at his tomb.[28]

The competition between the saints and pagan healers is most pronounced in cases involving men. When the deacon Anisim invited a sorcerer into his house to rid himself of an illness, his wife Mariia—who had previously been freed from an evil spirit by Saints Zosima and Savvatii—

was dismayed at her husband's act and tried to persuade him that the saints were the true healers:

> When they sat down to dinner according to custom, and the sorcerer sat with them at the table, suddenly the sorcerer started to shout in absurd tongues and to roll his eyes. Suddenly Anisim's wife Mariia . . . became confused in her mind and jumped up from the table. She was frightened and wept. Anisim was bewildered. After some time Mariia gathered her wits again. Anisim asked her what had happened to her. She said: "When we sat down at the table to eat, suddenly the venerable men Zosima and Savvatii appeared. Zosima held a rod in his hand and suddenly started to beat the sorcerer with these words: 'Why did you come to God's servant, you damned and wretched man? It is not befitting to you to come here. Go to your own kind.' Leaving him alone Zosima came up to you. He held a small vessel in his hand and brushed some ointment out of it with a brush on your head and over your face. When I came to I did not see anybody." Hearing this from his wife Anisim became depressed. He grieved and wept about his sin.[29]

The fact that Mariia, not her husband, experienced the vision of the sorcerer's punishment and Anisim's cure by the saints suggests not only that women accepted the thaumaturgical activity of the saints more easily than men, but that they experienced the supernatural in a more sympathetic manner than their male counterparts. This affective relationship between women and the saints is also evident in the holy men's reaction to women who had let themselves be influenced by pagan religious concepts. Whereas the saints tended to punish men for their lapses into paganism, they showed more patience and mercy to women. In cases involving men, the miracle stories often present the Christian holy men of the Russian north as angry saints. Saints Grigorii and Kassian mercilessly punished those who disturbed their graves. Onisim, who probed their resting place for a pagan treasure, was hurled to the ground and suffered a stroke. Gavriil, who initiated the destruction of the saints' shrine, was struck by fear and terror and ran through the forest like a wild animal.[30]

In contrast, Saints Grigorii and Kassian took pity on possessed women. Not only did they release Mavra (who injured herself during her lamentation of her husband) from her demonic affliction, but they showed her additional kindness by removing any trace of injury from her face.[31] Clearly the saints displayed more compassion for her personal well-being than concern for her unchristian behavior. In turn, the female experience of the supernatural was more benign and cordial, emphasizing the healing capacities of the saints. It thus appears that in cults in a pagan environment Russian saints had a greater spiritual appeal among the female members of the local population.

In areas where a saint's cult was rooted in the monastic tradition, women's participation in it was visibly discouraged. Although we possess little information about the ways most shrines were managed, the monastic aspects of a cult can easily be established with the help of the form-critical method. Consistent references to the monastery as the place of the saint's dispensation of healing, the presence of the monks at the shrines, and their involvement in the supernatural act of healing, all can be viewed as indicators of the monastic control of a cult.

The posthumous cults of Muscovite saints who had been monks during their lifetime centered around the monastic institutions where they had lived. Therefore the monastic code to a large extent determined the degree of contact and manner of interaction of the local population with the sacred relics. The regulations governing the monks' behavior vis-à-vis the secular world were particularly disadvantageous to women, who in the Christian ascetic tradition were seen as a threat to salvation.[32]

The tension between women and the monastery in Muscovite Russia is reflected in the *topos* of the hostile behavior of living saints toward their female followers in the *vitae* of Russian saints from the late fifteenth and the sixteenth centuries. In the second redaction of the *vita* of Saint Dmitrii Prilutskii, a pious noblewoman who desired to see the famous saint in person, on the advice of one of his fellow monks, waited for the saint at the rear door of his cell shortly before vigils. At the sight of the woman Dmitrii grew angry. She was instantaneously struck with paralysis and was cured by the saint only after the monks' intercession and a long lecture by Dmitrii about her misplaced curiosity. Although her action was motivated by pious zeal and had the approval of the saint's cell mate, the *vita* chastised her for being shameless and for having too little faith.[33]

The saints' concern for the monastic code meant that women were denied access to the miracle workers. Prince Iaroslav Vasil'evich Sevastian of Pskov, who was a generous patron of Saint Savvas Krypetskii's monastery and often visited his spiritual father, took it for granted that Saint Savva would pray for his ill wife.[34] However, when Prince Iaroslav Vasil'evich took her to Saint Savva's monastery, he unexpectedly incurred the wrath of the saint for violating the monastic purity requirement. Saint Savva seems to have lacked compassion for the ailing woman. Only after the prince recognized and repented his sin was the saint willing to look after his wife. However, in keeping with the monastic code, he performed the cure of the princess outside the monastic gate:

> The holy elder sent one of his disciples to meet the prince . . . and he said: "The sinful elder Savva tells you: 'Prince, you must not enter this monastery of the saint with your princess. Here we keep the custom of the Lord; according to the tradition of the holy Fathers women must not enter a monastery. If you violate the command of the Fathers you trespass against the law, and your princess will not be cured by God from her illness'". . . [The saint] himself went out to the monastic gate with the hegumen and the brothers, and there they honored the princess with blessings.[35]

The *topos* in medieval Russian *vitae* of the saints' reserve toward women because of the perceived conflict with the monastic code foreshadows the problematic involvement of women in the posthumous cults of Muscovite monastic saints. In all cases studied here, the female-male ratio amounts to approximately one-fifth to one-fourth of the entire clientele of the saints. In some monastic cults female participation was under 20 percent.[36]

The ascetic code's restriction of women's participation in monastic cults is further evident in the themes associated with male and female petitioners at the shrines. Afflicted men usually addressed the monastic authorities, who arranged their visit to the saint's tomb and participated in the supernatural act of healing by performing liturgical services at the shrine. For women, access to the saint often depended on more than a verbal arrangement with the monastic staff. The only woman petitioner in the cycle of Ioasaf Kamenskii brought an icon as a liturgical gift.[37] In the cult of Aleksandr Kushtskii, where supernatural cures were usually achieved through incubation at the shrine, men often undertook the procedure in the presence of monks, who sang prayers or read the gospel over them. In contrast, women generally spent their time at the shrine alone.

The reserved attitude of the monastic shrine controllers toward women seems to have induced women to develop a close spiritual relationship to their protector saints. Female petitioners are often associated with a faith motif. Solomoniia's ability to pray with tears in the cycle of Ignatii Vologodskii expresses *umilenie,* a highly acclaimed spiritual disposition in medieval Russia, which combines piety and humility.[38] The exclusive association of this motif in Ignatii's miracles with the saint's female petitioners was hardly accidental. The faith motif also occurs in the first miracle of the cycle, where a paralyzed woman is healed in her home after praying to the saint with tears: "In tears she called to him while she was lying in her bed in her house, and suddenly she felt that she was healed from the illness of her legs with the saint's prayers."[39] Saints Grigorii and Kassian of Avnega, who readily punished men for impious acts, were partial to their female followers because of their ability to address the saints with tearful prayers. See, for example, the miracle stories of the blind Kseniia ("She came to the saints' tomb and shed tears and called in her prayers on the holy fathers that God would be kind to her for their sake") and of the blind girl Marina ("One day she had herself carried to the miracle-working tomb of the saints and poured out her prayer together with hot tears"). In this cycle the superior spiritual disposition of the female clientele is underscored by related motifs, which emphasize women's ability to see God in their hearts and minds even in case of physical blindness, and to maintain contact with him through continuous prayer.[40]

Monastic attitudes also affected the ways women experienced the miraculous healing of the saints. Generally speaking, the healing of males by monastic saints was performed in a public context and involved the presence of authority figures such as abbots or priests at the shrines and the application of sacred objects. Women, in contrast, tended to receive healing during a private spiritual experience such as a dream or a vision. In the miracle cycle of Ignatii Vologodskii, two out of the three healing miracles involving men occur during a liturgical service for the sick; the third man, a monk, is cured after he rubs the shroud on the saint's tomb between his hands. In contrast, the lame woman Dar'ia is healed in a vision.[41]

The spiritual isolation of women in the cults of monastic saints was also formally expressed in the different arrangement of motifs in the miracle stories. In the miracle cycles of Aleksandr Svirskii, Nil Stolbenskii, and Savva Krypetskii, the usual healing pattern for men involved a trip to the monastery where the relics of these saints were located, a liturgical service for the ill man at the holy shrine, and the final cure handed down by the saint at the shrine. In contrast, women tended to invoke the saint directly by praying at home or to send male intermediaries to procure a contact relic. The next step usually entailed a woman's cure at home, either by the saint himself in a personal vision or through the application of the acquired contact relic. A variant of this theme is the supernatural cure of women on the road to the saint's tomb. In most instances a final visit to the holy site represents an optional, voluntary act of thanksgiving.

The percentage of women participating in the cults of holy men controlled by white clergy and often fostered by the highest echelons of the church hierarchy is about twice as high as in the cults of monastic saints. In Ioasaf's miracle cycle of Saint Nikita of Novgorod, women experienced 58 percent of the healings. The cult of Saint Nikita was initiated by the Novgorodian ecclesiastical hierarchy in 1558. According to Ioasaf, Saint Nikita visited the archbishop of Novgorod, Pimen, in a vision and ordered him to establish his cult. The miracles occurring at the tomb of Saint Basil the Blessed in connection with the establishment of his feast day on August 2, 1588, involved women in 57 percent of the cases. The miracles happened over thirty years after the saint's death in 1552.[42] Of the miraculous cures taking place at Roman of Uglich's tomb during the period March 2–12, 1605, 63 percent involve women. (Prince Roman Vladimirovich of Uglich died in 1282. After his relics were found on February 6, 1595, they were verified the same year by the metropolitan of Kazan', Germogen. Patriarch Iov commissioned the composition of the saint's commemoration service. Roman's *vita* and the first posthumous miracles starting on February 3, 1605, were lost during the destruction of Uglich in 1609.) The location of Roman's relics in a cathedral church implies that the local priests determined access to the relics. The ecclesiastical character of the cult is further supported by the interest of Metropolitan Germogen and Patriarch Iov in the veneration of the saint.[43] The people in charge of the ecclesiastical shrines were in general willing to make liturgical services and objects available to petitioners regardless of their gender. In the second cycle of Saint Varlaam, for example, women have free access to the icon of the saint located at his tomb and do not encounter problems when requesting services or holy water from the shrine.[44]

Even though the overall opportunities of female believers to participate in the patronage of the Russian saints increased when clerical authorities controlled the cults, this does not mean that the priest was always a woman's best friend. Traditional clerical misogyny is well attested in a number of miracle cycles that contain stories of priests who neglected the spiritual care of female members of their flock. Ioasaf's miracle cycle of Nikita of Novgorod contains a particularly striking example. When the blind woman Kseniia implored archbishop Pimen of Novgorod to pray to Saint Nikita that he might cure her blindness, Pimen refused her request. After the saint restored her sight in one eye, and the woman again asked Pimen to pray so that her entire vision would be restored, the archbishop had unkind words for her: "Old woman, I see that you are old and have lived many years. One eye will suffice you to serve your body to the time of your death."[45]

The observed clerical reluctance to extend pastoral care to female petitioners is also reflected in the presence of themes found already in the miracle cycles of monastic saints, such as cures taking place in visions, at home, or before reaching the shrine. Women's experience of spiritual isolation in ecclesiastical cults is demonstrated in the second cycle of Varlaam, where three out of five female healings occurred at home or in a place other than the shrine. In one case preliminary healing was granted in a vision.[46]

As in the miracle stories of monastic saints, the arrangement of the healing themes in miracles involving ecclesiastical saints often depends on the gender of the recipient of the cure. In the miracle cycle of Saint Basil, seven out of twelve women were healed by the saint at home or on the way to his shrine, whereas the majority of male petitioners received curative treatment at the shrine.[47] In female healings the role of the clergy is markedly underemphasized. In some cases the shrine no longer plays the primary part in the dispensation of the cure but merely becomes a focus for liturgical thanksgiving and for propagating the saint's miracles. For example, Anna from Kolomna set out on a pilgrimage to Saint Basil's tomb to seek a cure for her heart problems. She had not traveled eight miles when suddenly she became well. She continued on her journey, gratefully sang the liturgy to the Lord at the saint's shrine, and professed the miracle she had experienced.[48]

As in the monastic cults, women were largely left to their own devices to deal with their physical and spiritual crises. This is expressed by the theme of the friendly saint who relates to women's problems and often compensates for their neglect by the priests. In their healing visions women uninhibitedly conversed with the saints, experienced their physical touch, and regained hope and confidence. So, for example, in the second cycle of Varlaam Khutynskii, the woman Mamelfa—who had been paralyzed for twelve years—took communion from Saint Nicholas of Myra and received an explanation from Saint Varlaam as to why she had been ill for so long.[49] As in monastic cults the pious attitude of women was characterized by the presence of a faith motif. In six out of the fourteen female healings in the miracles of Saint Nikita of Novgorod, the faith of the afflicted women is emphasized. Nine women are credited with the gift of tears. In two instances, the disposition of female petitioners at Saint Nikita's shrine is characterized outright as *umilenie*.[50] In a number of other episodes the same spiritual attitude is expressed through metaphors such as "seeing with spiritual eyes" and "hearing with ears of the heart," while the communication with the saint is called "sighing from the heart" and "praying from the mind."[51]

THIS STUDY HAS TRIED to show that Muscovite miracle stories respond to the form-critical approach in a similar way as do Western medieval miracle texts. This method offers us a useful tool for the scholarly exploration of medieval Russian society and culture. In particular, the application of the form-critical method to the miracle stories of medieval Russian saints can render new insights into the religious life of men and women in Muscovite Russia. The examination of three different types of saints' cults in sixteenth- and seventeenth-century Muscovy (those in a preponderantly pagan environment, those centered in monastic institutions, and those controlled by the clergy) demonstrates that the ratio of female to male petitioners at the holy shrines increased with the progress of Christianity in Russia and with endeavors of the church hierarchy to gain control of the tombs of the holy men. The frequency of women's visits to the holy shrines did not increase in areas where the ground had been prepared for the Christian message by monastic communities. The *topos* of the living Russian saint who refused to extend spiritual care to women out of fear of corruption is transformed into the theme of the reluctant monastic shrine controllers, who try to keep contact between female visitors and the saints to a minimum. The monastic double standard made women's access to the supernatural difficult and resulted in the neglect of their spiritual care. In contrast, the ecclesiastically sponsored saints' cults in the sixteenth century attracted a greater number of women to the holy shrines. In spite of the improved access of women to the official shrines, however, their spiritual experience continued to be shaped by misogynist clerical attitudes.

The socioreligious restrictions women had to endure shaped their spiritual relationship with the saints after the saints' physical death. In contrast to the official cures men experienced at holy sites, interaction between the saints and female members of their cult was cast in personal, often intimate terms. Women's spiritual closeness to the saints is often marked by exclusively female motifs, such as strong faith and the appearance of a miracle worker in a woman's healing vision. The notion of a kind and caring saint propagated by these visions represents a powerful corrective to the dispassionate and neglectful treatment of women at the shrines. Clearly Muscovite women did not simply suffer from the restrictions of the monastic code or ecclesiastical gender bias but were able to indulge in their own gender-specific experience of the Holy. The tolerance of women's religious experience is reflected in the hagiographers' willingness to accept their testimony to the power of saints and to integrate it into their miracle tales.

NOTES

I wish to thank Nancy Shields Kollmann, Samuel Baron, and all participants in the Second SSRC Workshop on Early East Slavic Culture for their useful comments. Research for this project was made possible by the support of the International Research and Exchanges Board and the Kennan Institute for Advanced Russian Studies in Washington, D.C.

1. V. O. Kliuchevskii, *Drevnerusskie zhitiia sviatykh kak istoricheskii istochnik,* ed. K. Soldatenkov (Moscow, 1871), 438.

2. Gerd Theissen, *The Miracle Stories of the Early Christian Tradition,* trans.

Francis McDonagh (Philadelphia, 1983). The original German monograph, *Urchristliche Wundergeschichten: Ein Beitrag zur formgeschichtlichen Erforschung der synoptischen Evangelien,* appeared in 1974. For an early study of the miracle stories of Christian saints, see C. G. Loomis, *White Magic: An Introduction to the Folklore of Christian Legend* (Cambridge, Mass., 1948). For a discussion of the work, see Pierre Delooz, "Towards a Sociological Study of Canonized Sainthood in the Catholic Church," in *Saints and Their Cults: Studies in Religious Sociology, Folklore, and History,* ed. Stephen Wilson (Cambridge, 1983), 216 n. 35.

3. For a detailed description of the form-critical method, see Theissen, *Miracle Stories,* 1–40.

4. Ronald C. Finucane, *Miracles and Pilgrims: Popular Beliefs in Medieval England* (Totowa, N.J., 1977), and Pierre-André Sigal, *L'homme et le miracle dans la France médiévale, XIe–XIIe siècle* (Paris, 1985). Benedicta Ward, *Miracles and the Medieval Mind: Theory, Record, and Event, 1000–1215* (Philadelphia, 1987).

5. Finucane, *Miracles and Pilgrims,* 127, 135.

6. Theissen was well aware of the dangers of comparing miracle motifs from different local traditions. See Theissen, *Miracle Stories,* 2 n. 3.

7. Few scholars have approached medieval Russian miracle tales as sources for religious history. Gail Lenhoff has employed primarily a literary approach to Muscovite hagiography in order to explore the cult of specific saints. See Gail Lenhoff, *The Martyred Princes Boris and Gleb: A Sociocultural Study of the Cult and the Texts* (Columbus, Ohio, 1989), and "Canonization and Princely Power in Northeast Rus': The Cult of Leontij Rostovskij," *Welt der Slaven,* nos. 1–2 (1992): 359–80.

8. See O. A. Belobrova and L. V. Sokolova, "Ioasaf," in *Slovar' knizhnikov i knizhnosti Drevnei Rusi,* ed. D. S. Likhachev, 3 vols. in 5 pts. to date (Leningrad, 1987–), 2, pt.1:407. There are twenty-five miracle stories in Rossiiskaia Gosudarstvennaia Biblioteka (RGB), f. 304, I., Collection of Trinity–St. Sergii Monastery, no. 673, fols. 374v–88 (hereafter referred to as Trinity–St. Sergii Monastery).

9. Rossiiskaia Natsional'naia Biblioteka (RNB), F.I.730, fols. 98–104v. All nine miracles recorded in the text are found in Trinity–St. Sergii Monastery, I., no. 673. The miracles of RNB F.I.730 sequentially relate to miracles nos. 1, 3, 2, 4 and 5, 6, 8, 11, 22, 12, 20 in Trinity–St. Sergii Monastery, I., no. 673. For the author of the second redaction, see R. P. Dmitrieva, "Vasilii," in *Slovar' knizhnikov,* 2, pt.1:114, and Kliuchevskii, *Drevnerusskie zhitiia sviatykh,* 267, n. 2.

10. For the first redaction, see Rossiiskii Gosudarstvennyi Arkhiv Drevnikh Aktov (RGADA), f. 201, M. A. Obolenskii Collection, no. 20, fols. 859v–67 (hereafter referred to as Obolenskii Collection). An example of the second redaction is found in RGADA, f. 196, F. F. Mazurin Collection, no. 1188, fols. 125v–205v (hereafter referred to as Mazurin Collection). See N. V. Ponyrko, "Zhitie Makariia Zheltovodskogo i Unzhenskogo," in *Slovar' knizhnikov* 2, pt.1:292. Miracles 2–8 in Obolenskii Collection, no. 20, correspond to miracles 1–7 in Mazurin Collection, no. 1188.

11. See RNB, Solovki Collection, no. 182/182, fols. 120–26v (hereafter referred to as Solovki Collection); RNB, Q.I.365, fols. 461–87; Solovki Collection, no. 182/182, fols. 127v–41v.

12. Kliuchevskii, *Drevnerusskie zhitiia sviatykh,* 266–67.

13. Solovki Collection, fols. 139v–41v.

14. This phenomenon is particularly evident in the case of Makarii of Zheltye Vody and Unzha. Manuscripts kept in the saint's monastery contain an additional thirty-three miracle stories and briefly list sixty-six more healings. See Ieromonakh

Makarii, *Skazanie o zhizni i chudesakh prepodobnago Makariia Zheltovodskago i Un-zhenskago chudotvortsa* (Moscow, 1850), pt. 2, 6 n. 36.

15. L. A. Dmitriev, *Zhitiinye povesti russkogo Severa kak pamiatniki literatury, XIII–XVII vv.* (Leningrad, 1973).

16. See Ward, *Miracles and the Medieval Mind,* 32 (215, on the question of whether miracles "really happened" in the Middle Ages).

17. For the rising interest in Muscovite miracle workers, see Paul Bushkovitch, *Religion and Society in Russia: The Sixteenth and Seventeenth Centuries* (New York, 1992), 89–90.

18. Sergii's miracle cycle included material from Varlaam's and Martinian's notes. It also made use of the documentary evidence gathered at the inquests of 1625 and 1627. For a detailed discussion of the evolution of the miracle cycle, see Dmitriev, *Zhitiinye povesti russkogo severa,* 213–34. Varlaam's notes are found in Solovki Collection, no. 182/182 (551/182), fols. 120–26 (eighteenth century), and RNB, St. Petersburg Dukhovnaia Akademiia Collection, no. 270/2, fols. 210–17v (seventeenth century). Solovki Collection, no. 182/182, fols. 126v–28v, 128v–41v, also contains the notes gathered at the inquests of 1625 and 1627, along with a copy of the letter by Makarii, metropolitan of Novgorod, which discusses the circumstances leading up to the investigation of the miracles of the two saints. Sergii's miracle cycle is located in RNB, Q.I.365, fols. 461–87.

19. For Ivan's testimony, see Solovki Collection, no. 182/182, fols. 132v–33; for Sergii's literary rendition, see RNB, Q.I.365, fols. 478v–79.

20. Dmitrieva, "Vasilii," 114. It is not clear whether we are dealing with the Danilov Monastery in Moscow or in Pereiaslavl' (O. A. Belobrova, L. A. Sokolova, "Ioasaf," 407–8). Ioasaf identifies himself in the first redaction of Saint Nikita's *vita:* "the story and *vita,* the ascetic life and the miracle-working activities of our venerable father Nikita . . . by the humble hieromonk Ioasaf, hegumen of the Danilov Monastery" (Trinity–St. Sergii Monastery, I., no. 673, fol. 360). The translations of all Russian passages cited are my own.

21. Varlaam is cited from RNB, F.I.730, fol. 103v. Miracles 1–10 in Varlaam's redaction correspond to miracles nos. 1, 3, 2, 4 and 5, 6, 8, 11, 22, 12, 20 in Ioasaf's cycle.

22. RNB, F.I.730, fol. 101 (Varlaam); Trinity–St. Sergii Monastery, I., no. 673, fol. 378 (Ioasaf).

23. Ivan Iakhontov, *Zhitiia sv. severnorusskikh podvizhnikov Pomorskago kraia kak istoricheskii istochnik* (Kazan', 1881), 37–84. Iakhontov establishes a connection between the *vita* and miracles of Saint Sergii of Radonezh by Pakhomii the Serb and the *vita* and miracles of Saint Aleksandr Svirskii by Hegumen Irodion of the Svirskii Monastery. Also see ibid., 334–76, "Prilozheniia," nos. 1–11, for Irodion's borrowings from the *vi-tae* of Saints Kirill of Beloozero, Feodosii Pecherskii, and Varlaam Khutynskii.

24. Ian N. Wood, "Forgery in Merovingian Hagiography," in *Fälschungen im Mittelalter, Internationaler Kongress der Monumenta Germaniae Historica, München, 16–19. September, 1986,* 33, pt. 5 of *Monumenta Germaniae Historica. Schriften,* (Hanover, 1988), 384.

25. For Evdokiia Donskaia, see *Polnoe sobranie russkikh letopisei,* 41 vols. to date (St. Petersburg and Moscow, 1846–), 21, pt. 2: 410–11. For Solomoniia Saburova, see RNB, F.XVII.16, fols. 681–82v. For Evfrosiniia of Suzdal', see M. V. Tolstoi, *Kniga glagolemaia Opisanie o russkikh sviatykh gde i v kotorom grade ili oblasti ili monastyre ili pustyni pozhive i chiudesa sotvori, vsiakogo china sviatykh* (1888; reprint, Moscow, 1995), 210; the miracles are published in "Zhitie i zhizn'

blagovernyia velikiia kniazhny Evfrosinii Suzdal'skiia," *Izdaniia Imperatorskago ob-shchestva liubiteli drevnei pis'mennosti* 91 (1888): 110–48.

26. Compare the following figures concerning women's participation in the cults of saints in northern Russia: Aleksandr Kushtskii cycle, 23 percent (Trinity–St. Sergii Monastery, I., no. 677; Sanktpeterburgskii Filial Instituta rossiiskoi istorii Rossiiskoi akademii nauk [SPbFIRI], f. 238, N. P. Likhachev Collection, opis' 1 [hereafter referred to as Likhachev Collection], no. 162); Grigorii and Kassian of Avnega cycle, 26 percent (Trinity–St. Sergii Monastery, I., no. 677; Biblioteka akademii nauk Rossii [BAN], Arkhangel'sk Collection [hereafter referred to as Arkhangel'sk Collection], no. D.233); Nil Stolbenskii cycle, 11 percent (BAN, So-branie Arkheograficheskoi Kommissii, no. 177 [326]); Aleksandr Oshevenskii cycle, 14 percent (RNB, Q.I.114; new miracles only). The only exception is the Sergii of Obnora cycle, where 58 percent of the saint's clients are women. Due to the unstable numbers of the miracles in each cycle, these figures represent only approximate values. Nevertheless, the generally low involvement of women in these saints' cults is striking.

27. Trinity–St. Sergii Monastery, I., no. 677, fol. 157v.

28. RNB, Pogodin Collection, no. 647, fols. 348v–49v. The miracle is said to have happened on July 29, 1584 (fols. 349v–350).

29. RGADA, f. 381, Rukopisnyi otdel biblioteki Moskovskoi sinodal'noi ti-pografii (hereafter referred to as RGADA, f. 381), no. 199, fols. 329–29v.

30. Trinity–St. Sergii Monastery, I., no. 677, fols. 159–60 (Onisim), 158 (Gavriil).

31. Arkhangel'sk Collection, no. D.233, fol. 556v. Excessive lamentation was considered an impious act by the church Fathers.

32. Two major Russian monastic reformers of the early sixteenth century—Evfrosin of Pskov and Iosif of Volokolamsk—stipulated in their respective monastic rules that women should not be allowed to set foot within male monasteries. For the passage in Evfrosin's monastic rule, see Fairy von Lilienfeld, *Nil Sorskij und seine Schriften: Die Krise der Tradition im Russland Ivans III* (Berlin, 1961), 305–6. The monastic restrictions concerning women are included in *Slovo* 11 of the short rule of Iosif of Volokolamsk; see David Maurice Goldfrank, *The Monastic Rule of Iosif Volotsky* (Kalamazoo, Mich., 1983), 127, 153, 189, 200.

33. Trinity–St. Sergii Monastery, I., no. 790, fols. 128–30. The second redac-tion of the *vita* was composed in the later part of the fifteenth century; see T. N. Ukrainskaia, "Zhitie Dimitriia Prilutskogo," *Slovar' knizhnikov,* 2, pt.1:260; Kli-uchevskii, *Drevnerusskie zhitiia sviatykh,* 188–89.

34. RGADA, f. 181, Rukopisnyi otdel biblioteki Moskovskogo glavnogo arkhiva Ministerstva inostrannykh del, opis' 1, no. 676 (hereafter RGADA, f. 181), fol. 45. The Pskov monk Vasilii/Varlaam composed the *vita* in 1555 at the request of the monks of the Krypetskii Monastery (ibid., fols. 26v–29v). See also Dmitrieva, "Vasilii," 113–15. Saint Savva died in 1495.

35. RGADA, f. 181, opis' 1, no. 676, fols. 45–46v.

36. Out of the nineteen of Savva Krypetskii's posthumous healings only three benefited women (ibid., fols. 60v–106v). Women are found in miracles 15, 16, and 19. The original cycle of Makarii Koliazinskii, which contains sixteen episodes, makes reference to women only four times.

37. Likhachev Collection, opis' 1, no. 162, fols. 57–57v.

38. RGB, f. 310, Undol'skii Collection (hereafter Undol'skii Collection), no. 302, fols. 88v–89. On the concept of *umilenie* and its connection with the gift of

tears, see George P. Fedotov, *The Russian Religious Mind,* 2 vols. (Cambridge, Mass., 1946), 1:393 and 2:249.

39. Undol'skii Collection, no. 302, fols. 86v–87. The theme of prayer with tears occurs only once in connection with a male monastic who suffers from a toothache (ibid., fol. 93v).

40. Trinity–St. Sergii Monastery, I., no. 677, fols. 163 (Kseniia), 165 (Marina). A colorful example of male disbelief in the saints is related in the story of the hegumen Ilarion, who had little faith in Saints Grigorii and Kassian and therefore felt little enthusiasm in following his archbishop's orders to visit the site of the recently discovered miracle workers. The saints punished him by causing him to fall off his animal (ibid., fols. 155v–56v). The reference to a donkey in the text seems to have been taken from the *vita* of the holy fool Andrei where it forms part of an idiom. See I. I. Sreznevskii, *Materialy dlia slovaria drevne-russkago iazyka,* 3 vols. (1893–1912; reprint, Moscow, 1989), 3, col. 1063, s.v. "T"shchetina." A Slavonic translation of the *vita* of Andrei first appears in Russia in the late fourteenth century. See O. V. Tvorogov, "Zhitie Andreia Iurodivogo," in *Slovar' knizhnikov,* 1(1987):131–33.

41. Undol'skii Collection, no. 302, fols. 87v, 90v–91 (service for the sick), 94 (monk), 92v–93 (Dar'ia). A fourth episode involving a man represents a punishment miracle, which is eventually reversed (fols. 88–88v).

42. Trinity–St. Sergii Monastery, I., no. 673, fol. 373v (Pimen). A. M. Panchenko, "Zhitie Vasiliia Blazhennogo," in *Slovar' knizhnikov* 2, pt.1:250 (Saint Basil the Blessed).

43. Undol'skii Collection, no. 363, fols. 22–38, and Kliuchevskii, *Drevnerusskie zhitiia sviatykh,* 316 (Roman of Uglich).

44. See miracles 3, 6, 9, in RNB, F.I.730, fols. 300, 302, 303v.

45. Trinity–St. Sergii Monastery, I., no. 673, fols. 375v–76. The saint eventually cured her entire affliction.

46. Miracles 3 (vision), 10, 11 in RNB, F.I.730.

47. Only four out of nine men were visited by the saint before getting to the shrine (miracles 4, 5, 15, 21, in RGADA, f. 381, no. 199; the corresponding female miracles are nos. 1, 2, 8, 9, 11, 12, 13). The visions of male believers portray either an angry saint (nos. 4, 15) or a saint who demands attention and liturgical gifts (no. 5). The content of these visions contrasts sharply with the visionary experience of women, which emphasizes compassion and a supportive attitude in the saint (see particularly miracles 1, 2, 7, 12).

48. Ibid., fol. 565v.

49. RNB, F.I. 730, fols. 297v–99.

50. For Saint Nikita of Novgorod, see miracles 2, 3, 6, 10, 18, 23 (Trinity–St. Sergii Monastery, I., no. 673, fols. 376, 376v, 378, 384v, 386v). For the gift of tears, see miracles 2, 3, 6, 10, 18, 23 (ibid., fols. 376, 376v, 378, 384v, 386v). For *umilenie,* see miracles 5, 10 (ibid., fols. 378, 380v).

51. Miracle 4, in ibid., fols. 377 (spiritual eyes), 378 (ears of the heart), 376, 378 (sighing), 384 (praying). Only three out of eleven men in Saint Nikita's miracles are associated with a faith motif; see miracles 9, 13, 15 (ibid., fols. 380, 382, 383).

ROBERT O. CRUMMEY

THE
MIRACLE
OF MARTYRDOM

REFLECTIONS ON EARLY OLD BELIEVER HAGIOGRAPHY

The true Orthodox faith . . .
is sealed with the blood of the martyrs. . . .

AVRAAMII

This I consider to be great and truly miraculous *[divno]*,
that God would find me worthy to be burned in His name. . . .

The Tale of Boiarynia Morozova

HAGIOGRAPHY FORMS an integral part of the cultural life of Old Belief. Like other Christians in the East and the West, the Old Believers have treasured the stories of the lives and the martyrdom of defenders of the faith. When they rejected the reforms of Patriarch Nikon and began their struggle to preserve rigorous and authentic Russian Orthodoxy as they understood it, the Old Believers not only continued the cultural traditions of Russian Orthodoxy but also added to them works honoring the memory of the saints and martyrs of their own movement.[1]

The Old Believer variant of Muscovite Russian culture was the creation of a group of conservative clergymen and a few lay supporters in the mid-to-late seventeenth century. Judging by their works, the first Old Believer writers struggled to defend the Russian Orthodox culture of their time, which they equated with the timeless ecumenical Orthodox tradition. At the same time, in defending Muscovite Orthodoxy, they had to define and codify it—a process that consisted in part of setting themselves in opposition to the liturgical enactments and theological arguments that Patriarch Nikon and his allies advanced in support of their program of liturgical and administrative reform in the church. Thus their act of negation was simultaneously an act of creation.

The polemical writings of the first generation of Old Believers were part of a larger design. From the beginning, they and their followers aspired to maintain an authentically Christian way of life. Their polemical attacks on the Nikonian reforms directed attention to the liturgical observances that their words defended. For in their view liturgy, not theological conviction, was the center of Christian life. Moreover, by implication (and to some extent explicitly), their polemics told followers how they should live in the apocalyptic circumstances they found themselves in. Thus, within a generation or two, the Old Believers created their own liturgical cycle, elaborate institutional structures, ideological and polemical statements, a rigorous moral code, and a distinct artistic culture. In short, they built a separate world with its own culture.[2]

In creating a cultural world of their own, the early Old Believers drew heavily on Muscovite ecclesiastical culture of the mid-seventeenth century.[3] As they defined the canon of acceptably Orthodox texts, the early Old Believers included writings of the Eastern Church Fathers available in Russian translations or miscellanies and many classics of the Russian Orthodox tradition. To this collection of acceptably Christian works, they gradually added defenses of their own position and edifying works for their followers.[4] Similarly, they made the classic tradition of Russian icon painting and the plainchant of the pre-Nikonian church their own.

This remarkable burst of creativity took place in circumstances of deprivation and persecution. The official church and the state gave the first Old Believers ample reason to believe that the apocalyptic expectations common in seventeenth-century Russian Orthodoxy applied to them—that they were martyrs and that their sufferings were the prelude to the End Time. Driven into the "desert" or the catacombs, the first Old Believers adopted ever more rigorous tests of true Orthodox belief and practice since their very souls depended on holding correct belief and observing precisely the forms of worship that embodied it.

To illustrate these propositions, I propose to examine selected works of the early Old Believer canon, which were not ideological texts or polemics in the strict sense. Like all groups of Christians, the Old Believers defined themselves not only by liturgical observances or theological propositions but also by their stories. The Eastern Orthodox tradition provided them with a large repertoire of biblical and patristic stories and saints' lives.[5] To this canon, the first Old Believer writers added their own narratives, usually written in a direct manner in a mixture of exalted and popular language (in contrast to the convoluted complexity of their formal treatises and polemics). Although none of these works follows strictly the usual pattern of the saint's *vita*, all of them are in some sense works of hagiography, for they describe the saintly lives, the sufferings, and the martyrdom of defenders of the Old Faith.

How is a scholar to read texts of this kind? First, we should heed Paul Bushkovitch's advice to read each text in its entirety, and if its primary theme and purpose are religious, to concentrate on elucidating the religious messages rather than mining it for information on political events or social conditions.[6] Second, readers (even those inclined to view cultures as systems) must be sensitive to the inconvenient facts and discordant notes in any text so as not to become prisoners of their own interpretative structures, for all cultures contain their own inconsistencies and paradoxes. Finally, readers must read the text in its political, social, and cultural context, measuring its contents and style against the realities of the day and the textual traditions that may have shaped it.

The Old Believers' urge to write their own hagiography is not difficult to understand. Since they regarded themselves as the faithful remnant, the last bastion of true Orthodox Christianity, they needed to convince themselves and others that they possessed all the important attributes of an authentic Christian community, including edifying stories of suffering and death for the faith. Hagiographic tales served both as proof texts demonstrating the truth of the Old Believers' convictions and as examples of holy behavior for the edification of the faithful.

By far the best known of the early Old Believer hagiographic works is the "Life of Avvakum," whose title explicitly links it to the genre of saints' lives.[7] This paper, however, will concentrate on the hagiographic narratives of the Moscow center,[8] in particular the short narrative works of Avraamii and *The Tale of Boiarynia Morozova*. The discussion will focus on the ways in which these texts treat the theme of martyrdom, their authors' use of the miraculous, and the ways in which these two elements intertwine. Implicit in the task are two further questions—the extent to which Old Believer treatment of these central issues of Christian hagiography differed from earlier Russian Orthodox writings and the degree to which these narratives reflect prevailing currents in Orthodox high culture in mid- and late-seventeenth-century Muscovy.[9]

Before discussing the works themselves, we need to adopt definitions of the most important terms, "martyrdom" and "miracle." Literally a "witness," the term "martyr" was traditionally reserved for those who were put to death for the Christian faith. "According to the traditional view, a miracle is a sensible fact . . . produced by the special intervention of God for a religious end, transcending the normal order of things." In the history of Christian devotional writing, miracles have taken a wide variety of forms and played many different roles in edifying literature and popular devotional practice.[10]

Any discussion of pre-modern literary, polemical, or devotional writings raises important but vexing questions about the date of their composition, the readership they reached, the speed with which they reached it, and the ways the readers "received" and understood their contents. The dating of the texts we will examine poses no significant problems: serious textological studies date all of them to the years between 1669 and 1675. The time and pattern of their spread throughout the scattered Old Believer communities of the empire is much more complicated. Unlike the *vitae* of Avvakum and Epifanii, which have come down to us in the authors' own hands, the works of Avraamii and *The Tale of Boiarynia Morozova* survive in later copies, the earliest of which date from the end of the seventeenth and beginning of the eighteenth centuries.[11] The vast majority of extant manuscripts date from the latter half of the eighteenth century and the nineteenth. Any suggestions about the identity of the readers or hearers of these compositions are at best highly speculative.

FOR A BRIEF PERIOD, as the 1660s became the 1670s, the monk Avraamii was one of the most prominent spokesmen of the Old Belief in Moscow. Avraamii was the name in religion of the fool-in-Christ, Afanasii. After the arrest of several other leaders of the ecclesiastical opposition in 1666 and 1667, Avvakum, who greatly admired Avraamii's rigorous asceticism, convinced him to take the tonsure.[12] Avraamii's new status allowed him to serve as leader of the Moscow Old Believers (including Boiarynia Morozova and her household) and to collect an arsenal of devotional and polemical writings with which he and his allies could fight the Nikonians. Avraamii also wrote his own compositions, which became treasured contributions to the emerging Old Believer canon of sacred texts.[13] Such a prominent opposition leader could not for long work openly in Moscow. He was imprisoned on February 6, 1670, and was burnt at the stake in April 1672.

Two of Avraamii's compositions and a third sometimes attributed to him can be considered hagiographic. The first of the three, the fictional tale of the torture of the elders Petr and Evdokim, was probably written between February 17, 1669, and February 13, 1670.[14] Scholars have offered different hypotheses about its author: N. Subbotin published the text as a work of Deacon Fedor, but more recently N. Iu. Bubnov has convincingly attributed it to Avraamii.[15] While imprisoned in the Mstislavskii Dvor in Moscow in the summer of 1670, Avraamii wrote the longest of the three, the "Question and Answer" *(Vopros i otvet).*[16] The very short and as yet unpublished "Tale of the Dispute of Kondratii with the Ecclesiastical Authorities" was probably written in prison in 1671.[17] Unlike the tale of Petr and Evdokim, the "Question and Answer" and the tale of Kondratii are at their core autobiographical. At the beginning of the "Question and Answer," Avraamii explicitly identifies himself as the central figure in the story. The fact that the hero of the tale of Kondratii is also a prisoner in the Mstislavskii Dvor and undergoes interrogation by representatives of the church hierarchy suggests that he is Avraamii in disguise.[18]

In all three cases, Avraamii uses the narrative to present central propositions of early Old Believer ideology in a comparatively simple and popular
manner. In each, the story centers on the interrogation of the hero by representatives of the ecclesiastical hierarchy, sometimes joined by powerful lay officials. As he responds to the inquisitors' questions, the central character
makes many of the same polemical points as Avraamii did in his longer,
more complex polemical works, the "Petition" and the "Christian's Secure
Shield of Faith."[19] At the center of the debate lies the contrast between the
authentic Orthodox faith of the Russian church before the Nikonian reforms
and the heretical changes in belief and practice through which Nikon and his
ally, Arsenius the Greek, destroyed that faith and set off the Apocalypse. To
illustrate this central conviction, the heroes of the stories offer concrete evidence. Petr and Evdokim insist, for example, that Nikon brought heresy into
the Russian church by introducing the three-finger sign of the cross: this usage, they argue, is the sign of Satan since it implies an unspeakable heresy,
namely that Christ has three natures. In the "Question and Answer,"
Avraamii defends the traditional eight-point cross as distinct from Nikon's
four-point variant and attacks Nikon's decision to change the stamp of the
cross on communion wafers. Petr and Evdokim and Avraamii also criticize
the deletion of the epithet "true" *(istinnyi)* from a passage referring to the
Holy Spirit.[20]

Aggressive defense of the true faith invariably leads to suffering and martyrdom. Angered by Petr and Evdokim's attacks on Nikon's reforms and their
proclamation that the reign of Antichrist has begun, the tsar orders them
boiled in a huge kettle. Like the young men in the fiery furnace,[21] the heroes
accept their fate confidently, praying that they might share in Christ's resurrection and that, through their sacrifice, their tormentors might be con-
founded and brought to the true faith. After several minutes in the boiling
water, a miracle saves them: with great noise, fire descends from heaven and
smashes the kettle so that the martyrs emerge unscathed. So shaken is the
tsar that he lets Petr and Evdokim go free.[22]

The autobiographical central figures in the "Question and Answer" and
the tale of Kondratii find no such escape. When Avraamii stubbornly insists
on defending the old faith, the Metropolitan of Krutitsa pulls him around by
the beard, slaps his face, and in the process knocks off his cloak, cowl, and
skull cap. As physical abuse and persuasion fail to convince Avraamii to submit, his frustrated interrogators threaten him with strangling, a suitable fate
for an intransigent heretic. Kondratii is similarly beaten and put in chains. In
the end, the ecclesiastical authorities defrock Avraamii and prepare to hand
him over to the civil authorities. Later readers would have had no difficulty
remembering or imagining the unwritten final chapter of the story—
Avraamii's death at the stake.[23] Other than the example of the heroes' remarkable strength of character, the only reference to the miraculous in these stories
is ironic: Avraamii's inquisitors chide him for stirring up the people with tales
about men who survive boiling in a kettle or who have had their tongues cut
out, yet speak.[24] Avraamii himself experienced no miraculous rescue.

What, then, were the central messages of these stories and to whom did they speak? Although questions of authorial intention and probable readership or audience are risky, the simple language and narrative structure suggest that Avraamii composed these works for a comparatively large and varied public—the women and men, for example, who made up Morozova's large household. In telling the stories, he drew on the store of familiar Jewish and Christian images that he and his readers shared. The heroes resemble the Old Testament prophets and Christ in standing courageously before the mighty of this world and speaking the truth. Like these illustrious precursors, Petr and Evdokim are wanderers who have no earthly home. Like Christ before his interrogators, Petr and Evdokim and Avraamii bear physical abuse and humiliation silently. At the same time, they carry out the biblical injunction to preach the Gospel, contradicting the heretical statements of their adversaries.[25] As the fate of their predecessors makes clear, their unbending devotion to the faith leads inevitably to martyrdom.

The central image of the stories, then, is martyrdom. In a moment when the soul of Russia and indeed the fate of the whole world hung in the balance, God called faithful Christians to stand firm in the true faith, confront the powers of heresy resolutely, and relive the sacrifice of the prophets, the martyrs, and Christ himself. While Christ might use miraculous means to spare them suffering, the true miracle was their strength to remain faithful until the end.

OLD BELIEVER HAGIOGRAPHY flourished in the mid-1670s. Avvakum and Epifanii wrote their autobiographical saints' lives in prison in Pustozersk and, in Moscow, *The Tale of Boiarynia Morozova* carried on the tradition of Avraamii. In his thorough study of the *Tale*, A. I. Mazunin argues that Andrei, the steward of Morozova's household, composed the first version of the work between the end of 1675 and the middle of 1677.[26] Mazunin divides the extant manuscripts into three redactions—the Extended, the Abridged, and the Short. He argues that the Extended Redaction is the oldest and represents a condensation of the lost original text made in Moscow in the late seventeenth century and preserved in the manuscript tradition of the Russian north. This version of the *Tale* has close connections to Avraamii's work: several manuscripts of the Extended Redaction also contain Avraamii's writings. Moreover, Mazunin has noted a number of passages that the author appears to have borrowed from the "Question and Answer." The Abridged Redaction, Mazunin argues, was composed in the Old Believer settlements in Kerzhenets at the very beginning of the eighteenth century. According to his analysis, Semen Denisov, the leader of the Vyg community, used the Extended Redaction to create the Short Redaction in the 1720s as a chapter for his martyrology, the *Vinograd rossiiskii,* and later to recast it as a separate composition.[27] Thus, if Mazunin's conclusions are correct, the evolution of the *Tale* from one redaction to the next provides an interesting type case of changing perceptions of holiness and examples of evolving literary taste among the Old Believers in the seventeenth and eighteenth centuries.

Like other Old Believer narrative and devotional writings, *The Tale of Boiarynia Morozova* is not easy to classify. In the manuscript tradition, copyists usually labeled the text a "story" *(skazanie)*. Among a variety of other labels, the choice of the modern editor—"tale" *(povest')*—occurs only once, as does the term "saint's life" *(zhitie)*. Nevertheless, the three redactions all bear a resemblance to the ideal type of Byzantine or old Russian saint's life.[28] The Extended Redaction has a heading that begins with the date of the saint's feast and gives her name, accompanied by epithets attesting to her sanctity.[29] The Abridged Redaction, but not the other two, opens with a lengthy preface by the author. All three versions then provide a brief biographical sketch of the heroine's family background and her life up to the moment when her latent saintly qualities become fully manifest. As was customary, the author or editor devoted most attention to the events that fully revealed the heroine's sanctity and ended the composition with an account of her martyrdom and a description of the miracles she performed. Although the Extended Redaction ends abruptly, the two later versions of the text both conclude with a traditional paean of praise to the martyrs Morozova and her companions.[30]

In outline, the events narrated in the *Tale* are well known.[31] Boiarynia Morozova, widow of the boyar Gleb Ivanovich Morozov, made her household in Moscow a center of opposition to the Nikonian reforms. Up until that time, the events of her life did not distinguish her from other prominent noblewomen of the tsar's court. She had married, borne one son, Ivan, and lost her husband. When Nikon began his reforms, she and her sister Evdokiia, by marriage Princess Urusova, followed the teachings of Avvakum. Their stand attracted the attention of the ecclesiastical and secular authorities; eventually, even the tsar and the Boyar Council debated what to do with her. A succession of distinguished visitors unsuccessfully attempted to persuade her to accept the three-finger sign of the cross. When she remained intransigent, the authorities increased their pressure; after a period of house arrest, she and her sister and a third woman named Mariia were imprisoned in a succession of convents in Moscow. Repeated interrogations, torture, and threats of execution failed to intimidate them. The martyrs attracted a great deal of sympathetic attention and, in a manner dramatized in Surikov's painting, used every opportunity to bear public witness for the Old Belief. To put an end to the embarrassment, the authorities confined the three women in an underground prison in Borovsk and starved them to death.

At the center of the story is a series of confrontations between Morozova and her companions and the authorities. Again and again, gently or harshly, the representatives of the Nikonian church and the state demand that Morozova submit to the new order: each time she firmly refuses. When forced to attend a liturgy celebrated according to the reformed canons, she refuses to cooperate and upbraids the nuns around her. When the patriarch attempts to anoint her to heal her presumed psychiatric illness, she defends herself like a wrestler and pushes his arm away. Even while hanging on the *triaska,* she upbraids her torturers, conduct that serves only to lengthen her time in agony. As her end nears, she resolutely prepares herself and her companions for death, attempting only to win a few favors from sympathetic jailers in order to relieve her sufferings a little.

In short, the story once again is a tale of martyrdom. The author repeatedly emphasizes Morozova's sacrifice in giving up her wealth and social standing, her stubborn determination to defend the Old Belief, her deliberate choice of a martyr's fate (as illustrated, for example, by her repeated expressions of joy at being kept in chains like St. Paul), and her determination to die for her convictions. The most moving passages are those in which a starving Morozova begs a frightened guard for a few scraps of food and asks him to wash her shift in the river so that she will have clean clothes to meet Christ, her bridegroom.

The *Tale* poses a second problem of classification. To what extent, if any, can it be read as a source on female spirituality, since, like the early seventeenth-century tale of Uliianiia Lazarevskaia, it is probably the work of a man who knew the heroine well?[32] A number of themes or emphases in the text differ from Avraamii's hagiographic tales or the "lives" of Avvakum and Epifanii. First, in her confrontations with the authorities, Morozova, unlike her male counterparts, makes little attempt to discuss the theological and liturgical issues that separate the Nikonians and Old Believers.[33] Perhaps then, as among Old Believers today, theologizing was men's work. Second, among the issues that she and her interrogators do debate is her duty as a mother. Although she makes no attempt to hide her love for her son, Ivan, whose marriage she had hoped to celebrate, she makes it clear that her only ultimate love is Christ. If necessary, she would watch her son being torn apart by dogs at the place of execution and still not recant. Third, unlike their male counterparts, Morozova and her companions use passive resistance in the most literal sense. Morozova pretends to be ill in order to avoid attending the second marriage of Tsar Aleksei Mikhailovich. Later, she and Urusova take this tactic to extremes: pretending to be disabled, they force their persecutors to carry them everywhere on stretchers and bast mats or drag them on sleds. Only when Nikonian clergy attempt to minister to them against their will do they abandon the pretense, stand up and defend themselves vigorously.[34]

Morozova's most important worldly loyalties are to the community of women who assist her in serving Christ—first, the holy women who gather in her house; then her confessor, Melaniia, and her companions in martyrdom. In spite of many obvious inconveniences, she begs Melaniia to agree that she be tonsured a nun and regularly consults her about the best ways of fulfilling her monastic vows in the horrible circumstances she finds herself in. When the authorities separate Morozova, Urusova, and Mariia, the three women and their supporters take extraordinary risks to visit and comfort one another. If anything, the need for mutual support is even greater than that experienced by the male martyrs in the other works of early Old Believer hagiography. Nevertheless, the heroines' boldness and determination equal that of men. In the pun that occurs repeatedly in Old Believer hagiography, the women stood up for Christ courageously *(muzhestvenno).*

As in Avraamii's stories, the miraculous plays a comparatively minor role in the *Tale*. Indeed, the relative absence of miraculous episodes is surprising, since in the Western and Eastern hagiographic traditions, miracles provide one of the reliable proofs of sanctity. In the Extended Redaction, there are only three miracles, two of which occur in the afterword.[35] In the first, at the moment of Morozova's death, Melaniia sees a vision of her in shining monastic garments (the *skhima* and *kukol*), with radiant face, kissing an icon of Our Lady and with a cross sewn on her robes. The other two miraculous episodes seem to refer to Morozova's active life. When the priest, Dorofei, gives the three martyrs Holy Communion, they are transfigured and their faces glow like those of angels. As with Christ, transfiguration prefigures suffering and death. On another occasion, the prayers and tears of the three martyrs cure Melaniia of a grave illness.

The Abridged Redaction of the text places greater emphasis on the miraculous. In place of the stories of transfiguration and healing, its creator substituted Deacon Fedor's vivid account of a flood in his underground cell in Pustozersk. Each year, when spring reaches the Arctic, the prisoners' cells fill with water. On this occasion, however, Avvakum—who has quarreled with Fedor over questions of doctrine—convinces the guards to build a ditch so that all of the water pours into Fedor's cell. Standing on his knees in the flood, the latter prays for the intercession of Morozova, who has only recently died, and within a quarter of an hour the water has disappeared.[36]

In contrast, although the Short Redaction follows the literary conventions of the saint's life particularly closely, Semen Denisov incorporated few miraculous elements into his version of the story. In addition to the description of an unburied body (in this case, Morozova's), which remains white and does not decay, Denisov added one new story. When the jailers take away Morozova's cross and prayer beads, she has a vision of an angel carrying an icon of the Crucifixion and, from that moment, regards herself a nun.[37]

As the writer of the *Tale* makes clear, however, the most important miracle of all is the heroines' resolution in defending the faith. As Morozova responds to the tsar's message asking her to submit, the luxury and power of a noblewoman's life no longer appeals to her. "This I consider great and it truly is miraculous [*poistinne divno*] that God would allow me to be burned in His name at the stake that has been prepared for me at the place of execution [*na Bolote*]."[38]

In contrast, miracles and the supernatural loom much larger in the hagiographic autobiographies of Avvakum and Epifanii. Epifanii's "Life" consists largely of a succession of encounters with devils, over whom he is ultimately victorious.[39] In Avvakum's work, some of the miracles are extraordinary occurrences that can ultimately be explained in human terms.[40] At the same time, many events in Avvakum's story are miraculous by any standard. The "Life" describes many miracles of healing. The best known, about which Avraamii's interrogators complained, are the healing of Fedor, Lazar', and Epifanii, who rediscover how to speak after the executioner has cut out their tongues. Moreover, Epifanii's severed fingers heal remarkably quickly. On a number of occasions, Avvakum himself heals the sick and demon-possessed through prayer and anointing.[41] These miracles—particularly those retold together toward the end of the text—demonstrate Avvakum's sanctity and the rightness of his cause; unlike the lists of miracles at the end of other saints' lives, however, God works these wonders through a living saint, not a dead one.

Supernatural forces intervene in other ways as well. God communicates with men through dreams and visions. Avvakum's call to his mission takes the form of a vision of three golden ships, two for Avvakum's spiritual children and the third for him and his family as a sign that he should continue his pastoral work. Like Epifanii, Avvakum fights against devils; the stories of these struggles play a far less prominent role in Avvakum's "Life" than in his cell mate's, however.[42]

The contrast between *The Tale of Boiarynia Morozova* and the lives of Avvakum and Epifanii, all written in the mid-1670s, illustrates once again the richness and variety of early Old Believer culture. In its emphasis on the earthly activities of the heroine rather than on the miraculous, Morozova's life more closely resembles the early seventeenth-century life of Uliianiia of Murom than the vitae of Avvakum and Epifanii. That saints' lives of women differed from those of men is no accident. Since the Russian hagiographic tradition provided far more models for the lives of male saints than of their female counterparts, the male author of the original text of Morozova's life probably felt fewer constraints of tradition in telling a story whose central figures were all women.[43] Moreover, as Carolyn Walker Bynum has argued in her analysis of western European materials, the lives of female saints reflect the social relations and customs of the societies from which they emerged: as described in their lives, female saints lived more respectable and predictable lives, without dramatic breaks, conversions, or outbursts of inspired eccentricity, because their position in society simply did not allow them to engage in the more radical conduct of some saintly men.[44]

The *vita* of Morozova and Avraamii's writings also support, in their own ways, Paul Bushkovitch's interpretation of the elite religious culture of seventeenth-century Muscovy as being less centered on the miraculous than on the moral dimension of Christian teaching.[45] The author's emphasis on the personality of the heroine and the details of her daily life reflects another feature of seventeenth-century Russian writing—the stress on human individuality, exemplified above all by the life of Avvakum.[46] Taken together, these observations suggest that early Old Believer hagiographic writings reflect many of the characteristics of high ecclesiastical culture of the middle and late seventeenth century. These compositions serve as one illustration of the extent to which early Old Believer culture encapsulated the attitudes, values, and literary conventions of the time and society in which it took shape.

TO CONCLUDE, the first Old Believer hagiographic narratives stressed the resolute defense of pre-Nikonian Russian Orthodoxy. Except for stereotypical situations dictated by the requirements of the hagiographic tradition, the miraculous plays a relatively small role in Avraamii's hagiographic tales and

The Tale of Boiarynia Morozova. In their autobiographical works, Avvakum and Epifanii place greater emphasis on the miraculous; and Avvakum in particular, like Christians in many other places and times, tended to see God's hand in fortuitous events that could be explained in natural or human terms. Yet, for the writers of all these compositions, the greatest miracle of all was the strength to endure martyrdom for the Old Faith.

The first Old Believer writers had every reason to carry on the tradition of Christian hagiography. Since the blood of the martyrs demonstrates the truth of the faith, the Old Believer communities needed their own prophets and martyrs to show that they—and they alone—still carried on the authentic Christian tradition. Moreover, unlike their more narrowly ideological treatises, hagiographic compositions provided compelling examples of saintly conduct for the faithful to emulate.

In the late 1660s and 1670s, Old Belief produced its first martyrs and established its own tradition of martyrology. From that time forward, the lives of the martyrs became an enduring feature of Old Believer cultures. Life and literature reinforced each other. The struggle for survival of a persecuted minority produced many genuine martyrs in Imperial and Soviet times. Moreover, the hagiographic tradition provided the martyrs with an interpretative lens through which they could understand their sufferings. In many instances, miracles in the usual sense played a minor role in their hagiographic writings. Like all conservative Christians, Old Believers did and do believe that God intervenes in the natural order on behalf of the faithful. At the same time, the central emphasis of much Old Believer hagiography, including the earliest examples, lies in the lesson and examples *(exempla)* of martyrdom, the requirement that the faithful remain resolute, vigilant, and willing to suffer death in defense of the faith.

NOTES

1. When Old Belief took shape as a distinct movement is a subject of debate. Most historians have assumed that one can legitimately consider Old Belief in the late 1660s, 1670s, and 1680s to be a mass movement of religious and social protest. In his stimulating dissertation, "Myths and Realities of the Russian Schism: The Church and Its Dissenters in Seventeenth-Century Russia" (Ph.D. diss., Harvard University, 1991), Georg Michels argues that "Old Belief" in the late seventeenth century consisted, in reality, of a number of fragmented and diverse phenomena, which were united only in the imaginations of later polemicists. In his view, Old Belief became a movement only in the first decades of the eighteenth century, largely in response to the policies of Peter I.

2. In my recent work, I have tried to use Geertz's definition of "cultural system" as a conceptual approach to the complex phenomenon known as Old Belief. The concept is useful in its comprehensiveness, in that, once the movement reached its full development, it gave its adherents a complete way of life—liturgy, beliefs (or, if you prefer, an ideology), a moral code, rules, and taboos to govern day-to-day life. See Clifford Geertz, "Religion as a Cultural System," in his *Interpretation of Cultures*

(New York, 1973), 87–125. Robert L. Moore and Frank E. Reynolds, eds., *Anthropology and the Study of Religion* (Chicago, 1984) contains helpful essays on the theories of Geertz and Victor Turner.

3. Following the helpful suggestions of Natalie Zemon Davis in "From Popular Religion' to Religious Cultures," in *Reformation Europe: A Guide to Research,* ed. Steven Ozment (St. Louis, 1982), 321–42 (esp. 323), I have argued that Old Believer culture should be viewed as a multitude of closely interrelated subcultures. See Crummey, "Old Belief as Popular Religion," *Slavic Review* 52 (1993): 700–712.

4. For a discussion of the canon on which one early Old Believer polemicist based his own work, see Crummey, "The Origins of the Old Believers' Cultural Systems: The Works of Avraamii," *Forschungen zur osteuropäischen Geschichte* 50 (1995): 121–38. On the process of establishing a canon of authoritative texts, see E. R. Curtius, *European Literature and the Latin Middle Ages* (New York, 1953), 48–54, 256–72.

5. The must useful introduction to Russian hagiography remains V. O. Kliuchevskii, *Drevnerusskie zhitiia sviatykh kak istoricheskii istochnik* (Moscow, 1871; reprint, Moscow, 1988).

6. Paul Bushkovitch, "The Life of Filipp: Tsar and Metropolitan in the Late Sixteenth Century," in *Medieval Russian Culture,* vol. 2, ed. Michael S. Flier and Daniel Rowland (Berkeley and Los Angeles, 1994), 29–46.

7. Archpriest Avvakum, *The Life Written by Himself,* trans. Kenneth N. Brostrom, Michigan Slavic Translations, no. 4 (Ann Arbor, 1979). The most useful of the many Russian editions are *Zhitie Protopopa Avvakuma im samim napisannoe i drugie ego sochineniia,* ed. N. K. Gudzii (Moscow, 1960), and *Zhitie Avvakuma i drugie ego sochineniia,* ed. A. N. Robinson (Moscow, 1991). See also Priscilla Hunt, "A Penitential Journey: The Life of the Archpriest Avvakum and the Kenotic Tradition," *Canadian-American Slavic Studies* 25 (1991): 201–24.

8. N. Iu. Bubnov, in *Staroobriadcheskaia kniga v Rossii vo vtoroi polovine XVII v.* (St. Petersburg, 1995), divides early Old Believer writings into three groups based on the location in which they were written—Moscow, Pustozersk, and the Solovetskii Monastery.

9. See Paul Bushkovitch, *Religion and Society in Russia: The Sixteenth and Seventeenth Centuries* (New York and Oxford, 1992).

10. Definitions are taken from *The Oxford Dictionary of the Christian Church,* 2d ed., ed. F. L. Cross and E. A. Livingstone (London, 1974), 881, 920. The following recent works on miracles are particularly helpful: Peter Brown, *The Cult of the Saints* (Chicago, 1981); Benedicta Ward, *Miracles and the Medieval Mind* (Philadelphia, 1982); Pierre-André Sigal, *L'Homme et le miracle dans la France médiévale, XIe–XIIe siècle* (Paris, 1985); and, for the Russian context, Bushkovitch, *Religion and Society,* chaps. 4 and 5.

11. One of the two extant autograph copies of the *vitae* of Avvakum and Epifanii is reproduced in *Pustozerskii sbornik* (Leningrad, 1975). As far as I am aware, the earliest extant manuscripts of Avraamii's three compositions—"Vopros i Otvet," "Muchenie nekoikh starets ispovednik, Petra i Evdokima," and "Povest' o prenii Kondratiia s dukhovnimi vlastiami"—are in, respectively, the State Historical Museum, Moscow (GIM), Collection of Khludov, no. 148; the Russian State Archive of Ancient Documents (RGADA), f. 181, opis' 5, no. 434/893, fols. 291–98; and the Russian State Library (RGB), f. 732, Gor'kovskoe Collection, no. 47. All date from between the 1670s and the early eighteenth century. See Bubnov, *Staroobriadcheskaia kniga,* 139; V. S. Kuznetsova, "Povest' o muchenii nekoikh starets Petra i

Evdokima," in *Literatura i klassovaia bor'ba epokhi pozdnego feodalizma v Rossii* (Novosibirsk, 1987), 206–15; N. Subbotin, ed., *Materialy dlia istorii raskola za pervoe vremia ego sushchestvovaniia,* 9 vols. (Moscow, 1874–1890), 7:xxviii; A. I. Mazunin, ed., *Povest' o boiaryne Morozovoi* (Leningrad, 1979), 29, 110. The earliest extant manuscripts are the Russian National Library (RNB), O.I.341, and the Library of the Academy of Sciences (BAN), Collection of G. F. Nefedova, no. 4, both of which date from the very end of the seventeenth century.

12. Robinson, *Zhitie Avvakuma,* 59, 319.

13. On Avraamii's life and works, see Crummey, "Origins."

14. Bubnov, *Staroobriadcheskaia kniga,* 158. In Russian, the concepts "torture" *(muchenie)* and "martyrdom" *(muchenichestvo)* cannot be neatly separated. In this text, the word *muchenie* is used in the title, but in some versions the answers of the two heroes are labeled *"otvet muchenicheskoi"* (the martyrs' answer). Of the two manuscripts I have used, RGB, Viazemskii Collection, Q.53, repeatedly uses this phrase, but RNB, Collection of the Obshchestvo liubitelei drevnei pis'mennosti, 8°, no. 72, does not.

15. Subbotin, *Materialy* 6:302–9; Bubnov, *Staroobriadcheskaia kniga,* 158–59. Bubnov bases his attribution on the style of the work and the convoy in which it is found in the manuscripts. V. S. Kuznetsova leaves the question of authorship open in her recent edition of the earliest manuscript of the text, "Povest' o muchenii nekoikh starets Petra i Evdokima," in *Literatura i klassovaia bor'ba epokhi pozdnego feodalizma v Rossii* (Novosibirsk, 1987), 206–15.

16. For a recent textological study of the "Question and Answer," and its later reworkings in the manuscript tradition, see N. V. Shukhtina, "Pererabotki Voprosa i otveta' i Poslaniia k nekoemu bogoliubtsu' inoka Avraamiia v rukopisiakh, XVIII–XIX vv.," *Trudy otdela drevnerusskoi literatury* (hereafter *TODRL*) 44 (1990): 403–8.

17. Bubnov, *Staroobriadcheskaia kniga,* 169–71.

18. Subbotin, *Materialy* 7:386; RGB, f. 732, Gor'kovskoe Collection, no. 47, fols. 30v–31.

19. See Crummey, "Origins."

20. Subbotin, *Materialy* 6:306–7, 7:396–97, 402–3 (Apocalypse); 6:304–8 (heresy); 7:407–8 (communion wafers); 6:304, 7:399–401 (Holy Spirit).

21. Dan. 3 (Kuznetsova notes the similarity, in "Povest'," 206–7).

22. Subbotin, *Materialy* 6:307–9.

23. Ibid. 7:391, 404–5, 410, 415; RGB, f. 732, Gor'kovskoe Coll., no. 47, fols. 30v–31.

24. Subbotin, *Materialy* 7:409. The references are clearly to the tale of Petr and Evdokim and the stories about the Pustozersk martyrs Epifanii, Fedor, and Lazar', which appear in a number of Old Believer compositions. See Bubnov, *Staroobriadcheskaia kniga,* 158.

25. Subbotin, *Materialy* 6:302–4, 7:386–87, 391–92, 405–6, 414. The passage in the "Vopros i otvet" describing Avraamii's arrest closely resembles the Gospel stories of Christ's arrest.

26. Mazunin, *Povest',* 66–70, 75–77. See also H. W. Dewey, "The Life of Lady Morozova as Literature," *Indiana Slavic Studies* 4 (1967): 74–87.

27. Mazunin, *Povest',* 29–33, 49–50, 82–84 ("Question and Answer"), 49–51 (Abridged Redaction), 56–58 (Extended Redaction). Mazunin's argument rests in part on the absence of any mention of Avvakum (whose teachings the Kerzhenets Old Believers rejected) and the prominence accorded Deacon Fedor.

28. Ibid., 110–24. L. A. Dmitriev, *Zhitiinye povesti russkogo severa kak pamiatniki literatury, XIII–XVII vv.* (Leningrad, 1973), 4.

29. Mazunin, *Povest'*, 127. The other redactions have simpler headings (pp. 156, 186).

30. Ibid., 185, 206–7.

31. Except when noted, this summary is based on the Extended Redaction.

32. M. O. Skripil', "Povest' ob Uliianii Osor'inoi: Istoricheskie komentarii i teksty," *TODRL* 6 (1948): 256–323.

33. The Short Redaction differs somewhat in this respect. On one occasion, Morozova explains to her captors the theological significance of the two-finger sign of the cross and, on another, lists for them a number of the Old Believers' objections to the Nikonian reforms (Mazunin, *Povest'*, 193–95).

34. Unlike the Life of Uliianiia Osor'ina, the life of Morozova pays comparatively little attention to her acts of Christian charity.

35. Stylistic peculiarities suggest that the afterword, which in most extant manuscripts has a separate cinnabar heading, may be a later addition to the core of the text.

36. Mazunin, *Povest'*, 184.

37. Ibid., 204. In simplifying the story, Semen Denisov left out the character of Melaniia and needed another way of explaining how Morozova became a nun.

38. Ibid., 146.

39. *Pustozerskii sbornik*, 80–91, 112–38; A. N. Robinson, *Zhizneopisaniia Avvakuma i Epifaniia* (Moscow, 1963), 179–202.

40. Among the examples are two failed attempts at murder because guns fail to fire, escapes from drowning, Avvakum's hen that continues to lay eggs under the most unpromising circumstances, and miraculously large catches of fish for his hungry family (Robinson, *Zhitie Avvakuma*, 33, 40, 46, 49, 53, 75–76).

41. Ibid., 64–65, 35, 46, 48, 68–73.

42. Ibid., 32–33, 73–75.

43. I am most grateful to Natalie Zemon Davis and other participants in the 1993 summer workshop on Early East Slavic Culture for this insight.

44. Caroline Walker Bynum, "Women's Stories, Women's Symbols: A Critique of Victor Turner's Theory of Liminality," in *Anthropology and the Study of Religion*, ed. Moore and Reynolds, 105–25 (esp. 110–15).

45. Bushkovitch, *Religion and Society*, esp. chaps. 4, 5, 6.

46. See M. B. Pliukhanova, "O nekotorykh chertakh lichnostnogo soznaniia v Rossii XVII v.," in *Khudozhestvennyi iazyk srednevekov'ia* (Moscow, 1982), 184–200.

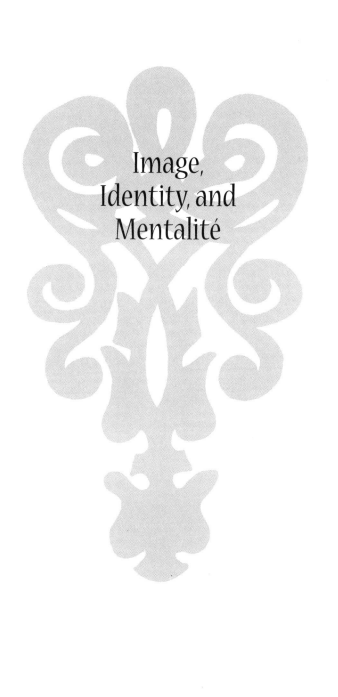

Image,
Identity, and
Mentalité

D A V I D   A .   F R I C K

MISREPRESENTATIONS, MISUNDERSTANDINGS, AND SILENCES

PROBLEMS OF SEVENTEENTH-CENTURY RUTHENIAN AND MUSCOVITE CULTURAL HISTORY

IN A PASSAGE strategically designed to offend the sensibilities of his compatriots, the Polish novelist, playwright, and essayist Witold Gombrowicz wrote that the Polish plain was the scene of the great loosening of European culture; here, he wrote, "against the Polish sky, against the sky of a paling, waning Europe, one can see why so much paper coming from the West falls to the ground, into the mud, onto the sand, so that little boys grazing their cows can make the usual use of it."[1] If we overlook the scatological aspects of this statement, there is nothing in it that is necessarily shocking: a cultural community that has a center or centers must also have its peripheries, and Poland could be considered peripheral. And yet, Gombrowicz, who knew the precise location of every sore spot on the body of the Polish self-image, had succeeded once again in causing discomfort. The problem was that this statement corresponded to the sorts of private insecurities harbored by many Poles in the face of programmatic statements about their mission in the world. Over the centuries the Poles—like many other self-consciously peripheral peoples—had developed a sense of their special place in Europe's spiritual and cultural geography: they were the bulwark, the *antemurale christianitatis,* the protector, the savior, the sacrificial lamb, the crucified Christ of the European nations. This image was a mixed blessing; it carried with it not only the exalted public image but also the private insecurities. The Poles were publicly certain of, perhaps even overly insistent upon, their membership in a European cultural community because of their daily defense of those perceived values against the enemies to the East: Turks, Tatars, Muscovites, and Bolsheviks. But they also had private doubts, because they were, after all, on the frontier, and the barbarians were just beyond the gate.

Students of the cultural history of the East Slavic world in the seventeenth century often suffer from maladies similar to those of Gombrowicz's Poles. We deal with a document base that is in many regards stingy, mendacious, opaque, and noncommunicative; yet we often forget that these testimonies cannot tell the story completely or directly. In describing figures, movements, and events we employ traditional sets of exclusive concepts: Orthodoxy and heresy; East and West; Slavonic, Greek, and Latin; Muscovite, Ruthenian, and Pole; faith and betrayal; patriotism and treason. But we often grant tacit objectivity to these terms; rarely do we acknowledge their instability and contingency. Could it be that this behavior stems in part from a sort of subconscious paradox? from a sense that this sort of epistemological doubt frequently encountered in studies devoted to western Europe is a luxury we can ill afford in dealing with a document base several degrees more spotty and witnesses equally unreliable? If we (and these comments apply to Slav and Slavist alike) suffer a nagging sense of insecurity from occupying the peripheries of shifting fields of authority, if we feel at some private level that everything is ad hoc, does it not make all the more sense to insist in public on the objective truth of our provisional solutions?

Gombrowicz's diagnosis of the Polish spiritual maladies also offered a sort of a cure. The writer took perverse pleasure in admonishing his fellow Poles to embrace their second-rated-ness, to exploit their position at the periphery, to use this self-aware and self-reliant liminality to effect a revision of Europeanness.[2] His diagnoses and prescriptions may offer some relief to cultural historians who work at the peripheries. It is this methodological intuition I would like to follow in this essay: tensions between the public certainties and the private doubts that coexisted in the minds of those who occupied Europe's eastern edge may offer us some insights into the creation of official and private identities among the East Slavs in the early modern period, that is to say, in the period of their first coming to terms with the West. I would like to suggest we try making a virtue out of necessity. Is there not something to be gained by exploiting the ad hoc nature of our objects of investigation? by focusing on the peripheral quality and the shifting centers that characterize our areas of interest? and by facing directly the thinness of the document base and the mendacity of the testimonies?

My ultimate object of interest here is the process that led to the creation of official, early modern, Orthodox Slavic national cultures in Rus' and Muscovy during the course of the seventeenth century. In attempting to encourage the sometimes reluctant witnesses to speak of the formation of this official culture, I make several working assumptions. (1) That, in the course of the seventeenth century, the Orthodox Slavs of the Polish-Lithuanian Commonwealth and those of Muscovy underwent, at different times and in different ways, a crisis of confidence occasioned in part by their various encounters with the culture of the early modern West, in its Polish version above all, but also in other guises. (2) That, in their various responses to external and internal challenges, Ruthenian and Muscovite cultural figures were forced to operate with a pronounced discrepancy between public programs and private consciousness. (3) That the Orthodox came to accept more and more the Western rules of the game, and that as a consequence the Orthodox often allowed themselves to be forced to provide "Orthodox" answers to questions they had either not posed before or had not posed with the kind of intensity attached to them in the Protestant-Catholic debates of the sixteenth century.[3] (4) That Rus' and Muscovy entered into the debates well after the initial stages, which meant that Orthodox Slavs faced the difficult task of finding "third ways" in opposition to well-defined, practically rigid and frozen, mutually dependent Protestant and Catholic cultures. (5) That in general the West (and this, for my purposes here, included Poland) was characterized by its highly codified authorities, the East by the practical lack of that codification. This larger scheme applied in smaller scale to the cultural sphere of Poland, Rus', and Muscovy. Polish culture was better defined at the explicit, public level than those of Rus' and Muscovy, the culture of Rus' better than that of Muscovy.[4] Thus Orthodox cultural figures often suffered a sense of insecurity in facing challenges from the West because of an awareness of a discrepancy between their public stances (which insisted that there existed an Orthodox culture that could be opposed to those of the West) and private doubts as to the precise definition of that culture. And finally, I also make the assumption (6) that it can be useful to compare groups and individuals of varying power and authority—the better defined with the less well defined, the stronger with the weaker.

Hints about the structures of cultures and about the attitudes of human beings toward those structures are often to be found in the moments of internal contradiction, of conflict between individuals and between individuals and structures. This model says that part of human behavior—often an important part—is characterized by seeking strategies to live with, negotiate, co-opt, or subvert a set of structures informed by authorities of varying gravity and degree of definition. Our job is to recreate the rules of the game and to follow individual players as they seek to exploit both the rules and the loopholes in attempts to impose their own type of play.

The nature of this model may perhaps be perceived better if I say a few words about its relationship to other, better-established and more familiar methodologies and models in the Slavic field. The structuralist model remains perhaps the most authoritative approach to specifically Muscovite and Russian cultural history. The model I am describing differs from this approach in a few key points.

One influential type of structuralist approach to Russian cultural history has focused upon continuities and upon grand schemes; it has posited an underlying set of binary oppositions, to which it has recourse in order to explain and predict surface-level phenomena; and it has made Russia's cultural uniqueness both a point of departure and a goal of proof. This structuralist approach seeks continuities in disruptions and revolutions, and it views the crisis of the seventeenth century as a moment between one order and the adoption of an antithetical order (which it views, at the deeper level, as a restoration of the same thing); it seeks continuities in the behavior of Russians on both sides of the divide and in the willingness to make an about-face. The crisis, in short, was brief and resulted in a *renaming* of the same old thing.[5]

I have found it useful to focus upon the disjunctures, dissonances, and misunderstandings. Seventeenth-century cultural figures both exploited and were made to act by binary oppositions, but I doubt their explanative and prognostic usefulness. I would locate them nearer the surface level, as a part of the rhetoric of cultural invective. The crisis was characterized by an attempt to make old names—or, often, names that are alleged to be old— fit new situations and things in ad hoc manners, in ways that are subject to interpretation but not always to explanation. The crisis lasted considerably longer than a moment, and there were elements of crisis on both sides of the "critical moment."[6]

I focus on these things in part to supplement the structuralist approach. That line of investigation seeks one grand truth to explain a collective mentality; I suggest that it may prove useful to investigate the many, more private truths that partially adhere to, partially deviate from the grand scheme. But I also do this out of a suspicion that binary oppositions located at some base level do not adequately explain the "laws of history," and that an important part of the human drama is to be found in the gray areas on the fringes of or even outside those oppositions. My suspicions go something like this: human beings (and I include in this category both men and women of the seventeenth century and their twentieth-century interpreters) like to impose dual models upon their reality in order to control it, to make sense of it. But human beings also feel uncomfortable, limited, frustrated with neat binary oppositions, and they seek areas for negotiation, third ways, means to escape the control of the either/or situations to which they have become voluntarily or involuntarily subject. This, too, was true of seventeenth-century Ruthenians and Muscovites, and it can also apply to their twentieth-century interpreters.

The Russian structuralist model has argued that the first way of thinking, the habit of acting according to dual models, is typically Russian; the second, which accommodates third areas, is typically Western.[7] I would argue that there is nothing non-Western about recourse to dual models and nothing non-Russian about seeking to subvert or escape the control of those models. It may ultimately prove useful to investigate this version of Russian structuralism itself as a recent chapter in a long series of attempts by the Russian intellectual elite to establish its relationship to the West.

The proposed model implies a number of shifts in focus. The sets of binary oppositions that, in structuralist approaches, lie at the foundation of Russian culture (and, in the case of some Russian structuralists, that of Russian culture alone) become a part of the rhetoric of argumentation. Human actors move on the object-subject spectrum a few degrees in the direction of becoming partial subjects of these binary oppositions: they continue to be manipulated by them, but they also manipulate them. The scale of interest shifts, from grand schemes that find their justification in the actions of small people, to a series of episodes that tell the story of how individuals at various places on the social ladder and in varying circumstances were able to make their ways in a world of greater and lesser—and, above all, fluctuating—authorities.

History in the Russian structuralist model is deterministic and static in the extreme. Change is explained in this model only in terms of sudden outside influences, and the only change possible is a flip-flopping of the values, plus for minus and minus for plus. As Lotman and Uspenskii put it:

> Given such a consistent and cyclically repeated "negation of negation," the possibility of forward development is determined by the appearance of a new perspective. At each new stage, changing historical conditions and, in particular, external cultural influences lead to a new perspective on cultural development that will activate one semantic parameter or another.[8]

But who changes these "changing historical conditions," and how do they do it? The model I am describing acknowledges the importance of structures, but it says that equally important for an understanding of both structure and change are the episodes of action and reaction in the areas of lesser authority. In other words, this model leaves more room for a limited free will. It employs (and I borrow here the words of Giovanni Levi on the methodology of microhistory):

> an action and conflict model of man's behaviour in the world which recognizes his—relative—freedom beyond, though not outside, the constraints of prescriptive and oppressive normative systems. Thus all social action is seen to be the result of the individual's constant negotiation, manipulation, choices and decisions in the face of a normative reality which, though pervasive, nevertheless offers many possibilities for personal interpretations and freedoms. The question is, therefore, how to define the margins—however narrow they may be—of the freedom granted an individual by the interstices and contradictions of the normative systems which govern him. In other words, an enquiry into the extent and nature of free will within the general structure of human society. In this type of enquiry the historian is not simply concerned with the interpretation of meanings but rather with defining the ambiguities of the symbolic world, the plurality of possible interpretations of it and the struggle which takes place over symbolic as much as over material resources.[9]

Rules in the structuralist model are something rigid, a collection of commandments and prohibitions internalized by all "native speakers" of a culture.[10] In the model I am describing, rules designate something less thoroughly delineated, a collection of tendencies to acknowledge certain authorities and strategies for negotiating them.

The structuralist approach to cultural history, especially in studies devoted to the so-called poetics of everyday life (but not only there), is caught in an unacknowledged circular argument. An extreme metaphorization of the language of linguistics tells us that life is text, and text is life. But this raises more problems than it solves. On the one hand, these treatments of life as text generally lack a more subtle appreciation for the contaminated qualities of the testimonies—in short, for the social nature of the texts. Our testimonies are a variety of texts that were written by various people, under varying circumstances, and with their own particular goals in mind. On the other hand, although these studies make implicit claims—sometimes quite strong claims—to say something about the historical reality they allegedly examine, they rarely make it clear what story they are telling. We are caught here in a semiotic game that shuttles between text and reality and is never quite willing to declare against which set of values the results are to be verified—those of some historical reality, those of the texts, or those of the scholarly game.[11]

The approach for which I am arguing obviously shares with the so-called linguistic turn in historical studies the conviction that the sources do not communicate any truths directly, and that an objective historiography, a recreation of the past "as it was" is an impossibility. But it differs just as emphatically from the extreme versions of epistemological relativism in a number of its other convictions and assumptions. First, that it is the job of the cultural historian not just to document the ways in which the testimonies are noncommunicative, deceitful, opaque, full of holes, contradictions, silences (although, I would argue, this is still an important task in most cases for Slavic materials), but to attempt to find means to make those testimonies speak about the past, even if we discover that they tell not one large truth but many partially conflicting smaller truths. This model recognizes that the truths to be told, the past to be recreated, will be partial and in some ways subjective, contingent upon the experience and inclinations of the historian and upon the quantity and qualities of the testimonies; but it also presumes that these truths will be offered as such, subject to supplementation or correction by a stronger interpretation of the testimonies.

The model I am describing here is not a methodology as such, but an open set of strategies for coping with a bad situation. This observation applies both to the world I am attempting to recreate in small parts and to the set of strategies I am attempting to develop for examining that world. In fact, I believe, we can learn something about possible approaches by observing the people we are studying. We often complain of a lack of standard authorities for this period—historical grammars and dictionaries, definitive statements of Orthodox doctrine, biographical dictionaries, authoritative lists of Orthodox saints, and so on—but we are not alone in this complaint, and we can begin to recreate some of these things by watching the Orthodox Slavs of the seventeenth century make do, borrow, adapt, and recreate in offering to the public world an early modern Orthodox Slavic culture.

This model also implies a somewhat different approach to the question of the "secondariness" versus the "uniqueness" of Muscovite culture. This approach posits that in the seventeenth century, as a part of what, by analogy with the Catholic Reform, we might term an Orthodox Slavic Reform, members of Ruthenian and Muscovite society began to pose to each other some of the questions about a modern national culture that western European nations had posed and answered in the Age of Reform. It was this act of playing the game by Western rules—not the precise answers to the questions posed—that was the real influence, the mark of secondariness. In fact, I would argue, cultural figures of seventeenth-century Rus' and Muscovy were much less fearful of the taint of influence from their Western neighbors than their nineteenth- and twentieth-century students have been. Aspects of the uniqueness of Ruthenian and Muscovite culture are to be sought in the ways members of those societies borrowed and adapted a variety of elements belonging to Western Protestant and Catholic cultures, as well as to what they perceived to be Eastern Orthodox spirituality, in order to create Orthodox national cultures.

The general outlines of the model I am describing are certainly familiar to readers of microhistorical studies such as those by Carlo Ginzburg and Natalie Zemon Davis, or to students of the strategy- and game-theory analyses of social encounters put forth by sociologists such as Erving Goffman.[12] These strategies first suggested themselves to me (though in much less precise form) when I was attempting to make do with the bad situation I faced in evaluating the sources for a biography of Meletii Smotryts'kyi. In the course of that work, by a very roundabout way, I began to suspect that strategies similar to those developed to write "history from below" in western Europe might prove well suited to an investigation of elites and official cultures on Europe's eastern periphery at the beginning of the early modern period in that part of the world.

But, again, this model is not a methodology: there are no rules here for either subject or observer, only strategies and tendencies, and a will on the part of the historian to seek means to falsify the results; it may therefore prove useful to pass to a few concrete examples. This material stems from my work on Meletii Smotryts'kyi and from an ongoing inquiry into "borderlands and border-crossings."[13] This general approach first suggested itself to me when I noticed that Meletij Smotryts'kyi was a student and a practitioner of what was called at the time the *ars dissimulandi*. One of my questions then became, To what extent were the players in the seventeenth-century cultural games aware of a shift in the rules, from truths that were eternal, "natural," divinely given, to those that were contingent, conventional, socially constructed? I found that a growing number of the Orthodox Slavic elite were playing by the new rule book, and I began to take this as one of the marks of entry into the early modern West. This first step suggested a further question, Could I exploit the knowledge that my objects of interest sometimes lied to identify those moments when they did not lie, or lied a little less? In other words, could I make use of an awareness of the presence of rhetorical masks in order to search for holes in those masks that might reveal something deeper?

In my current investigation of "border-crossings," I envision an examination of the lives of individuals of mid-seventeenth-century Rus' and Muscovy who crossed over one or more of the boundaries—cultural, confessional, or political—that defined their lives. In this period, before the new boundaries of Poland, Ukraine, and Muscovy had been more clearly drawn, we find many examples of people who converted from one church to another, who chose new political and confessional masters, who shifted cultural orientations, or who simply had hesitations about offering exclusive allegiances; some of these people conducted most of their business in public, but many of them, so the documents would seem to indicate, engaged in a certain amount of dissimulation in the course of fashioning their new selves. The lives of these cultural-confessional spies and double agents will tell us much about the creation of cultures and identities in early modern Rus' and Muscovy and about the eastern delimitation of Europe.

Let me begin with the players' own understanding of the rules of the game. Can we find any evidence, direct or indirect, that the people we are studying had any awareness of the ad hoc nature of their culture? of the contingency and constructedness of the truths they expressed about it? The answer, it seems to me, is clearly yes, and this awareness was expressed in a number of ways.

Consider the case of Meletii Smotryts'kyi, the Ruthenian archbishop whose conversion from Orthodoxy to the Uniate church was one of the scandals of the age. On July 6, 1627, Smotryts'kyi addressed three letters to Rome. One was to Pope Urban VIII asking forgiveness for his sins and reception into the church. A second went to Cardinal Ottavio Bandini (an influential member of both *Propaganda Fide* and the Holy Office of the Inquisition), declaring Smotryts'kyi's desire "not to depart by a hair's breadth from the will of Our Most Holy Lord [that is, as we can see from the larger context, Pope Urban VIII] and of Your Domination." A third went to the Holy Office, in which, among other things, he specifically requested permission to remain for some time a covert Uniate, and to practice a number of types of dissimulation in the interim, in the hope of remaining in close contact with his former coreligionists and finally of leading them into Union with Rome.[14]

All three letters, directly or indirectly, raised questions of conformity and dissimulation. Specific aspects of Smotryts'kyi's requests to the Holy Office in particular betrayed a familiarity with codified techniques of lying. Especially interesting in this regard is his petition that he be allowed to continue mentioning out loud the patriarch of Constantinople when he celebrated the liturgy, but with the understanding that he would silently be praying to God for Cyril Lukaris's conversion. This was nothing more than a request for permission to employ a type of dissimulation known as *reservatio mentalis*.

Mental reservation was only one of the more frequently practised types of licit lying that were described in the many handbooks on the *ars dissimulandi* produced throughout Europe in the age of confessional debate. In the *Tractatus Quintus: De juramento et adjuratione* of his commentary on Saint Thomas Aquinas, the Spanish Jesuit Francisco Suárez (1548–1617) gave examples of the practice of mental reservation: among other things, one could swear "I did not do it," followed by an inaudible "today"; or one could say "I swear," then say inaudibly "that I am swearing," and complete the oath with an audible "I did not do it."[15]

This particular example of "lying by the book" (and there were several others) came from Smotryts'kyi's Uniate—or, more correctly, covert-Uniate—period. I have found evidence, however, that he had been studying the rule book earlier in his career. In a polemical tract of 1621, the Orthodox Smotryts'kyi devoted (as far as I have been able to determine) his only lines to the theory and practice of the art of lying. Here he argued that his Catholic and Uniate opponents had been lying, and he rejected their lies in these terms:

> But they say that there are three sorts of falsehoods (for that is how the apostate theologians, who were rebuked for this malice, defend themselves): *officiosum, jocosum, perniciosum* [helpful, humorous, malicious]. Does any one of these three allow one to lie against the honor and the blood of your neighbor? Are humorous and helpful lies of the sort that cause harm?[16]

He then went on to cite several biblical passages directed against lying. And he concluded: "their theology allows them these things. We and the Church of God do not have that custom."

Smotryts'kyi had engaged here in confessional stereotyping: "Your apostate theologians [read: pupils of the Jesuits] justify lying; the Church [read: our side] rejects it." But in so doing he also showed himself well versed in the theory of this sort of casuistry. After all, the standard tripartite taxonomy of lies that he attributed to the "apostate theologians" *(officiosum, jocosum, perniciosum)* must actually have stemmed from his own reading of the handbooks. Thus, as an Orthodox churchman, Smotryts'kyi had been reading some works justifying lying, which he attributed to the theologians of the other side. And once he had gone over to that other side, he would show himself an adept practitioner of the theory that, when an Orthodox, he had attributed to the Catholics and the Uniates. This would seem a sort of confessional stereotyping at the level of self-representation.

In reading, then, of Smotryts'kyi's desire not to depart a "hair's breadth" from the will of Cardinal Bandini and of Pope Urban VIII, we are permitted to question whether he was not actually expressing his sincerely held desire not to *appear* to have departed from the party line. And, similarly, we are also entitled to wonder whether the statements of subjection to the pontiff were in any way conventional pieties, which he hoped he believed (or hoped he seemed to believe) but which actually expressed much more ambivalent feelings toward the holder of an office he had earlier described as a spiritual tyrant, a peer of the Turkish sultan. Smotryts'kyi made clear his use of the art of dissimulation only once he had joined the Uniate and Catholic side, but an examination of the contradictions in his arguments will show that he must have been aware at some level that he lived in a world in which "truths" from the realms of culture, faith, and politics were (like those he sometimes offered concerning his own persona) contingent upon the needs of the moment and regularly used in campaigns to manipulate public opinion.

Was lying a more widespread practice among the Orthodox? or was it limited to those, like Smotryts'kyi, who were tainted with Jesuit learning? A broader investigation will reveal that allegations that the other side had resorted to the art of dissimulation were a part of the rhetoric of cultural invective, which could be directed toward vulnerable parties—by Orthodox toward Catholics and Uniates, and by Muscovites toward Ruthenians (and Greeks). But an investigation of the dissonances in the lives and works of other Ruthenian and Muscovite cultural figures of the seventeenth century will show that for them too (even the Muscovites), the "truth" was not necessarily what was true but what would help make a point in the public debate at a given moment, even if the individual arguments were mutually contradictory. Although we may not necessarily wish in every case to discount the truth-value of public and semi-private statements, we need to take into consideration not only what was said, but—just as important for us—under what circumstances it was said, against whom, and to what end.[17]

In that same set of letters written to Rome on July 6, 1627, Smotryts'kyi placed himself firmly at the edges of Western culture. He introduced himself to Pope Urban VIII as one who was by chance of birth "situated in the most remote appendage of the sinful world."[18] To the Holy Office of the Inquisition he argued that Lithuania and Ukraine occupied a position in the moral geography of the Counter-Reformation similar to that of India (and he might have added China, Japan, and the New World), where Jesuits were allowed a certain latitude in the prosecution of their mission.[19] Taken at face value, these statements would place Rus' in Meletii's mind on the eastern peripheries of the West. And probably he did think this way most of the time, but the situation was really much more complicated than this. In this instance Smotryts'kyi was writing as a recent convert, a penitent, and a covert Uniate to his new masters in Rome, seeking to convince them, on the one hand, of his bona fides and, on the other hand, of the necessity for treating Ukraine as a missionary territory where the rules of the game could be adapted to the needs of the moment. That is, he was simultaneously declaring his allegiance to a particular spiritual community and seeking to loosen the hold of that authority over him.

Other inhabitants of the Lithuanian and Ukrainian outback would play similar games when they looked to the West. In a letter dated Kleck, April 18, 1563, Szymon Budny—the most interesting of the Polish radical Antitrinitarians, at this point in his career still a mainstream Protestant—introduced himself to Zwingli's successor in Zürich, Heinrich Bullinger, in the following terms:

I have long held a great desire to write to Your Piety, Most Illustrious Man; nay rather, as will soon be made clear, I was compelled to write by a great necessity. And yet, it was due to the great distance of the places that I did not yield to the desire and the necessity, since, indeed, it has been my lot to dwell in a region in which no couriers from Your lands, but Scythians, Moschi [Muscovites], and other barbarians are only too often seen. . . . But until now there remained a much greater obstacle to writing: namely, the awareness of my insignificance. For this alone easily deprived me of my courage, until finally, having forgotten my own insignificance, I began to consider Your candor, kindness, and great learning, all of which both shine forth abundantly in all Your writings and are proclaimed loudly by those who know You personally. For these qualities easily persuaded me to expect that You will excuse me and pardon me if anything should be said not entirely correctly. I am also certain that You will be far from expecting either eloquence or a thorough education in a man of this region, since no muses ever resided under our cold star.[20]

Here too a certain amount of dissimulation and flattery was at play. This was a type of *topos modestiae*, a way of evening the playing field between the authority of the capital and a very cosmopolitan provincial: Budny was a consummate sacred philologist; he had a mastery of Hebrew, Greek, and Latin (not to mention Church Slavonic), and of the fine points of contemporary doctrinal—especially Trinitarian and Christological—debate; and he suffered no private doubts about his self-worth or ability to conduct a serious discussion with the better-known scholar.

Smotryts'kyi, for one, would change his story, depending upon the audience and his goals at the moment. The edge of the world in representations to Rome would become, in open letters to Rus', a sort of center, the vanguard of a renewal of Orthodox spirituality. In this view, it was Rus' alone of the contemporary Orthodox Slavic nations that was both free and learned; Muscovy was free but ignorant; and the rest of the Orthodox Slavs suffered in both political and spiritual darkness.[21] To phrase it somewhat differently, Rus' now became in these representations the most western outpost of the East. There was no necessary contradiction here. Smotryts'kyi viewed Rus' as the intersection of two spiritual communities: that of the Latin West of late Humanism and that of Orthodox Slavdom. It was in some sense both East and West, and Smotryts'kyi would refer to it both ways: always as a periphery of the West; sometimes periphery and sometimes center (depending upon the needs of the moment) with respect to the East. A couple of decades later, in the course of the Khmel'nyts'kyi Rebellion, we can observe the attempts of the Ukrainian side to represent itself to Warsaw and to Moscow (whichever center was the more useful at the moment) as the last outpost of that particular civilization.

The point I wish to make here is that the so-called borderland phenomenon existed at a great many levels and in a great many ways in this part of the world. The borderland itself was in part a social construct. We can speak of an odd sort of competition between Poles and Ruthenians for position on the far eastern border of Latin culture. Ruthenians, moreover, would also play a game of shifting centers—setting Polish king against Muscovite tsar, and vice versa, or Roman pope against patriarch of Constantinople, and vice versa—depending upon which authority was becoming too demanding of their allegiance at the given moment. As Andrzej Potocki, a Polish observer of the Khmel'nyts'kyi Rebellion, reported to the Polish king, "it is [the Ruthenians'] *summa ratio status* to be neither under Your Royal Majesty nor under the tsar; and they expect to bring this about by misleading and frightening Your Royal Majesty with the tsar and the tsar with Your Royal Majesty."[22] And Muscovy—despite growing tendencies to represent itself to the world as a new spiritual and political focus—continued to suffer private insecurities and to view itself as peripheral to a variety of centers: Constantinople, Jerusalem, Kiev, and the West.

One of my main working assumptions here is that we can come closer to this process of creating new private and corporate identities by examining episodes of misrepresentation and misunderstanding across perceived cultural, confessional, and political boundaries. Here Ukraine—that borderland of borderlands—stands central. Before the upheavals of the midcentury, it had begun to define its identity in opposition to both its neighbors, but especially, at least at the practical level, in opposition to Poland. By the middle of the century, when Kievans began to arrive in Moscow in greater numbers, they had already developed an early modern Orthodox Rus'ian culture that (by borrowing and adapting) answered the questions posed by the Protestants and the Catholics.

The Ruthenian-Muscovite encounter was to be decisive for the future shape of both cultures and thus for the definition of Europe's eastern boundary. This was an encounter quite definitely across some sorts of borders that were cultural, confessional, and political, in which, nonetheless, participants could at times and in an atmosphere of mutual distrust, pretend for a variety of reasons that no borders had been crossed, that "we are all Rus'." And it was in these moments of dissonance between overt oneness and almost hidden conflict that we may be able to discover something about the shape of both cultures and the ways individuals negotiated them.

Interesting here are those cases of border-crossing when a representative of the one culture sought residence in the other, took up a position of authority, and began to explain to his new masters what they really ought to have held true all along. Such encounters include the famous ones such as Simiaon Polacki and Epifanii Slavynets'kyi, both products of Ruthenian culture, who offered competing versions of early modern Muscovite Orthodoxy from positions of high authority. But equally interesting are those less well known encounters recorded in distorted and fragmentary form that nonetheless offer us small glimpses into this process of mutual forming and deforming.

Consider the curious story of Lavrentii Zyzanii's trip to Moscow in 1627. Zyzanii was a Ruthenian archpriest, a man somewhat older than Smotryts'kyi; he was to lead the challenge of the lesser clergy against the more famous archbishop after his conversion to the Uniate church. Smotryts'kyi had traveled to Constantinople in 1623, Ruthenian catechism in hand, ostensibly for the purpose of having Patriarch Cyril Lukaris act as censor. When he "discovered" (or was this still a genuine discovery at this point?) that the patriarch was a crypto-Calvinist, Smotryts'kyi—at least according to his own later representations—decided to lead the movement in Rus' for a united church in union with Rome and under an independent Kievan patriarchate. When Smotryts'kyi returned to Kiev from Constantinople, Zyzanii set off for Moscow—likewise Ruthenian catechism in hand. His purpose in traveling eastward seems to have been to gain the approval of Patriarch Filaret of Moscow for his own statement of Orthodox doctrine of the faith. Perhaps he already hoped to find a way to oppose Smotryts'kyi. The encounter had aspects of the tragicomic. A Muscovite protocol of the three-day-long debate between Zyzanii and the correctors of his work shows many instances of mutual misrepresentation and misunderstanding. Zyzanii seems, in fact, to have been under some kind of house arrest and in danger of punishment depending on his performances. Although the catechism was printed in Moscow, it seems to have been simultaneously suppressed. The year 1627 marks an official Muscovite ban on Kievan and all Ruthenian books, and the encounter with Zyzanii may have been a contributing factor (if not the final straw).[23]

Let us examine one instance of misrepresentation and misunderstanding that arose in this encounter, in this case over the question of the status of Greek authorities. The Muscovite correctors seem to have suspected that Zyzanii belonged to a nation that accepted the new Greek texts. Echoing Maksim Grek, the Muscovite correctors told of new Greek texts that agreed neither with the old Greek nor with the Slavonic texts, and which they did not accept because, "although they are indeed printed in the Greek language, . . . the Greeks now live under great oppression in infidel countries and are not able to print them according to their custom." Asked by Lavrentii whether they knew Greek, the Muscovite correctors responded that "we know enough Greek that we do not add any syllable to any phrase, or take one away."

Lavrentii was clearly searching for some authority to support his side of the argument, and he attempted twice to make Greek texts his authority. Apparently he suspected that the Muscovites might bow before Greek authority; even better, that they did not know Greek, and that he might thus be able to gain a polemical advantage. "In the Greek language it is said thus," Lavrentii began his challenge, and he continued, "Who among you knows Greek?" But the Muscovites managed to maintain the authority of *genuine* Greek texts and still undermine Lavrentii's argument: we adhere to old Greek texts and to the Slavonic texts translated from them; you adhere to the new Greek texts that have been corrupted by the "Latins." Twice Lavrentii retreated after some argument, agreeing that these texts were indeed corrupt. And not only did he concede that this was the case, but he asserted that "we [Ruthenians], too, do not accept the new translations of books in the Greek language."[24]

But was this true? The prefaces to the Kievan editions of liturgical and patristic texts published in the 1620s (on some of which Zyzanii had, himself, collaborated as corrector) explicitly defended recourse to precisely those new Greek texts published in the Latin West. Zyzanii himself had served as corrector of the 1623 edition of the sermons of St. John Chrysostom, and he had carried out his correction according to "the most reliable Greek archetype, which was most excellently imprinted in the city of Eton" (that is, in Protestant England).[25]

This exchange calls in doubt Zyzanii's claims that he had come to Moscow for spiritual enlightenment. In my reading, on both occasions Zyzanii first argued one way, expressing views that were in keeping with the Kievan program; and both times he finally gave in, not because he had been convinced (he attempted twice, after all, to make the same point) but because he despaired of convincing the Muscovite authorities with this argument. That is, Zyzanii shifted his statements on Orthodox belief—both subtly and not so subtly—whenever he felt the need to do so during his interrogation by the Muscovite authorities. The truth here was not what was true, but what was useful. Greek authority could be useful to both sides, but it could also be difficult to control, especially in Muscovy.

This shifting of position in the course of public polemics also shaped what we call orthodoxy and heresy. It may be nothing more than a truism that orthodoxy is ultimately what the stronger side holds, heterodoxy the position of the weaker. But we should be aware that in the middle of the seventeenth century in Rus' and Muscovy, even the side that was stronger (or would ultimately prove itself the stronger) was genuinely unsure of what was Orthodox faith and what was heresy. It would decide what was correct faith only in the course of the seventeenth century as it came to terms with the various internal and external challenges: from the Latin West in various forms, from Kiev, from the Greeks, from the Old Believers.

Consider the following example. Zyzanii's Muscovite interlocutors denied the licitness of baptisms performed by non-priests when no priest was present. This situation often arose for Orthodox Christians living in the Polish-Lithuanian Commonwealth; it was thus a matter of great concern for Lavrentii, who had written that "if no priest was present, a person can be baptised by a deacon, or a clerk, or a monk, or a layman." The Muscovite correctors responded with apparently unfeigned amazement: "What city is there where there are deacons and clerks, but there is no priest?" Zyzanii's response was eloquent in its terseness: "there is much of this in the world." The Muscovite side was apparently ignorant of the realities of life on the western boundaries of Orthodox Christendom, and they argued that "without a priest, not only is it not proper for the faithful to be baptised, but even to be born or to die." In this particular instance it was Zyzanii who argued for what would eventually become Orthodox doctrine in Muscovy.[26]

Both sides manipulated the truth in an effort to gain from the other side something useful and to discover and neutralize what was potentially threatening. This was at the beginning of the Ruthenian-Muscovite encounter, and the debate was informed by a surprisingly large amount of mutual ignorance and mistrust. Both sides seem to have thought they had something to gain:

Zyzanii, perhaps, the authority of the patriarch's approbation, and the Muscovite authorities, perhaps, the fruits of Kievan learning. In this particular instance both sides seem to have been disappointed.

From the point of view of students in the late twentieth century, the record of Ruthenian and Muscovite cultural history is even more full of silences than those of the contemporary Western cultures. Some of these silences were fortuitous, some perhaps not entirely so. It might be useful to begin the laborious task of collecting and evaluating the gaps in the testimonies. Can we learn something about a society by finding those things about which it does not talk? Can we describe a rhetoric of cultural and societal taboos? But how are we to identify a silence? Can we tell a meaningful silence from a meaningless one?

Let me begin with a concrete example. Although we know something about Zyzanii's role in the official condemnations of Smotryts'kyi's catechism in 1628, as far as I know (and there is always the danger that a new witness will suddenly speak out), the Ruthenian sources are silent on Zyzanii's own catechism, even about his trip to Moscow in general. What are we to make of this? Is it possible to make cautious arguments on the basis of what should have been said but was not said? In other words, can we use a type of argument from silence?

In this particular instance, we can never know whether it is significant or fortuitous that Ruthenian documents directly reflecting Zyzanii's Muscovite experience are not available to us. But what about other extant documents such as Smotryts'kyi's own protestation against the treatment he received at Zyzanii's hands in Kiev in 1628? Should Smotryts'kyi have mentioned Zyzanii's trip to Moscow and the very tentative approval he had received from Filaret? This would, after all, have suited Smotryts'kyi's polemical purposes ideally, since he could have represented Zyzanii—to the Polish-Lithuanian Commonwealth in general, and to Orthodox readers in particular—as a Muscovite agent, both political and cultural, one who for his own purposes had enlisted the support of a foreign and enemy power and sought enlightenment from the benighted. There were all sorts of polemical points to be made here, but Smotryts'kyi did not make any of them.

This seems to indicate that Smotryts'kyi did not know of the trip. But this would then raise still more questions. How did this event remain secret? Did Zyzanii go to Moscow on his own? or was he sent? Was this another of the attempts of the Orthodox Metropolitan of Kiev, Jov Borec'kyj, to play off Moscow against Warsaw and Rome?

There are probably many other silences and half-silences to which we could become attuned. Consider, for example, the account of Vasilii Vasil'evich Buturlin's embassy on behalf of Tsar Aleksei Mikhailovich to the Ukraine in 1653 and 1654. This lengthy document makes frequent use of a formula to describe the alleged universal joy of the locals at the coming of Muscovite authority: "and at that time there was a great multitude of people in the Church, of the male and female sex, and they cried from great joy, that the Lord God has judged all of them worthy to be under the sovereign high hand."[27] This formula is suspicious for a number of reasons. First, it is a formula; it appears in the same form over and over, as one local community after another greeted Buturlin's embassy. Second, we know from a variety of sources that the joy was not universal, often not even particularly joyful. Third, it mentions women, who rarely appear in these official tales. Why do Ruthenian women suddenly speak out here?

The answer in each case is probably that the vexed question of the willingness of Rus' to be under Muscovite rule was already at that time an object of competition for public control. What can the witnesses tell us? Here again we find that the contemporary testimonies were conditioned by power relationships between speaker and audience. One interpretative camp will point to documents such as Buturlin's account or to the secret reports of Father Maksym Fylymovych, who wrote to his Muscovite correspondent begging that the tsar impose his order on Ukraine and urging him not to listen to any of the opposing voices.[28] Another camp will cite the letter of the archpriest of Chernobyl, who wrote, "Khmel'nyts'kyi has yielded us all up into the slavery of the Muscovite tsar."[29] Those who wish to discredit the first witness will point out that his letter could be read as a plea for order of any sort after the anarchy of the early 1650s, that the author himself indicated here and elsewhere that not all were happy with the prospect of Muscovite rule, and that he seems to have been positioning himself as a Muscovite agent in expectation of the new order. Those who wish to discredit the second witness (including the nineteenth-century editor of the letter) point out that his letter was written from the other side of the border, that the author's son remained in Polish territory, and that he was concerned for his son's well-being. As usual, the truth was probably much more complicated than the traditional either/or question. Probably many Ruthenian men and women, made to speak out here in favor of one power or another, had quite complicated and contingent reasons for choosing one side over the other; and many of them, like many of the leaders, may have hoped to find some third way.

When Khmel'nyts'kyi was asked to swear his oath of loyalty to Tsar Aleksei Mikhailovich, he countered by asking the tsar's envoy, Buturlin, to pledge on behalf of the sovereign to uphold the Ruthenians' privileges and freedoms, and he cited the precedence of his dealings with the Polish king and his senators. The Muscovite response was internally contradictory. It sought to discredit appeal to the Polish model first on Polish terms, by arguing that the Polish king was not good for his word, and then on Muscovite terms, by arguing that the Polish king was not a sovereign—as was the tsar.[30] We do not know directly from these testimonies what the people of Rus' thought about this issue because they were either silent or were required to shape their answers with the various authorities in mind. The history of the Treaty of Pereiaslav can be interpreted as a long series of cross-cultural misunderstandings.[31]

Questions of orthodoxy and heresy became implicated in this political game. As long as Khmel'nyts'kyi needed Moscow and the tsar still wished to employ persuasion in his dealings with Rus', both sides would begin much of their correspondance with a formula that spoke of the need to defend "God's holy Churches and Orthodox Christians from the Polish king and from Lithuanian people." And in one particularly fulsome moment, Khmel'nyts'kyi urged Tsar Aleksei Mikhailovich "not to grant peace to his [the tsar's] enemies, the pagan Poles."[32] And yet, as we know, on the one hand Ruthenian leaders in fact could find areas of agreement with the "pagan" Poles, and on the other hand the Orthodoxy of Ruthenian cultural leaders, including men of the church, would be viewed with suspicion in Moscow. In this atmosphere of mistrust, assurances of sincerity and genuineness were frequent and must have been counterproductive the more insistently they were made. A subject that deserves our attention in this regard is the frequent reference by Ruthenians and Muscovites in this period to the theory and practice of rumor and slander. Many of the letters, public announcements, polemical pamphlets, and other documents of the period seem to have been, in part, attempts to control the rumor mill.

Finally (and I leave this last comment in the form of a question for now), can we take morphology—that is to say, typological invariants and structural similarities—into consideration in historical studies?[33] We should be aware, after all, that in examining cross-cultural misunderstandings between Ruthenians and Muscovites, we will encounter similarities and differences of a different order from those that crop up, for example, in Jacques Gernet's study of Jesuit missions in China.[34] The Latin West and the Byzantine East shared a long-distant past and were not entirely closed to each other in the interim. Similarities and differences that arose in response to the same questions in the seventeenth century may be the result of cross-cultural influences, but they may also result from similar responses to similar structural challenges. Similarities in structure may result from a common past, and they may then facilitate the acceptance of outside cultural influences. An examination of the overdefined West may provide some clues to an understanding of the underdefined East. A consideration of the comparative morphologies of the cultures of the Latin West, of Rus', and of Muscovy may offer us some hints about where to look for telltale misrepresentations, misunderstandings, and silences.

NOTES

1. Witold Gombrowicz, *A Kind of Testament,* ed. Dominique de Roux (Philadelphia, 1973), 55.

2. Ibid., 63: "I was virtually sure that the revision of European Form could only be undertaken from an extra-European position, from where it is slacker and less perfect." See also ibid., 56–57.

3. What, for example, was the Orthodox position on the authority of Scripture? on penance? on justification?

4. Once again Gombrowicz: "A Pole, when confronting the East, is a Pole delineated and known in advance. A Pole with his face turned toward the West has a turbid visage, full of unclean angers, disbelief, and secret sore spots" (*Diary,* 3 vols. [Evanston, Ill., 1988–1993], 1 [1988]: 14). To what extent can we, for various historical periods, substitute "Ruthenian" and "Muscovite" (or "Ukrainian" and

"Russian") for the word "Pole" in Gombrowicz's statement?

5. I am reacting here in specific terms to the highly influential article by Iurii M. Lotman and Boris A. Uspenskii, "Binary Models in the Dynamics of Russian Culture (to the End of the Eighteenth Century)," published in English in *The Semiotics of Russian Cultural History: Essays by Iurii M. Lotman, Lidiia Ia. Ginsburg, Boris A. Uspenskii,* ed. Alexander D. Nakhimovsky and Alice Stone Nakhimovsky (Ithaca, N.Y., 1985), 30–66.

6. Nicholas Riasanovsky writes in his *History of Russia,* 4th ed. (New York, 1984), 11, that "Continuity is the very stuff of history." And here many adherents of the Russian structuralists would agree with him. But is this necessarily so for everyone involved? This statement, which appears before the chapters on Kievan Rus', elides the question of a Kievan-Muscovite continuum. A Ukrainian historian might be tempted to write that "Disjuncture is the very stuff of history." In the cases of both Ukraine and Russia, it might be useful to study both continuity and change, and especially the troublesome and underexamined disjunctures of Russian history. For example, we might consider investigating the degree to which it was the Ruthenians who, for their own perhaps short-term goals, helped teach the Muscovites to think of Kievan-Muscovite continuity in the mid-seventeenth century. If Russia was the natural home of structuralism (as the argument of Uspenskii and Lotman seems to suggest), was the Ukraine postmodern already in the early modern period?

7. See Lotman and Uspenskii, "Binary Models," 31–32.

8. Ibid., 33.

9. Giovanni Levi, "On Microhistory," in *New Perspectives on Historical Writing,* ed. Peter Burke (University Park, Pa., 1992), 94–95.

10. See Lotman and Uspenskii, "Binary Models," 30.

11. What are we to understand, for example, from the following statement (ibid., 60): "The binary structure of Russian culture was significantly more stable than any of its concrete realizations." Is this statement falsifiable? If so, according to what set of criteria?

12. For methodological discussions of microhistory, see Levi, "On Microhistory"; Edward Muir, "Introduction: Observing Trifles," in *Microhistory and the Lost Peoples of Europe,* ed. Edward Muir and Guido Ruggiero (Baltimore, 1991), vii–xxviii; Carlo Ginzburg, "Clues: Roots of an Evidential Paradigm," in *Clues, Myths, and the Historical Method* (Baltimore, 1989), 96–125. Microhistorians are reluctant theorizers. Classics of the genre of practical microhistoriography include Carlo Ginzburg, *The Cheese and the Worms: The Cosmos of a Sixteenth-Century Miller* (Baltimore, 1980); Natalie Zemon Davis, *The Return of Martin Guerre* (Cambridge, Mass., 1983); Giovanni Levi, *Inheriting Power: The Story of an Exorcist* (Chicago, 1988); Pietro Redondi, *Galileo: Heretic* (Princeton, 1987). Of Erving Goffman's works, I have found especially suggestive, *The Presentation of Self in Everyday Life* (New York, 1959); "Expression Games: An Analysis of Doubts at Play," in his *Strategic Interaction* (Philadelphia, 1969), 1–81; and *Frame Analysis: An Essay on the Organization of Experience* (New York, 1974).

13. I have written about some of this material before in other contexts, where the focus was not on questions of methodology. See David A. Frick, *Meletij Smotryc'kyj* (Cambridge, Mass., 1995); and "Zyzanij and Smotryc'kyj (Moscow, Constantinople, Kiev): Episodes in Cross-Cultural Misunderstanding," *Journal of Ukrainian Studies* 17, nos. 1–2 (1992): 67–93. An important example of a study devoted to a member of the elite caught between competing definitions of corporate identity on Europe's eastern edge is Frank E. Sysyn's *Between Poland and the Ukraine: The Dilemma of Adam Kysil, 1600–1653* (Cambridge, Mass., 1985).

14. Athanasius Velykyj, ed., *Litterae episcoporum historiam ucrainae illustrantes, 1600–1900*, vol. 1, *1600–1640*, Analecta Ordinis Sancti Basilii Magni, series 2, sectio 3, Documenta Romana Ecclesiae Catholicae in Terris Ucrainae et Bielarusjae (Rome, 1972), 127, 128 (127).

15. On the history of casuistry and the *ars dissimulandi* in the early modern period, see Perez Zagorin, *Ways of Lying: Dissimulation, Persecution, and Conformity in Early Modern Europe* (Cambridge, Mass., 1990), passim (p. 183, for the example from Suárez); Carlo Ginzburg, *Il Nicodemismo: Simulazione e dissimulazione nell'Europa del '500* (Turin, 1970).

16. Meletii Smotryts'kyi, *Verificatia niewinności* (Vilnius, 1621) 42v, facsimile edition, *Collected Works of Meletij Smotryc'kyj*, Harvard Library of Early Ukrainian Literature, Texts, vol. 2 (Cambridge, Mass., 1987), 367.

17. This rule from the handbook of microhistorical detection is a rephrasing of a much older guide to philology and exegesis. Erasmus offered these suggestions for the interpretation of Holy Scripture: "Accedet hinc lucis nonnihil ad intelligendum scripturae sensum, si perpendamus *non modo quid dicatur, verum etiam a quo dicatur, cui dicatur, quibus verbis dicatur, quo tempore, qua occasione, quid praecedat, quid consequatur* [emphasis added]" (No little light will be added in this way for understanding the sense of Scripture if we will weigh carefully *not only what is said, but also by whom it is said, to whom it is said, with what words it is said, at what time, on what occasion, what precedes, what follows*). See Jerry H. Bentley, *Humanists and Holy Writ: New Testament Scholarship in the Renaissance* (Princeton, 1983), 180.

18. Velykyj, *Litterae*, 125.

19. Ibid., 128.

20. Theodor Wotschke, *Der Briefwechsel der Schweizer mit den Polen: Archiv für Reformationsgeschichte*, Ergänzungsband 3 (Leipzig, 1908), 172–73.

21. Meletii Smotryts'kyi, *Apologia* (L'viv, 1628), 2v–3r (facsimile edition, *Collected Works*, 519).

22. Andrzej Potocki, *Pamiatniki izdannye Vremennoiu kommisieiu dlia razbora drevnikh aktov*, 3 vols. (Kiev, 1845–1852), 3 (1852): 300.

23. See K. Kharlampovich, *Malorossiiskoe vliianie na velikorusskuiu tserkovnuiu zhizn'* (Kazan', 1914), 108.

24. See "Prenie litovskogo protopopa Lavrentiia Zizaniia s igumenom Ilieiu i spravshchikom Grigoriem po povodu ispravleniia sostavlennogo Lavrentiem katikhiziza," in *Letopisi russkoi literatury i drevnosti*, ed. Nikolai S. Tikhonravov, 5 vols. (Kiev, 1859–1863), 2 (1859): 95, 88, 95, 99.

25. Khv. Titov, *Materiialy dlia istoriji knyzhnoii spravy na Vkraiini v XVI–XVIII vv.: Vsezbirka peredmov do ukraiins'kykh starodrukiv*, Ukraiins'ka Akademiia Nauk. Zbirnyk istorychno-filolohichnoho viddilu, no. 17 (Kiev, 1924), 57. (Facsimile edition, with an introduction by Hans Rothe, Bausteine zur Geschichte der Literatur bei den Slaven, vol. 16 [Cologne, 1982].)

26. "Prenie litovskogo protopopa Lavrentiia Zizaniia," 97.

27. *Akty, otnosiashchiesia k istorii iuzhnoi i zapadnoi Rossii (hereafer, AZR)*, 15 vols. (St. Petersburg, 1863–1892), 10 (1878): 228 (cf. also 192–93, 214).

28. Ibid., 4 (1863): 31.

29. I cite this hybrid text (part Polish, part Ruthenian-like in Latin letters) as an indication that the reluctance to make either/or choices extended even to the linguistic realm: "Prosiłem sleznie hospodara moiego, żeby dobre rzeczy stały, ale jako wiżu, źle; bo wydał Chmielnicki wszech nas w niewolu Moskiewskiemu Caru po Wlodymer, po Turow, i ieszcze co daley. Sam z woyskiem swoim przysiąhl, i miesto Kijow syloiu pod miecznym karaniem do teho prywioł, że przysięhli. Nie wiem szczo

i z Czarnobylem budiet się deialo, bez mało koniecznie toż budet musiał uczynit" (I asked my Lord tearfully that good things might happen, but as I see, it is bad. For Khmel'nyts'kyi has betrayed all of us into the slavery of the Muscovite tsar as far as Volodymyr, Turov, and even further. He himself swore allegiance, along with his army, and he brought the city of Kiev by force, under punishment by the sword, to swear allegiance. I do not know what will happen with Chernobyl; it is all but certain that it will have to do the same). "Kopia listu iego mości oyca protopy czarnobylskiego," *Chteniia v imperatorskom Obshchestve istorii i drevnosti pri moskovskom universitete* 3 (1861): 1.

30. *AZR* 10 (1878): 226.

31. For some episodes in the history of the bilateral misinterpretations of this event, see Orest Subtelny, "Mazepa, Peter I, and the Question of Treason," *Harvard Ukrainian Studies* 2 (1978): 158–83.

32. Ibid., 342.

33. For a discussion of this methodological problem, see Carlo Ginzburg, *Ecstasies: Deciphering the Witches' Sabbath* (New York, 1991), 14–30.

34. Jacques Gernet, *China and the Christian Impact: A Conflict of Cultures* (Cambridge, 1985).

ENGELINA S. SMIRNOVA

Translated by Michael S. Flier

SIMON USHAKOV—
"HISTORICISM" AND "BYZANTINISM"

ON THE INTERPRETATION OF RUSSIAN PAINTING
FROM THE SECOND HALF OF THE
SEVENTEENTH CENTURY

SIMON USHAKOV (1626–1686) long served as head of the royal icon painters who worked in the Moscow Kremlin, filling the orders of Tsar Aleksei Mikhailovich, his family, the patriarch, members of the court, and prominent hierarchs. His art is known for its characteristic incorporation of individual devices from European painting into the old Byzantine Russian system of icon painting. Ushakov and his followers began to convey depth in facial features through gradual chiaroscuro modeling, to depict to a certain extent the volume of figures, and to make broad use of modern European architectural motifs (columns and arches) for settings. His oeuvre shows the most important processes at work in Russian painting in the second half of the seventeenth century. For this reason Ushakov's painting offers the best examples for assessing the essence of Russian artistic culture of that period.

The bibliography on Ushakov's work is quite small, consisting primarily of published information taken from written sources,[1] and of the publication and attribution of the works themselves.[2] When it comes to interpreting his art and evaluating his place in the history of culture, a binary division prevails. Ushakov is treated simultaneously as a traditionalist and an innovator (even a "naturalist"), and his work is considered a combination of both tendencies.[3] In this regard his art has been evaluated in both positive and negative terms. Ushakov's oeuvre often serves as a convenient example for illustrating the antagonism between the adherents of naturalism in art (for example, Iosif Vladimirov in his treatise on icon painting) and their critic, archpriest Avvakum.[4] Additionally there are a number of studies that investigate the western European models used in Ushakov's works. I share the view that the way these patterns were employed depended entirely on the specific artistic tastes of the Russian icon painters, with the result that European motifs acquired a completely different resonance.[5] The basic idea that emerges from the many pronouncements about Ushakov is that he took a giant step—successful or unsuccessful—from a medieval toward a modern conception of art. It is the dynamism that is emphasized in the development of seventeenth-century Russian painting, in which, as in all of Russian culture of that period, the foundations seem already to have been laid for the reforms of Tsar Peter I at the juncture of the seventeenth and eighteenth centuries.

My purpose here is to show, on the contrary, that the painting of Simon Ushakov and his pupils in the Kremlin workshops does not provide evidence of any serious move toward a new artistic epoch in the second half of the seventeenth century. Whereas the European influences and motifs in his painting are undeniably important, his art on the whole belongs to the old system and remains fully within the medieval artistic tradition. This idea was already formulated in the 1920s by Vladimir Nechaev but has not yet been developed.[6] By taking into account the quite successful studies of Byzantine and Post-Byzantine art in the second half of our century, we are now in a position to compare the art of Ushakov with other phenomena of medieval Orthodox culture and affirm their very close relationship, indeed their parallelism.[7]

The present study examines only one aspect of Ushakov's work, the repetition of old "Orthodox" models in subject matter and in iconography. It is meant as a preliminary statement, merely an outline of the main thematic contours. It is fairly difficult to evaluate the kinds of subject matter that dominated the interest of one or another medieval master. The information about Ushakov's work gleaned by Filimonov from documentary evidence shows that only a handful of the many icons painted by Ushakov have survived. Nonetheless these very icons are sufficiently representative for our purposes. As a rule, they are works from the lower tiers of iconostases or from those areas of the church where the subject matter was determined by the concrete situation: church dedication, requirements of the patron's commission, and so on.

In some ways Ushakov's activity was similar to that of Patriarch Nikon, who tried to transfer to Russia the essence of the holiness of Christian history. Nikon founded the Holy Cross Monastery in the north of Russia to house fragments of the True Cross. He placed a copy of the highly venerated Athonite icon the *Iverian Mother of God* in a newly erected eponymous monastery. He also founded the New Jerusalem Monastery, which was an imitation of the real Jerusalem and its Church of the Holy Sepulcher.

Among the surviving icons of Simon Ushakov, it can be shown that the predominant ones were those called upon to underscore the antiquity and glory of the Orthodox world's sacred treasures, the wealth of the historical memory of the Russian state and the Russian church, and in a number of cases, the involvement of Moscovite Rus' in the sanctity of other areas of the Greek and Slavic world. Ushakov's icon painting apparently presents a certain program, a kind of "historicism" characteristic of him. Ushakov copied many famous Russian icons of the twelfth through the sixteenth centuries and miraculous icons from other Orthodox countries. Additionally, he reconstructed Byzantine iconographic schemes.

The subjects of his copies depended primarily on patrons, but the iconography depended primarily on the painter himself. This point is well illustrated by Ushakov's famous icon from the Church of the Trinity in Nikitniki, *In Praise of the Vladimir Mother of God* (1668), in Tret'iakov Gallery, Moscow.[8] The icon of the Vladimir Mother of God is represented in an oval frame in the center of the composition. This palladium of the entire Russian State is kept in the Kremlin Cathedral of the Dormition in Moscow. Prominent figures of the Russian church and Russian history are placed within the twisted branches of a large tree on either side of the oval framing the icon: metropolitans, patriarchs, certain pious tsars, Tsarevich Dmitrii (innocently murdered in 1591), famous monks, founders of monasteries, and glorified fools-in-Christ as well. In the clouds above, Christ entrusts angels with a cloth, which they prepare to extend over the great heroes of Russian history. The Kremlin is depicted below with the Cathedral of the Dormition inside. Its fourteenth-century builders, Metropolitan Peter and Prince Ivan Kalita, water the tree growing out of the cathedral, with Tsar Aleksei Mikhailovich (1645–1676), his wife, and children standing at the sides. Some analysts are correct in noting a similarity in compositional structure and symbolism between Ushakov's icon and Ukrainian engraving from the second half of the seventeenth century, namely, the frontispieces in a number of Kievan publications.

Certain details of the Muscovite composition lead one to suspect that the icon might be responding to the burning issues of the 1660s, especially the correlation of secular and ecclesiastical power.[9] But much more important than any current, contextual, or circumstantial motifs in the Muscovite icon is the eternal theme of intercession, protection of the Russian Land, the protective cover of the heavenly veil, the theme of the miracle-working power of the *Vladimir Mother of God* icon from the Cathedral of the Dormition. This fundamental idea is linked with the theme of Russian piety and its zealots, the theme of Russia as a blessed garden, the theme of duty and service to country and to church. Among the many other shades of meaning present in Ushakov's icon, I might single out the prayers of the dead for the living, the praying of the great zealots of Russian holiness for the Muscovite tsardom.

Aside from the icon under discussion (a one-of-a-kind work conceptually), Ushakov made copies of many other famous icons. He copied the *Vladimir Mother of God* several times. We might mention the icon of 1652 in Tret'iakov Gallery, Moscow; the icon of 1662 in the Russian Museum, St. Petersburg; and the icon of 1676 (?) from the Sergiev Posad Museum (unpublished).[10] In 1668 he made a copy of the *Don Mother of God* for the Don Monastery, the original of which is kept in the Cathedral of the Annunciation in the Moscow Kremlin.[11] He copied the *Kazan' Mother of God* at least twice, in 1674 and 1676, and restored the *Blachernae Mother of God* from the Cathedral of the Dormition in the Moscow Kremlin in 1675.[12]

These copies are either identical in size to the originals or close to them. The inscriptions on the icons of the 1652 *Vladimir Mother of God* and the *Don Mother of God* directly indicate that these works were done "to the exact dimensions" *(v tu zhe meru)* of the originals. In some cases even artistic peculiarities are reproduced, for instance, the facial expression in the *Don Mother of God*. Ushakov makes true copies, in what is very close to our own understanding of the word, and not iconographic replica repetitions. The abundance of such copies says something about the subtleties in attitude toward miracle-working icons at the time. The economic growth of the provinces and the stronger role of townspeople and merchants altered social consciousness; furthermore, the grace of miracle-working icons had to extend not only to the most important churches in Moscow and the ancient centers of ecclesiastical life, but to the more modest towns and dwellings as well. Hence the tendency toward documentation, the desire to reproduce not only the internal truth of the copied icon but its external likeness as well.

Certain works of Ushakov and his students apart from the miracle-working icons may be viewed as copies of venerated icons. To begin with we have the upper torso representations of Christ Emmanuel *(Spas Emmanuil)* in a particular composition where only the head and the upper part of the shoulders are shown. One of the icons of Christ Emmanuel from 1668 is in the Russian Museum in St. Petersburg; another, still unpublished, is in a museum in Irkutsk.[13] Apparently one other icon with this subject, also from 1668 and known from old descriptions, was in the collection of Count Aleksei Musin-Pushkin in Moscow at the beginning of the last century.[14] Among art works of the seventeenth century we also find ensembles of three icons—Christ Emmanuel in the center flanked by Archangel Michael and Archangel Gabriel—in a particular composition in which the torso is cut off very high. The Siia icon pattern book has tracings of three such icons, presumably by Prokopii Chirin, an artist of the "Stroganov School" from the beginning of the seventeenth century.[15] Iconography of this type is also found in the works of followers and students of Ushakov working within his stylistic tradition. The three icons by master Mikhail Miliutin from 1697 in the New Convent of the Virgin in Moscow provide good examples.[16]

Compositions of the "abridged" type are completely atypical for the painting of the Russian late Middle Ages. In the sixteenth–seventeenth centuries they occur in Cretan icon painting but are possessed of a somewhat different configuration: the shoulders are cut off not only from below, but along the sides as well, making the represention appear to be a fragment of a larger composition with a full-length or half-length figure.[17] As far as subject matter is concerned, the seventeenth-century Russian icons with Emmanuel and the two archangels are without parallels either in later Russian icon painting (except for the Kremlin masters) or in Post-Byzantine icon painting. Only one iconographic prototype suggests itself: the famous twelfth-century icon from the Cathedral of the Dormition in the Moscow Kremlin, apparently brought there from some Russian city in the sixteenth century.[18] This icon was venerated in Moscow. Such a composition on the walls of Kremlin buildings is represented in miniatures from the *Book of the Coronation of Tsar Mikhail Fedorovich Romanov* (1613). It is likely that a number of seventeenth-century masters—Simon Ushakov among them—copied this icon but produced the copy on three separate boards, rather than on one, as in the original.

In this context one has to inquire about the sources of numerous depictions of the Savior Not-Made-by-Hands, the Mandylion, painted by Ushakov for various churches and monasteries. We have the 1658 icon from the Church of the Trinity in Nikitniki (Tret'iakov Gallery, Moscow); the 1673 icon from the sacristy of the Trinity–St. Sergii Lavra (Tret'iakov Gallery, Moscow); the 1674 icon in the Cathedral of the Trinity at the same monastery; and the 1678 icon of unknown intention that came from Smolensk (Tret'iakov Gallery, Moscow).[19] There are many references in documents to the icons of the Savior Not-Made-by-Hands painted by Ushakov. Meanwhile we should mention that neither in the painting of local seventeenth-century Russian schools nor in post-Byzantine art did the theme of the Savior Not-Made-by-Hands ever become as widespread as it did in the work of Ushakov. These icons by Ushakov could very well be copies of one of the most venerated icons of this type in Moscow, that is, a twelfth-century icon from the Kremlin Cathedral of the Dormition (Tret'iakov Gallery, Moscow)[20] or, less likely, the local church icon of the Savior-Andronik Monastery, which has not survived.

Let us now turn to Ushakov's copies and replicas of icons that are revered outside Russia. First and foremost, we have the *Kykko Mother of God,* a 1668 icon from the Church of Gregory of Neocaesarea in Moscow (Tret'iakov Gallery, Moscow). Interest in the history and sacred objects of Cyprus rose in Russia in the seventeenth century for a number of political reasons.[21] In his icon Ushakov does not reproduce any of the variants of this iconography, but a somewhat later type, whose face is known to us from rather late Post-Byzantine replicas.[22] What is special about this late variant is that Christ holds an open—rather than a closed—scroll with the Greek text from Luke 4:18. Ushakov very accurately copies the Cyprian composition, but he introduces two changes: he uses a mirror image with the scroll in the left rather than the right hand of Christ, and on the background next to the scroll he provides a Russian translation of the Greek text so carefully rendered on the scroll: "The spirit of the Lord is upon me, because he hath anointed me." The iconography adapted by Ushakov in imitation of late Cretan painting is repeated by masters from his circle—as, for example, in the anonymous icon from the Church of Nikola in Golutvino (Historical Museum, Moscow; see fig. 1).

The type reproduced in the icon *Dormition* from the Trinity–St. Sergii

Fig. 1   Painter from Ushakov's circle. *Kykko Mother of God.* Church of Nikola in Golutvino. Historical Museum, Moscow. Reproduced by permission.

Fig. 2   Simon Ushakov. *Dormition*. 1671. Trinity–St. Sergii Lavra Collection, Sergiev Posad Museum. Reproduced by permission.

Lavra done for Bogdan Matveevich Khitrovo in 1671 (Sergiev Posad Museum; see fig. 2) can be assigned to the category of "non-Muscovite" sacred objects.[23] Ushakov's signature is on it, but it is difficult to say to what degree the icon actually belongs to him. The painting is poorly preserved and the earlier work has been overpainted in many places. Nonetheless, the overall composition has survived. The iconography is unique for art from the second half of the seventeenth century: a horizontal composition, a stern group of apostles, no bishops, no women from Jerusalem. Two large figures of flying angels are represented flanking the slightly inclined head of Christ. The symmetrical structures ("basilicas") are simply outlined. This composition bears a striking resemblance to those of the Byzantine Dormitions of the eleventh–twelfth centuries, whereas the gestures of the upraised hands of the apostles, spare and expressive, bring to mind the fresco at Asinou, Cyprus, from 1105–1106.

The unusual composition is because the icon was copied from the primary icon of the Kievan Caves Monastery, as noted in the endowment book of the Trinity–St. Sergii Lavra under the year 1673: "The icon of the Dormition of the Most Holy Mother of God was copied from the icon in the city of Kiev, in the Caves Monastery, in the church; the image itself is represented

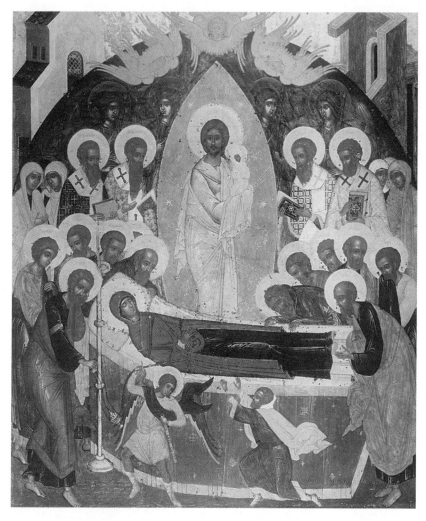

Fig. 3   Simon Ushakov. *Dormition.* 1663. Florishchevo Monastery. Tret'iakov Gallery, Moscow.
Reproduced by permission.

in the altar."[24] Probably Khitrovo or Ushakov had access to a tracing or engraving of the Kievan image, both of which enjoyed some currency in the
Ukraine and were distinguished by a special feature: the representation of a
container for relics at the side of the bier.[25] In other words, in these engravings and Ushakov's icon we see a reflex, albeit a weak one, of the iconography of the local church icon *(khramovaia ikona)* of the Church of the Dormition in the Kievan Caves Lavra, a building finished in 1077 and
consecrated in 1089. The history of this composition and its emergence in
the art of the seventeenth century merit special study.[26]

   Ushakov's *Dormition* of 1663 (Tret'iakov Gallery, Moscow; see fig. 3), the local church icon of the Florishchevo Monastery, has nothing in common with the great Dormitions created in Russia under different stylistic situations during the seventeenth century.[27] Smooth contours, massive forms, the self-assured pose, the "Byzantine" drawing of the buildings, all this presents a conception completely different from the exalted, overly detailed compositions of the Muscovite masters raised on Stroganov School traditions of taste. The iconography of the Florishchevo Monastery *Dormition* is symmetrical with four prelates, a Byzantine redaction from the Palaeologan period. The icon is copied from a Russian model unknown to us (possibly it reflects the composition of an ancient local church icon from Moscow's Cathedral of the Dormition) or from a Cretan model.

As a final example, Ushakov painted several large icons of the Pantocrator Enthroned for the local tiers of iconostases, where they were placed to the right of the royal doors. There is a 1672 icon from the Nikolo-Ugresha Monastery (Historical Museum, Moscow; see fig. 4), a 1682 icon in the New Convent of the Virgin, a 1684 icon from the Cathedral of the Trinity in the Trinity–St. Sergii Lavra, and several replicas as well.[28] Such monumental pictures, with the silhouette of Christ inscribed in an imagined oval and with a throne back straight across, did not follow the Russian tradition of the seventeenth century, with its complicated composition and scalloped throne back.[29] Rather they represent a new combination from Cretan models and early Russian-Byzantine iconography.

Ushakov's first inspiration was the monumental Cretan *Pantocrators* of this special type, like the icon of Thomas Vatas from circa 1596, in the Monastery of the Apocalypse on Patmos.[30] The other was an ancient treasure of the Cathedral of the Dormition, the *Savior of the Golden Robe* (see fig. 5), which repeats the old iconography in a later painting on a board from an eleventh-century icon found among the old appointments of Novgorod's Cathedral of the Holy Sophia. This icon includes a form of the throne dating to Byzantine art of the eleventh–twelfth centuries.[31]

As for style, Ushakov's reliance on older models was important not only for content. It had an effect on the artistic system of his painting as well. The simple, even monumental composition and the large generalized form provide the element of novelty that distinguishes Ushakov's icons from those of the Armory produced before his time. His icons—whether a *Mother of God, Emmanuel, Savior Not-Made-by-Hand, Dormition,* or *Pantocrator*—possess a quite singular, formidable rhythm as compared with the works of artists from the preceding generation. These new qualities do not rely on the influence of European art, but on Ushakov's orientation toward earlier models of Old Russian and Byzantine painting.

The fundamental tendency of Simon Ushakov's art is not toward realism, but toward the ideal, toward big, large-scale form, toward a majestic intonation of representation. In my view, western European motifs in his work are of much less significance than motifs from the Orthodox tradition proper. Western influences from the art of the fifteenth or early sixteenth centuries are shown most clearly in the icons of the Mandylion.[32] While it is true that

Fig. 4   Simon Ushakov. *Pantocrator Enthroned.* 1672. Nikolo-Ugresha Monastery. Tret'iakov Gallery, Moscow. Reproduced by permission.

at first blush these finely modeled faces of Christ unwittingly recall works from the circle of Hans Memling or Rogier van der Weyden, the depictions of the Savior in Ushakov's icons nonetheless lack the subtle and complex characteristics of the inner world inherent in their great models. Thus the Mandylions stand as only one of the episodes in the history of Ushakov's art, which was, on the whole, traditional.

The utter absence of any traces of the Baroque in Simon Ushakov's icons merits serious attention. He employed only pre-Baroque models and, on encountering Baroque works, remained free of their specific peculiarities: their heightened emotionalism, compositional accents, contrasts of light and shade. So, for example, in composing the icon *In Praise of the Vladimir Mother of God*, he used motifs from several Ukrainian engravings with obvious Baroque features. But in Ushakov's icon, these features are completely absent. Meanwhile, in other works of Muscovite painting (done after Ushakov, to be sure), echoes of the Baroque resound quite clearly, in the icons from the Church of the Intercession in Fili (1690s), for example.

One senses a kind of barrier between Ushakov and his European Baroque contemporaries, a barrier of orientation toward models. It is precisely the medieval basis of artistic thought that links Ushakov's icon painting with Post-Byzantine, especially Cretan, painting. Seventeenth-century Russian painting and Post-Byzantine painting both represent the medieval tradition, but with different European orientations. Post-Byzantine art relies mainly on Italian motifs, whereas Russian painting makes extensive use of northern European models as well as Italian, including the well-known Piscator Bible and so on. The peculiarities of Ushakov's oeuvre, the new tendencies of his art, were not only his "historicism" and "Byzantinism," but also his active use of Post-Byzantine, mainly Cretan, models. The close relationship between Russian and Greek culture in the second half of the seventeenth century encouraged a greater level of such interaction as opposed to earlier periods. Ushakov's *Trinity* (1671), a free paraphrase of Rublev's *Trinity*, was commissioned by Nicholas Nicoleta, a Greek merchant from Ioannina (Epirus) who was residing in Moscow.[33] Even the nuances of color in Ushakov's icons (the crimson-raspberry red, for example) recall similar color in Cretan painting dependent upon Venetian prototypes.

Ushakov's copying of early models provides firm evidence of the distance between the painter and earlier epochs. But his reconstructions are only imitations of early style. The "manneristic" Russian icons painted before Ushakov are actually better suited to Orthodox prayer than Ushakov's "Byzantine" paintings. It is in this sense—and only in this sense—that Ushakov can be said to have departed from strict medieval tradition.

At the same time, however, his "Byzantinism" is a mark of his belonging to the medieval age. This appeal to the past, this attempt of his to resurrect ancient subjects and old forms, is the final example of those "renaissances" that are well known to the art of the Orthodox Middle Ages. Simon Ushakov's work belongs to the Middle Ages to the same degree as do Patriarch Nikon's reforms, through which problems in the interrelations of Russia

Fig. 5 *Pantocrator Enthroned* ("Savior of the Golden Robe"). Eleventh-century iconography under the painting of Kirill Ulanov, 1698. Cathedral of the Dormition, Moscow. Reproduced by permission.

and the Orthodox countries of eastern Europe were resolved in the sphere of religion and ritual. Perhaps a new term is needed to designate the work of Ushakov and his followers along with other phenomena of sixteenth- and seventeenth-century Eastern European culture, phenomena neither classically medieval nor modern.[34] For the time being the most apt designation might be "late medieval."

NOTES

1. G. D. Filimonov, "Simon Ushakov i sovremennaia emu epokha russkoi ikonopisi," in *Sbornik na 1873 god, izdannyi Obshchestvom drevnerusskogo iskusstva pri Moskovskom Publichnom muzee* (Moscow, 1873), 1–101.

2. A. Uspenskii, *Piat' vnov' otkrytykh ikon kisti Simona Ushakova* (Moscow, 1901); D. Trenev, *Ikony tsarskogo izografa Simona Ushakova v Moskovskom Novodevichiem monastyre* (Moscow, 1901); D. Trenev, *Pamiatniki drevnerusskogo iskusstva tserkvi Gruzinskoi Bogomateri* (Moscow, 1903); V. P. Gur'ianov, *Ikony Spasitelia pis'ma Simona Ushakova* (Moscow, 1907); I. Grabar' and A. Uspenskii, "Tsarskie ikonopistsy i zhivopistsy XVII veka," in *Istoriia russkogo iskusstva,* ed. I. Grabar', vol. 6 (Moscow, 1915), 427–40; N. P. Sychev, "Ikona Simona Ushakova v Novgorodskom eparkhial'nom drevlekhranilishche," in *Sbornik nauchnykh trudov v chest' Dmitriia Vlas'evicha Ainalova* (St. Petersburg, 1915), 91–104; N. P. Sychev, "Novoe proizvedenie Simona Ushakova v Gosudarstvennom Russkom muzee," in *Gosudarstvennyi Russkii Muzei: Materialy po russkomu iskusstvu,* vol. 1 (Leningrad, 1928), 78–111; T. N. Kedrova, "Ikony Simona Ushakova v sobranii Zagorskogo muzeia," in *Soobshcheniia Zagorskogo gosudarstvennogo istoriko-khudozhestvennogo muzeia-zapovednika,* vol. 2 (Zagorsk, 1958), 46–54; T. A. Anan'eva, *Simon Ushakov: Mastera mirovoi zhivopisi* (Leningrad, 1971); T. A. Anan'eva, "Neizvestnoe proizvedenie Simona Ushakova," in *Soobshcheniia Gosudarstvennogo Russkogo muzeia,* vol. 10 (Moscow, 1974), 101–3; N. G. Bekeneva, *Simon Ushakov, 1626–1686* (Leningrad, 1984); O. A. Poliakova, "Novootkrytye ikony tsarskikh izografov iz sobraniia Muzeia Kolomenskoe," in *Pamiatniki kul'tury: Novye otkrytiia, Ezhegodnik 1985* (Moscow, 1987), 212–21; P. P. Balakin, "Ikona Makarii Zhetovodskii Simona Ushakova," in *Pamiatniki kul'tury: Novye otkrytiia, Ezhegodnik 1988* (Moscow, 1989), 246–53. This representative sample of publications is by no means exhaustive.

3. I. E. Danilova and N. E. Mneva, "Zhivopis' XVII veka," in *Istoriia russkogo iskusstva,* ed. I. Grabar', vol. 4 (Moscow, 1959), 368–89; V. G. Briusova, *Russkaia zhivopis' XVII veka* (Moscow, 1984), 38–42 (with bibliography).

4. E. S. Ovchinnikova, "Iosif Vladimirov: Traktat ob iskusstve," in *Drevnerusskoe iskusstvo. XVII vek* (Moscow, 1964), 9–61.

5. Cf. Sychev's studies noted above as well as E. L. Ostashenko, "Ikonostas Pokhval'skogo pridela Uspenskogo sobora Moskovskogo kremlia," *Gosudarstvennye muzei Moskovskogo kremlia: Materialy i issledovaniia,* no. 4, *Proizvedeniia russkogo i zarubezhnogo iskusstva XVI–nachala XVIII veka* (Moscow, 1984), 147–62; and I. L. Buseva-Davydova, "Prostranstvennye postroeniia v rabotakh Simona Ushakova," *Gosudarstvennye muzei Moskovskogo kremlia: Materialy i issledovaniia,* no. 8, *Russkaia khudozhestvennaia kul'tura XVII veka* (Moscow, 1991), 20–31.

6. V. N. Nechaev, "Simon Ushakov," in *Izobrazitel'noe iskusstvo* (Leningrad, 1927), 113–46. See I. L. Buseva-Davydova, "O kontseptsiiakh stilia russkogo

iskusstva XVII veka v otechestvennom iskusstvoznanii," *Gosudarstvennye muzei Moskovskogo kremlia: Materialy i issledovaniia,* no. 7, *Problemy russkoi khudozhestvennoi kul'tury* (Moscow, 1990), 107–17, esp. 108–9.

7. See, for example, M. Chatzidakis, *Icônes de Saint-Georges des Grecs et de la collections de l'Institut* (Venice, 1962); Chatzidakis, *Icons of Patmos: Questions of Byzantine and Post-Byzantine Painting* (Athens, 1985); M. Garidis, *La Peinture murale dans le monde orthodoxe après la chute de Byzance (1450–1600) et dans les pays sous domination étrangère* (Athens, 1989); M. Borboudakis, ed., *Eikones tēs krētikēs technēs* (Heraklion, 1993).

8. See V. I. Antonova and N. E. Mneva, *Katalog drevnerusskoi zhivopisi Gosudarstvennoi Tret'iakovskoi galerei,* 2 vols. (Moscow, 1963), 2: no. 912 (with bibliography), pls. 142–43; Bekeneva, *Simon Ushakov,* 29–56; E. S. Smirnova, *Moskovskaia ikona XIV–XVII vekov* (Leningrad, 1988), pls. 199–200, and *Moscow Icons: Fourteenth–Seventeenth Centuries* (Oxford, 1989), pls. 199–200.

9. V. G. Chubinskaia, "Ikona Simona Ushakova 'Bogomater' Vladimirskaia,' 'Drevo Moskovskogo gosudarstva,' 'Pokhvala Bogomateri Vladimirskoi': Opyt istoriko-kul'turnoi interpretatsii," *Trudy Otdela drevnerusskoi literatury* 38 (1985), 290–308, esp. 293–97, 304–6.

10. For 1652, see Antonova and Mneva, *Katalog,* no. 909, and Bekeneva, *Simon Ushakov,* 11 (pls.); for 1662, see Anan'eva, "Neizvestnoe proizvedenie," 101.

11. The copy is currently housed in the Tret'iakov Gallery, Moscow. See Antonova and Mneva, *Katalog* 2: no. 913; and Briusova, *Russkaia zhivopis',* 41, pl. 25.

12. For *Kazan' Mother of God,* see A. I. Uspenskii, *Tsarskie ikonopistsy i zhivopistsy XVII veka: Slovar'* (Moscow, 1910), 312, 356; and A. S. Kostsova and A. G. Pobedinskaia, *Russkie ikony XVI–nachala XX veka s nadpisiami, podpisiami i datami: Katalog vystavki* (Leningrad, 1990), no. 9. For *Blachernae Mother of God,* see Filimonov, "Simon Ushakov," 43.

13. Anan'eva, *Simon Ushakov,* pls.; Anan'eva, "Neizvestnoe proizvedenie," 101–3. Personal communication from I. Birnbaum and N. G. Bekeneva.

14. K. F. Kalaidovich, "Svedeniia o zhizni, uchenykh trudakh i sobranii drevnostei grafa A. I. Musina-Pushkina," in *Zapiski i trudy Obshchestva istorii i drevnostei rossiiskikh,* pt. 2 (Moscow, 1824), 21.

15. N. P. Kondakov, *Litsevoi ikonopisnyi podlinnik,* vol. 1, *Ikonografiia Gospoda Boga i Spasa nashego Iisusa Khrista* (St. Petersburg, 1905), 92 (tracings 39–41).

16. K. Onasch, *Ikonen* (Berlin, 1961), pls. 136–38.

17. Théano Chatzidakis, ed., *L'Art des icônes en Crète et dans les îles après Byzance* (Charleroi, Palais des Beaux-Arts, 1982), no. 30.

18. Now housed in the Tret'iakov Gallery, Moscow. See Antonova and Mneva, *Katalog* 1: no. 6, pls. 23–25; V. N. Lazarev, *Russkaia ikonopis' ot istokov do nachala XVI veka* (Moscow, 1983), 41, pl. 18; L. I. Lifshits, "Angel'skii chin s Emmanuilom i nekotorye cherty khudozhestvennoi kul'tury Vladimiro-Suzdal'skoi Rusi," in *Drevnerusskoe iskusstvo: Khudozhestvennaia kul'tura X-pervoi poloviny XIII veka* (Moscow, 1988), 211–30.

19. See Antonova and Mneva, *Katalog* 2: no. 909, pl. 144 (icon of 1658), no. 919 (icon of 1673); T. V. Nikolaeva, *Drevnerusskaia zhivopis' Zagorskogo muzeia* (Moscow, 1977), 28, 31 n. 67 (icon of 1674); Antonova and Mneva, *Katalog* 2: no. 921 (icon of 1678).

20. See Antonova and Mneva, *Katalog* 1: no. 7, pls. 26–27; Lazarev, *Russkaia ikonopis',* 35, pl. 5.

21. For the icon, see Antonova and Mneva, *Katalog* 2: no. 914, pl. 146. For interest in Cyprus, see O. A. Belobrova, *Kiprskii tsikl v drevnerusskoi literature* (Moscow, 1972); and O. A. Belobrova, "Hoi eikones tēs Theomētoros Kypriōtissas kai Kykkōtissas stē rōsikē logotechnia tou 17–archēs 18 aiōna," *Epeterida Kentrou meletōn Ieras monēs Kykkou* 1 (Leukōsia, 1990), 131–40, pls. 1–6.

22. L. Hadermann-Misguich, "La Vierge Kykkotissa et l'éventuelle origine latine de son voile," in *Euphrosynon: Aphierōma ston Manolē Chatzidakē* (Athens, 1991), 197–204; M. Chatzidakis, V. Djurić, and M. Lazović, *Les Icônes dans les collections suisses* (Bern, 1968), no. 131; M. Lazović and S. Frigerio-Zeniou, eds., *Les Icônes du Musée d'Art et d'Histoire Genève* (Geneva, 1985), no. 33, pl. 33.

23. Nikolaeva, *Drevnerusskaia zhivopis'* 28, no. 342.

24. E. N. Klitina, T. N. Manushina, and T. V. Nikolaeva, eds., *Vkladnaia kniga Troitse-Sergieva monastyria* (Moscow, 1987), 105.

25. *Ukrainskie knigi kirillovskoi pechati, XVI–XVII vv.: Katalog izdanii, khraniashchikhsia v Gosudarstvennoi biblioteke SSSR imeni V. I. Lenina*, no. 2, pt. 1, *Kievskie izdaniia vtoroi poloviny XVII v.* (Moscow, 1981), cat. nos. 164–65 (pp. 31–32), pl. 1629 (p. 284).

26. See V. Putsko, "Pechers'ka Icona Uspinnia Bogoroditsi: legenda i diisnist'," in *Rodovid*, vol. 9 (Kiev, 1995), 65–72.

27. For Ushakov's icon, see Antonova and Mneva, *Katalog* 2: no. 911; and G. H. Hamilton, *The Art and Architecture of Russia* (Harmondsworth, 1954), 156, pl. 106.

28. See Gur'ianov, *Ikony Spasitelia*, 6 (icon of 1672), 5–6 (icon of 1682), pl. II–2 (icon of 1684).

29. L. N. Savina, "Ikona Spas na prestole s pripadaiushchimi mitropolitom Filippom i patriarkhom Nikonom iz sobraniia Moskovskogo oblastnogo kraevedcheskogo muzeia," in *Pamiatniki kul'tury: Novye otkrytiia, Ezhegodnik 1988* (Moscow, 1989), 233–45.

30. M. Chatzidakis, *Icons of Patmos: Questions of Byzantine and Post-Byzantine Painting* (Athens, 1985), no. 65, pl. 121.

31. See E. S. Smirnova, V. K. Laurina, E. A. Gordienko, *Zhivopis' Velikogo Novgoroda, XV vek* (Moscow, 1982), 182–85.

32. This idea was formulated by Nikolai Sychev in 1915; see Sychev, "Ikona Simona Ushakova." For Western analogues to the face of Christ, see Jan Białostocki, "Fifteenth-Century Pictures of the Blessing Christ Based on the Rogier van der Weyden," *Gesta* 15, no. 2, pt. 2 (1976): 313–20 (with bibliography).

33. Sychev, "Novoe proizvedenie."

34. On the problem of Baroque style in Orthodox art, see Dejan Medaković, ed., *Zapadnoevropski Barok i Vizantijski svet: Zbornik Radova sa naučnog skupa održanog od 10. do 13. oktobra 1989* (Belgrade, 1991).

VICTOR   M.   ZHIVOV

RELIGIOUS REFORM AND THE EMERGENCE OF THE INDIVIDUAL IN RUSSIAN SEVENTEENTH-CENTURY LITERATURE

THE SEVENTEENTH CENTURY was an epoch marked by cultural changes so radical that the very principles by which Russian culture defined itself were transformed. Regrettably, most cultural historians continue to ignore this transformation and to divide the culture and literature of Russia into two periods, juxtaposing the period between the eleventh and seventeenth centuries to the modern period. This periodization is based upon the cultural myth that Peter the Great created the new Russia, a myth that was as relevant for the Slavophiles and westernizers as for the radical revolutionary intelligentsia and conservative populists. The old, pre-Petrine Rus' was seen as the domain of "nature" and the new, post-Petrine Russia as the domain of "culture," in spite of ample evidence documenting the continuity of social and economic changes in the seventeenth and eighteenth centuries. The notions of the "old Russian"—or (synonymously) "pre-Petrine"—culture, art, or literature continue to function as general unifying concepts. The progression from "nature" to "culture" may be interpreted in different ways: as a positive or negative development; as a new, more advanced stage in the process of civilization; or as the destruction of an organic tradition. In any case, the binary opposition as such persists and continues to determine the structuring of cultural and literary history.

Operating on this tacit assumption, literary historians lump together unrelated phenomena from different historical epochs. The result is a confused and inadequate typology of these epochs where misleading comparisons and contrasts are drawn. One consequence of this distorted picture is the widespread view that Old Russian culture replicated Byzantine culture. According to this view (formulated with some insignificant differences by Nikolai Trubetskoi, Dmitrii Likhachev, and Dmitrii Obolensky), Old Russian culture was the result of a transplantation of Byzantine culture.[1] It is evident, however, that only a fragment of Byzantine culture was brought to Russia, a fragment both relatively limited in its content and structurally simplified. It was not the culture of Constantinople, highly differentiated and sophisticated, but the culture of a provincial Byzantine monastery that was the most probable home of the Greek missionaries who ventured to distant and "barbaric" Kievan Rus'. As was convincingly demonstrated by F. Thomson, the corpus of Byzantine literary texts known in Kiev (in Slavic translations) was roughly similar to the library of a provincial Byzantine monastery.[2] In Byzantium, classical authors were studied, cited, and imitated, and the classical tradition was preserved—albeit in a mutilated and dilapidated form. By contrast, in Kievan Rus', the classical tradition was perceived as pagan, anti-Christian, and unworthy of any attention.[3] Thus, only fragments of the Byzantine cultural system were reproduced in its Russian counterpart.

As far as we can determine, Kiev did not intend to replicate Byzantine culture as a whole but, by building on heterogeneous sources, to create a new Christian culture. The Kievans exploited both Byzantine and Western models, especially those of the recently Christianized Scandinavian and Western Slavic barbaric states. The cult of martyred princes (Boris and Gleb, in the Russian case) may be regarded as direct evidence of this non-Byzantine orientation.[4] All of the evidence suggests that it would be futile and unreasonable to describe Old Russian culture exclusively in terms of Byzantine models and patterns. At the same time, comparison with Byzantine culture reveals specific features of Old Russian culture and literature, helping to clear the ground for the study of later developments and to determine what was traditional and what was new in different epochs.

In Byzantium, secular and spiritual cultures constituted two different traditions; they interacted and influenced each other but, nevertheless, remained separate. In ancient Russia there was no similar dichotomy, at least in the area of bookish culture. Elements of the Byzantine secular tradition placed in the Russian context were perceived as part and parcel of the general Christian spiritual tradition. For instance, the penal legislation of the Procheiron (a Byzantine legal codex of the tenth century) was regarded as belonging to the sacred patristic tradition; in some Russian manuscripts its translation was entitled "Commandments Concerning Punishments—According to the Instructions of the Holy Fathers and the Decrees of the Holy Emperors."[5] Similarly, *The History of the Judaic Wars* by Joseph Flavius, considered by the Greeks to be a continuation of classical historical writings, was misconstrued in the Russian context as a text describing sacred history. In the same way, the *Christian Topography* of Cosmas Indicopleustes was perceived not as a modification of classical geographical treatises but as a description of the Christian universe. Russian readers, who perceived themselves as citizens of this universe, were understandably interested in the description of the whole.

Such examples can be multiplied. The most important inference to be drawn, however, is that there was no opposition of secular and spiritual cultures in Kievan Rus' and therefore that the definition of various Old Russian texts as secular is fundamentally anachronistic (and, one suspects, attributable to an inordinate fondness for binary oppositions). The Old Russian cultural and literary system as a whole was structured on different principles. Due to the absence of an opposition between secular and spiritual traditions, no clear-cut internal subdivisions existed in the cultural or literary spheres. Byzantine culture and literature were to some extent based on the classical heritage, which may be regarded as a germ of the Byzantine secular tradition and also had some influence on the spiritual tradition. The rhetorical organization of cultural activity, a classical practice, was part of this heritage. Russian culture and literature, in contrast to their Byzantine counterparts, were not rhetorically organized.

Up to the seventeenth century, Russian Christian writers did not distinguish between poetic and prosaic texts, a distinction that constitutes the basis for the perception of cultural values as essential in their own right. In my opinion, all efforts to discover some kind of poetic organization in various Old Russian texts—be it metrical or topical—have not as yet brought any convincing results. The properties of the material account for the futility of such efforts. Genre distinctions seem to be no more productive in dealing with Old Russian texts than the distinction between poetry and prose. The features differentiating various types of texts are elusive, and this elusiveness does not derive from inadequate analytical procedures but first and foremost from the properties of the texts. In other words, we may classify them according to their function but not according to generic criteria.[6] The same narrative can function in a variety of ways, thus crossing the boundaries of any imaginable system of genres. For instance, "The Tale of Russian Letters"—in which the history of the Slavic alphabet and the Cyrillo-Methodian mission was described—was written in the beginning of the twelfth century as an anti-Catholic pamphlet, but it later functioned both as a tale in the Chronograph and as a reading in memory of Saint Constantine-Cyril.[7] A striking example of this kind of boundary crossing is the use of historiographical notes on the martyrdom of Saints Boris and Gleb as a liturgical lection from the Old Testament.[8] This kind of polyfunctionality would not have been permitted in Byzantine literature or, for that matter, in any rhetorically organized system. The most widespread type of book in medieval Russia was the miscellany. Such compilations combined texts of different types and may be taken as evidence that all writings were perceived as parts of a unique and undivided corpus of literature characterized by its Christian content and didactic value rather than by any formal distinctions.[9]

The Russian cultural background as described above unambiguously marks the seventeenth century as an age of crucial changes. These changes were not produced solely through Western influence (an explanation favored by many scholars). Indeed, the notion of influence is loosely defined and one can speak of Western influence while dealing with the fifteenth and sixteenth centuries as well as with the seventeenth.[10] The seventeenth century, in contrast, is characterized not by disparate instances of Western influence but by a far-reaching transformation of the cultural system, for only at the beginning of that century can we speak of oppositions between secular and spiritual culture, and secular and spiritual literature. Not only were some manifestly secular texts produced (F. Gozvinskii's 1607 translation of Aesop's *Fables,* for example), but the culture's attitude toward the religious sphere changed.[11] The spirit of religious austerity and moral reform manifested primarily by the so-called zealots of Piety *(Bogoliubtsy)* became one of the major factors in the reassessment of the Orthodox tradition. This reassessment introduced distinctions between secular and spiritual, Orthodox and non-Orthodox, in all cultural activity, calling into question not only contemporary phenomena but the legacy of the past as well.

The conception of the seventeenth century as an organic part of traditional Russian culture is based on the mythology of the new Russia created by Peter the Great, but also on the formulations of some seventeenth-century authors who, in the period following the Time of Troubles, represented their innovations as original features of Russian Orthodoxy. They issued declarations that can be characterized as programmatic, for they strove to reconstruct the traditional culture, to rebuild Holy Russia after its destruction during the civil wars and the Polish invasion. Misreading of this material has too often led students of Old Russian culture to conclude that attitudes and notions unknown prior to the seventeenth century are age-old. For example, unequivocal evidence concerning the perception of bookish (Church Slavonic) language as sacred belongs only to the seventeenth century, contrary to the opinion of B. Uspensky who regards this attitude as an essential feature of traditional Russian linguistic consciousness.[12] Similar anachronistic thinking manifests itself in studies on the jongleurs *(skomorokhi).* The tsar's and patriarch's decrees of the mid-seventeenth century banning their activities are presumed to be characteristic of traditional Russian attitudes. A resolute struggle against the *skomorokhi*—attested in the lives of such Bogoliubtsy as Archpriests Avvakum and Ioann Neronov (who were beaten to within an inch of their lives in the process)—is also mistakenly seen as a sign of their fidelity to the original Russian tradition. Actually, their antipathy to the *skomorokhi* was part of their reforms.[13]

In George Florovsky's estimation, the seventeenth century was a "critical," not an "organic," epoch in Russian history, "a century of lost equilibrium, . . . harsh personalities and colorful characters." The destruction of moral norms and social institutions during the Time of Troubles produced a sense of the need to "repair" or to "restore" the society; this "reparation" was understood by a significant part of Russian society (Florovsky had in mind the efforts of Ioann Neronov and Avvakum) as "repentance, moral transformation, and concentration of will."[14] The focal point of the moral reform was the perfection of Russian society and the eradication of pernicious customs and habits. However, the discourse in which these reforms were proclaimed and popularized corresponded to the traditional mentality. The customs to be abandoned were declared to be recent inventions, whereas the order to be established was described as an ancestral legacy. This discourse is especially characteristic of the polemic between Patriarch Nikon and the Old Believers. In the 1640s, the leaders of both parties belonged to the same reformist circle, the *Bogoliubtsy*. Though the relative nature of the terms "old" and "new" could have become evident in the preceding years, the ensuing struggle was based on different understandings of what was new and what was old. Thus, one of the important questions was the correct spelling of the name Jesus: Iisus" or Isus". The historical evidence was ambiguous but both parties claimed that the spelling they defended was the original and the other the corrupted. And in both cases the principal goal was not the preservation of the old order but rather the correction of the mixed and, therefore, "corrupted" practice.[15]

Any reformist movement changes attitudes toward personality. The struggling reformer is always a highly individualistic person, and his life and deeds are presumed to deviate from established social or cultural norms. From the beginning of the seventeenth century the individual and his unique fate became an object of constant cultural reflection. D. S. Likhachev explains this phenomenon as a delayed development of the Renaissance in Russian culture, asserting that the medieval religious mind-set gave way to a more modern and at least partly secularized mentality. A new interest in the fate of individuals encouraged Russian writers to borrow Hellenistic plots (for example, stories about selling one's soul to the devil). Likhachev claims that the so-called secular tales of the seventeenth century (*The Tale of Savva Grudtsyn, The Tale of Frol Skobeev,* and so on) illustrate his point. He sees another instance of the same development in the autobiography of Avvakum, which he regards as a baroque narrative that functions as a Renaissance text in the Russian literary process. Writers approached their texts as individuals and created individualistic literary characters.[16]

This could have been an acceptable scheme, though it is difficult to imagine what—in the Russian context—was meant by a Renaissance personality or a baroque narrative. The problem is that secular tales were written in the second half (most probably in the last decades) of the seventeenth century and that the protagonists of these tales were somehow connected with the Devil, who is represented as the instigator of their individualistic wanderings.[17] The single exception is *The Tale of Frol Skobeev,* but this narrative is a late specimen of the genre and was probably written at the beginning of the eighteenth century. All in all, secular tales were marginal in the literary system. The manuscript copies are not numerous and only a small number of them belong to the seventeenth century. Their prominence in literary histories must be attributed to scholars who, in hindsight, seek to represent belletristic texts as the most important element of the literary canon. All of the evidence suggests, therefore, that secular tales were a secondary product of the process of cultural change: the origins and first significant results of this process must be sought elsewhere.

In the seventeenth century, the main corpus of Russian literature remained spiritual or ecclesiastical. The Scriptures, liturgical hymnography, various *vitae,* and sermons were, as before, the usual reading for all social groups. Even more important, these texts still defined literary and cultural norms, continuing to serve as the only models. This does not mean, however, that there was no development, for a single model could be conceived in different ways and reinterpreted. Moral reform could not help but stimulate such reinterpretations. Indeed, the first signs of the new cultural consciousness can be discerned in the spiritual literature of the first half of the seventeenth century. Thus, for instance, the portrait of Boris Godunov in the "Skazanie" of Avraamii Palitsyn (a history of the Time of Troubles with special attention to the siege of the Trinity–St. Sergii Monastery by Polish troops) is unexpectedly dynamic: his sagacity, greatness, and renown were described, together with his vices; his life was represented not as a manifestation of a good or evil nature but as a personal drama. There is a strong similarity between some passages of the "Skazanie" and later biographical writings of the *Bogoliubtsy.* Thus, Palitsyn described his encounter with the Russian troops led by Pozharskii and Minin—who were encamped in Iaroslavl', some three hundred miles from Moscow, and who were not especially eager to march to the capital and liberate it from the Polish invaders. Palitsyn regarded this unwillingness as the product of evildoers: "mutineers and flatterers and lovers of feasts, but not lovers of God *[miatezhniki i laskateli i trapezoliubiteli, a ne bogoliubtsy],* who generated hatred and discord among the leaders and the soldiers."[18] Palitsyn expostulated with them and persuaded them to move forward, an action represented as a moral contest, a kind of "reparation" of the type that Florovsky attributed to the *Bogoliubtsy.*

A new concern with personality—the first glimpses of which are discernible in Palitsyn's "Skazanie"—is particularly pronounced in the writings of the *Bogoliubtsy* and in their *vitae.* A well-known example is the autobiography of Avvakum, whose individualistic character has been thoroughly investigated and widely discussed. Especially significant in this respect is the passage in which Avvakum narrated his dream: Avvakum saw himself in the dream as a body in which the entire world was contained, that is, as an eschatological figure of cosmic dimensions. In his perception, the destiny of the world became dependent on his individual sanctity or righteousness (that is, on his individual choice); it was thus transformed into an existential problem.[19]

These features of Avvakum's narrative were evidently new, but they were not unique. There are traces of the same new mentality in a voluminous treatise of Avvakum's archenemy, Patriarch Nikon, called the "Refutation or Excoriation of the Boyar Simeon Streshnev's Questions."[20] This treatise was written in 1663–1665 when Nikon lived in the New Jerusalem Monastery, which he had founded ten years before. In 1659 Nikon protested against the tsar's interference in church affairs, resigned his patriarchal office, and left Moscow for the monastery. He described his conflict with the tsar's counselors partly in traditional terms, as a struggle of a righteous man with a hostile secular power, but partly as a personal contest between himself and the tsar, preserving in this way the biographical nature of the event. He reminded the tsar of their joint efforts to "repair" the country and spoke several times of the tsar's vow to be guided by Nikon in spiritual matters. Nikon referred not only to the tsar's usurping of spiritual power, not only to the dangers of vacillation in enforcing the spiritual reforms, but also to his personal disappointment and his disillusionment with the tsar's policy. His style is vehement and sometimes sarcastic, so that a new kind of discourse is created. He portrays himself as a reformer, a suffering individual who tries to save his people by his own efforts; he is opposed by the hostile and conservative evildoers who are indifferent to the moral cause and aggressive in their desire to preserve their sinful customs.

The theme of personal struggle is particularly noticeable in the life of Ioann Neronov, written in the late 1670s. Neronov belonged to the circle of *Bogoliubtsy* and made his career as a popular preacher.[21] Together with Avvakum and others, he opposed Nikon's innovations, was excommunicated, and exiled. In his later years, he repented and was reconciled with the official church. Admired by many people for his personal piety, he was not perceived as a follower of the Nikonian party or as an Old Believer. His *vita* reflects his ambiguous status as a saintlike figure on the one hand and as a historical personality on the other. There were two models for writers of biography: annalistic (as in the chronicles) and hagiographical. The opposition between the two was not clear-cut; there are some well-known examples of annalistic texts that are also works of hagiography. However, the features characteristic of a hagiographical approach are readily recognizable: historical details are omitted or generalized and topical abstract formulas are used. These formulas identify a saint as a martyr, a confessor, a founder of a monastery, or such and in this way demonstrate the essence of his sanctity. The events of a saint's life are selected with reference to his type. In the case of Neronov's *vita,* the historical approach took precedence over the hagiographical approach and an individual biography was produced, that is, a narrative focused on Neronov's personality and his unceasing conflicts with various authorities, both secular and spiritual, as well as with his colleagues and the general public.

In his youth, Neronov left his native village and came to Vologda. As he entered the city, he caught sight of a band of masked revelers coming from the archbishop's residence. With no thought of the consequences, Neronov denounced the revelers and then began to scold the archbishop's servants. For his pains, he was severely beaten.[22] After this experience, he left Vologda for a village, where he arranged to study the art of reading with a priest named Titus. According to his *vita*, Ioann Neronov was a slow learner and worked on the primer for half a year without discernible success. The boy went off by himself and offered ardent prayers for God to help him in his studies. When he returned and took up his primer, "the light of understanding kindled in his heart" and by the grace of God he mastered the material and was able to understand the Scriptures. This event is portrayed as a revelation of Neronov's calling: the implication is that Neronov was elected by God in the same way as were the apostles, when the Holy Spirit descended upon them during Pentecost.[23] Neronov then became a priest and a popular preacher. Since there had been no tradition of public preaching in Russia, this vocation was perceived as a pernicious innovation. Neronov was repeatedly confronted by other priests, beaten, and eventually thrown into prison.[24] Patriarch Filaret defended him, however, and he was permitted to return to his parish in Nizhnii Novgorod. This part of the *vita* is entirely consistent with the hagiographical tradition: evil is punished, righteousness rewarded.

In the next episode, however, Neronov opposed the tsar and Patriarch Filaret. He preached against the war with Poland (1632–1633), representing it as a senseless shedding of Christian blood. This unwonted pacifism—a phenomenon very rarely mentioned in the lives of the medieval saints, regardless of nationality—greatly irritated the most pious tsar, and Neronov was exiled to a distant monastery on the shore of the White Sea.[25] This episode is by no means typical. Neronov's teaching was esteemed as highly moral and inspired by God, but his opponents were not punished for refusing to follow the saint's instructions: although the tsar's troops were defeated, the most pious tsar did not become less pious. The point of the story seems to be not the triumph of righteousness but rather the peculiarity of Neronov's position, his moral integrity and personal courage. And again he appeared to be a sufferer by his own choice (as did Avvakum in his autobiography). Neronov's nontraditional behavior is illustrated repeatedly in the narrative, especially in the section that recounts Neronov's conflict with Patriarch Nikon and the Nikonian bishops. Neronov was not a typical saint, and the author of his life did not attempt to portray him as such by obliterating his individual traits. He inserted only as many hagiographical *topoi* as were necessary to show the reader that the protagonist was a saint.

Traditional cultures usually do not provide individuals with a choice of cultural or religious values. Spiritual reforms create this choice. From the reformer's point of view, one must embrace the spiritual reform or perish. Usually some people declare their readiness to give up their lives or at least their intent to preserve their traditional lifestyle. The consequences for the literary canon are evident. Alongside the figure of a holy reformer there must appear his secular counterpart, the unholy one who prefers to be damned. This is why I consider the emergence of a profane hero in the secular tales of the seventeenth century (such as *The Tale of Savva Grudtsyn*) as a by-product of spiritual reforms. In this context, it is easily understandable that the profane hero should be in some way inspired by the Devil—just as his counterpart, the reformer, is inspired by God. The emancipation of the individual, now depicted as opposed to and struggling with society, gives rise to two types of hero: one portrayed primarily in religious literature and the other in profane stories. They never meet in the same narrative, but both are splinters of the cultural crisis and as such can be treated as interdependent innovations. The achievements of the reform spirit were not limited, however, to changes in the set of literary characters but encompassed the sociocultural system as a whole.

The most important outcome of the moral reform was the emergence of the opposition between spiritual and secular cultures. In the previous cultural system there was a broad transitional zone between the secular and the spiritual.[26] For instance, a wedding was a manifestly Christian ritual, actually one of the church's sacraments. However, it was usually accompanied by festivities and pageantry of a profane nature. These profane rituals originated in Slavic pagan practices and were not completely assimilated to Christian values. A bishop or priest who consecrated the marriage participated in the wedding feast and blessed the meal. In a way, his participation sanctioned the singing, dancing, and frolicking, so that the carnival or blasphemous elements in the nuptials were neutralized and legitimized. These traditional amusements were not perceived as conflicting with the essentially Christian nature of the ceremony. In the seventeenth century, however, this perception changed. In 1648 the young Tsar Aleksei Mikhailovich married Maria Miloslavskaia, and this time things went differently. As it is narrated in Neronov's life, Stefan Vonifat'ev—the Tsar's confessor, a supporter of Neronov, and a leading member of the *Bogoliubtsy*—protested against the impious mixing of traditions: "The Priest Stefan not only requested, but charged [all concerned] to refrain from laughter, blasphemy, devilry, [and] shameful songs during the wedding. . . . And the marriage of the pious tsar was consecrated in serenity and fear of God with the singing of spiritual hymns."[27] Thus, the age-old customs were reappraised, the boundary between the Christian and non-Christian or spiritual and profane was clearly drawn, and, at least in some of the most important official rituals, it was no longer permissible to mix the two spheres.

The same process of demarcation took place in the literary system. In a polemical pamphlet, "On the Visible Image of God," written in the 1630s, Ivan Begichev declared that his opponents were ignorant of theological literature:

> Your knowledge is not worth a wooden nickel. . . . You have read nothing except fabulous tales *[basnoslovnye povesti]* about prince Bova which you consider useful for your souls . . . and tales about the rooster and the fox and other fabulous tales and humorous texts *[basnoslovnye povesti i smekhotvornye pisma]*, but you know nothing about divine books and dogmatics *[bozhestvennye knigi i bogoslovnye dokhmaty]*.[28]

Existing literature was reclassified in this spirit of boundary fixing, and this reappraisal concerned not only the new texts but literature as a whole. Thus, chronicles that had been regarded as an extension of religious literature, recording the fulfillment of divine providence in human deeds, could now be viewed as simple descriptions of past events. Andrei Lyzlov, for instance, wrote *A History of the Scythians* in the last decade of the seventeenth century.[29] It was a compilation from various Russian chronicles and other sources, but the borrowed fragments functioned in his narrative as entirely secular descriptions and his *History* as a whole was obviously conceived and written without any religious intent.

This reappraisal extended to the entire sphere of cultural activity. Boundaries could be drawn in different ways, and ardent discussions were dedicated to the problem of what pertained to the secular domain and what to the religious. The opposition itself, however, was firmly maintained and became an indispensable element of the new discourse. The proponents of the new westernized or hellenized culture insisted that genuine Christian wisdom could not be obtained without philosophy, rhetoric, and grammar. The liberal arts were necessary, from their point of view, for the correct understanding of Scripture and hence for learning the path to salvation. Nikonian bishops claimed that the Old Believers were ignorant of the liberal arts and argued that the teachings of ignoramuses could not but lead to spiritual peril. Avvakum and his followers argued in response that the liberal arts were merely external wisdom that did not belong to the religious sphere, or Christian tradition, and hence had nothing to do with salvation. Avvakum in his autobiography declared that he had not studied dialectic, rhetoric, and philosophy but possessed the understanding of Christ.[30] In one of his sermons he urged his spiritual children "not to seek rhetoric and eloquence but to follow true and sound precepts because a rhetor and a philosopher cannot be a Christian." Christian knowledge, derived directly from the Scriptures and the writings of the Holy Fathers, is thus opposed to *vneshniaia bliad'* (literally "external delusion," that is, secular knowledge).[31] Salvation, in Avvakum's opinion, depends not on such external knowledge but on a personal relationship with God. Individual choice and individual charisma are set against social norms, though this time not the norms of traditional society but the norms of the culturally sophisticated elite.

Once a distinction between the secular and spiritual spheres is established, a principally new structure of culture and literature is created. The mechanism of differentiation starts to play its role and brings forth a rhetorically organized system. As already noted, one of the first results was the emergence of the opposition between prose and poetry. Many scholars have tried to ascribe metrical regularity to various Old Russian texts but their efforts are of dubious value. Folk songs certainly existed for many centuries, with rhymes and assonances as their structural base. However, bookish poetry in any recognizable form was not written before the seventeenth century. Its emergence may be connected with the important role that persuasion had to play in the new cultural system. Spiritual reforms necessitated the recruitment of followers and adherents, since religious convictions became an object of individual choice. Poetic expression could be regarded as effective means of persuasion.

It is worthy of note that one of the first instances of bookish poetry was verses by Ivan Nasedka, a bookman connected with the Trinity–St. Sergii Monastery and in many ways a predecessor of the *Bogoliubtsy* movement. These verses were included in his treatise "Exposition against the Lutherans" written between 1622 and 1625 in pursuit of the kind of "reparation" that Florovsky had attributed to the *Bogoliubtsy* after the Time of Troubles.[32] Previously, folk poetry stood in opposition to bookish prose; in the seventeenth century, religious culture took away the expressive potential from the popular tradition and used it for its own purposes. This transformation is analogous to the rise of public preaching as part of an effort to eradicate popular pageantry and buffoonery from the streets and squares, and to impose a universal social norm of piety and gravity.

This intrusion of poetry into the domain of spiritual culture signifies that artistic activity as such emerged as a distinct cultural phenomenon. Writing a literary text stopped being a purely pragmatic act dependent on a didactic or apologetic function and became a creative activity guided by aesthetic values. Literary activity acquired an element of reflection. As a result, texts with exclusively literary purposes (such as a literary epistle) made their appearance. In the second quarter of the seventeenth century, authors belonging to the so-called Chancellery School *(prikaznaia shkola)* wrote quite a number of poems of this kind.[33]

At this time a conception of individual authorship also gained ground. It was a significant innovation, since literary activity had previously been regarded as impersonal and literary texts as common property. Society was only interested in the divine—and hence impersonal—truth expressed by the text, not in the author's skill.[34] It is hardly coincidental that the notion of individual authorship came into being simultaneously with the individualistic protagonist in literary narrative.

The system of culture became differentiated, offering a choice between secular and spiritual, between prose and poetry. Literary activity ceased to be oriented according to "functions" and writers began to reflect on the choice of a particular type. Rhetoric served as a proper guide for such choices and hence rhetorical treatises appeared. The first manual of rhetoric compiled or copied in Russia is preserved in a manuscript dated from 1623 (probably copied from an earlier manuscript of 1617–1619), the so-called Makarii-Rhetoric.[35] This treatise was not an original production, but it testifies to the interest in restructuring the literary process. During the century, various manuals of rhetoric were distributed, in tens of copies. Considering the peculiar background of medieval Russian culture, rhetorical treatises could not help but function in a specific way. Rather than regulating well-established practices, they provided rules for new cultural and literary activity, and norms for new social behavior. Renate Lachmann introduced a notion of *Dekorum-Retorik* to designate this specific normative function.[36] Original rhetorical manuals appeared in the beginning of the eighteenth century, but the need was felt earlier and was met by translations and compilations. At any rate, Russian culture became rhetorically organized and the perception

THE EMERGENCE OF THE INDIVIDUAL   195

of cultural phenomena was now based on rhetorical models.

Rhetoric prescribed a system of genres as a means of classifying and regulating literary activity. From the seventeenth century onward, the notion of genre can be applied to Russian literary texts with a certain justification. A genre system made it possible to discern various types of writing and to consciously choose between them, that is, by taking into account the purpose of the text, its subject, and so on. At first the genre system was not full-fledged, but rhetorical organization acted as an incentive for its development. In the course of the seventeenth century previously unknown genres such as drama, meditative poetry, sermons, and historical narrative came into being. Rhetorical structuring dictated the opposition of the public and private spheres, the consequence being that the private sphere became an object of cultural reflection whereas previously it had not been assigned any cultural value. One of the results was that gradually there emerged a distinction between genres dealing with theological, philosophical, or political problems and genres specially designated to express personal experience and to describe individual properties of persons and events. Biographies and autobiographies, diaries and eyewitness accounts were written (such as, for instance, Matveev's account of the Musketeer rebellion of 1682); they were later followed by love songs (the first examples appeared at the end of the seventeenth century), and still later by elegies, sacred odes, versified prayers, and so on.[37] It is interesting that sacred odes, that is, poetical translations from the Psalter, became in the eighteenth century the main genre in which personal experience, anguish, resentment, and complaints were expressed. This development parallels the transformation of a saint's life into an individual biography. This "private" literature was clearly and consciously distinguished from the genres connected with the public sphere: panegyrical prose and poetry, political and theological discourses, spiritual instructions. A fully developed genre system was formed only in the second half of the eighteenth century, but its development began in the seventeenth century and this start should be considered as a real turning point.

All these processes—that is to say, the modernization of traditional Russian culture—are usually conceptualized in terms of their Europeanization and secularization. In my opinion, however, other forces caused the transformations we have observed in the seventeenth century. The initial impetus for a new cultural system was provided by the religious reforms in the first half of the century. Aimed at restoring moral values and religious order after the Time of Troubles, these reforms did not reinstate the traditional system but inspired a general reappraisal of traditional attitudes and activities. The role of these Russian religious reforms is, in part, comparable to the role of the Reformation and the Counter-Reformation in Western Europe in that it conditioned the emergence of the individual as an autonomous cultural value. This development, in turn, produced new spheres of cultural activity. From this perspective, the main factor in Russia's modernization was neither Western influence nor a belated, peculiar Renaissance caused by this influence, but the transformation of cultural consciousness—Russian culture's reappraisal of its own heritage. This reappraisal is based on a highly specific ancient Russian cultural foundation. For the first time the secular and spiritual cultural spheres are set in opposition to each other and the literary and artistic enterprises take on autonomous significance. By virtue of this autonomy, the culture undergoes radical changes. The culture's need to organize itself leads to its rhetorical disposition and those cultural strata whose absence was foregrounded by the new rhetorical standard are expropriated from external sources (the classical heritage, Western influence).

NOTES

1. N. S. Trubetzkoi, *Vorlesungen über die altrussische Literatur* (Florence, 1973), 19–28; D. S. Likhachev, *Razvitie russkoi literatury X–XVII vekov: Epokhi i stili* (Leningrad, 1973), 14–35; D. Obolensky, *The Byzantine Commonwealth: Eastern Europe, 500–1453* (London, 1974), 420 ff.

2. Fr. J. Thomson, "The Nature of the Reception of Christian Byzantine Culture in Russia in the Tenth to Thirteenth Centuries and Its Implications for Russian Culture," in *Belgian Contributions to the Eighth International Congress of Slavists, Zagreb, Ljubljana, September 1978, Slavica Gandensia* 5 (1978): 107–39; Fr. J. Thomson, "The Corpus of Slavonic Translations Available in Muscovy: The Cause of Old Russia's Intellectual Silence and a Contributory Factor to Muscovite Cultural Autarky," in *Christianity and the Eastern Slavs,* vol. 1, *Slavic Cultures in the Middle Ages,* ed. B. Gasparov and O. Raevsky-Hughes (Berkeley and Los Angeles, 1993), 181–82.

3. V. M. Zhivov and B. A. Uspenskii, "Metamorfosy antichnogo iazychestva v istorii russkoi kul'tury, XVII–XVIII vv.," *Antichnost' v kul'ture i iskusstve posleduiushchikh vekov* (Moscow, 1984), 204–85.

4. N. W. Ingham, "The Martyred Prince and the Question of Slavic Cultural Continuity in the Early Middle Ages," in *Medieval Russian Culture,* ed. H. Birnbaum and M. Flier (Berkeley and Los Angeles, 1984), 31–53; J. H. Lind, "The Martyria of Odense and a Twelfth-Century Russian Prayer: The Question of Bohemian Influence on Russian Religious Literature," *Slavonic and East European Review* 68, no. 1 (1990): 1–21.

5. Cf. the title of chapter 39 of the Procheiron in Gosudarstvennyi istoricheskii muzei, Collection of A. S. Uvarov, no. 578: "Zapoviedi po predaniiu sviatykh pravil izbrannaia o kaznekh, po poveleniiu sviatykh otets i po ustavu sv. Tsarei" (Arkhimandrit Leonid [Kavelin], *Sistematicheskoe opisanie slaviano-rossiiskikh rukopisei sobraniia grafa A. S. Uvarova* 1 [Moscow, 1893], 649). See also M. Benemanskii, *Zakon gradskii: Znachenie ego v russkom prave* (Moscow, 1917), 111; and V. M. Zhivov, "Istoriia russkogo prava kak lingvo-semioticheskaia problema," in *Semiotics and the History of Culture in Honor of Jurij Lotman: Studies in Russian,* ed. Morris Halle et al. (Columbus, Ohio, 1988), 46–128 (esp. 101–2).

6. G. Lenhoff, "Toward a Theory of Protogenres in Medieval Russian Letters," *Russian Review* 43 (1984): 31–54; W-H. Schmidt and K.-D. Seemann, "Erzählen in den älteren slavischen Literaturen," in *Gattung und Narration in den älteren slavischen Literaturen,* ed. K.-D. Seemann (Wiesbaden, 1987), 1–25; K.-D. Seemann, "Zum Verhältnis von Narration und Gattung im slavischen Mittelalter," in ibid., 207–21.

7. V. M. Zhivov, "Slavia Christiana i istoriko-kul'turnyi kontekst 'Skazaniia o

russkoi gramote'," in *La cultura spirituale russa: A cura di L. Magarotto e D. Rizzi* (Trent, 1992), 71–125.

8. G. Lenhoff, *The Martyred Princes Boris and Gleb: A Socio-Cultural Study of the Cult and the Texts* (Columbus, Ohio, 1989), 75–77.

9. See a new approach to the analysis of medieval Russian literary canon based on the manuscript tradition as a whole in the recent monograph by R. Marti, *Handschrift—Text—Textgruppe—Literatur* (Wiesbaden, 1989).

10. A. I. Sobolevskii, *Perevodnaia literatura Moskovskoi Rusi XIV–XVII vv.: Bibliograficheskie materialy* (St. Petersburg, 1903), 38.

11. R. B. Tarkovskii, *Starshii russkii perevod basen Ezopa i perepischiki ego teksta* (Leningrad, 1975).

12. B. A. Uspensky, "The Language Situation and Linguistic Consciousness in Muscovite Rus': The Perception of Church Slavic and Russian," in *Medieval Russian Culture,* ed. Birbaum and Flier, 365–85; and *Istoriia russkogo literaturnogo iazyka, XI–XVII vv.* (Munich, 1987).

13. D. S. Likhachev, A. M. Panchenko, and N. V. Ponyrko, *Smekh v drevnei Rusi* (Leningrad, 1984).

14. G. Florovsky, *Ways of Russian Theology,* trans. R. L. Nichols (Belmont, Mass., 1979), 87.

15. S. Zen'kovskii, *Russkoe staroobriadchestvo: Dukhovnye dvizheniia semnadtsatogo veka* (Munich, 1970).

16. Likhachev, *Razvitie,* 151; D. S. Likhachev, "Semnadtsatyi vek v russkoi literature," in *XVII vek v mirovom literaturnom razvitii* (Moscow, 1969), 299–328 (esp. 308–9).

17. E. V. Petukhov, *Russkaia literatura: Istoricheskii obzor glavneishikh literaturnykh iavlenii drevnego i novogo perioda. Drevnii period* (Petrograd, 1916), 332–34.

18. L. V. Cherepnin, ed. *Skazanie Avraamiia Palitsyna* (Moscow and Leningrad, 1955), 221.

19. M. B. Pliukhanova, "O nekotorykh chertakh lichnostnogo soznaniia v Rossii XVII v.," in *Khudozhestvennyi iazyk srednevekov'ia* (Moscow, 1982), 184–200.

20. Rossiiskii gosudarstvennyi arkhiv drevnikh aktov (RGADA), f. 27, no. 140, pt. 3.

21. Zen'kovskii, *Russkoe staroobriadchestvo,* 78–79.

22. N. Subbotin, ed., *Materialy dlia istorii raskola,* 9 vols. (Moscow, 1874–1890), vol. 1, 246–47. The manner in which this conflict is described is characteristic of the reformist mentality. The carnival procession is called "a devilish spectacle" *(besovskoe igralishche).* The participants who beat Neronov are likened to "wild beasts" *(zveri divii).* They beat Neronov "mercilessly" *(nemilostivo),* while he continues to censure them. Cf. similar expressions in the writings of Avvakum: *Pustozerskii sbornik: Avtografy sochinenii Avvakuma i Epifaniia* (Leningrad, 1975), 19, 25, 29, 51.

23. Subbotin, *Materialy,* 249–50.

24. Zen'kovskii, *Russkoe staroobriadchestvo,* 78–79.

25. Subbotin, *Materialy,* 267–68.

26. V. M. Zhivov, "Dvoeverie i osobyi kharakter russkoi kul'turnoi istorii," in *Philologia slavica: K 70-letiiu akademika N. I. Tolstogo* (Moscow, 1993), 50–59.

27. Subbotin, *Materialy,* 272: "protopop Stefan i moleniem i zapreshcheniem ustroi ne byti v ono brachnoe vremia smekhu nikakovomu, nizhe koshchunam, ni besovskim igraniiam, ni pesnem studnym. . . . I sovershisia toi zakonnyi brak . . . v

tishine i v strase Bozhii, i v peniikh i pesnekh dukhovnykh." The author evidently underlines the opposition between the two types of behavior.

28. A. I. Iatsimirskii, ed., "Poslanie Ivana Begicheva o vidimom obraze Bozhiem," *Chteniia v Obshchestve istorii i drevnostei rossiiskikh* (1898), bk. 2, sect. 2, I-X, 1–13 (esp. 4).

29. A. Lyzlov, *Skifskaia istoriia,* ed. A. P. Bogdanov (Moscow, 1990). Lyzlov named his sources in the beginning of his book (ibid., 7).

30. Avvakum, *Pamiatniki istorii staroobriadchestva XVII v. Kn.1, vyp.1* in *Russkaia istoricheskaia biblioteka* 39 (1927): 67; *Pustozerskii sbornik,* 60.

31. Avvakum, *Pamiatniki,* 547–48. In this sermon Avvakum insisted that, in accordance with the teaching of the Holy Fathers, rhetoric and philosophy were an "external delusion" *(vneshniaia bliad').* Collections of excerpts from various writings against liberal arts were popular among Old Believers; see a publication of one of this sort of manuscripts: Subbotin, *Materialy,* 484–90.

32. *Russkaia syllabicheskaia poeziia, XVII–XVIII vv.* (Leningrad, 1970), 56–59.

33. A. M. Panchenko, *Russkaia stikhotvornaia kul'tura XVII veka* (Leningrad, 1973), 34–77; L. S. Sheptaev, "Stikhi spravshchika Savvatiia," *Trudy otdela drevnerusskoi literatury* 21 (1965): 5–28.

34. Uspensky, *Istoriia russkogo literaturnogo iazyka,* 55–59.

35. *Die Makarij-Rhetorik,* ed. R. Lachmann (Cologne and Vienna, 1980).

36. R. Lachmann, ed., *Feofan Prokopovich: De arte rhetorica libri X: Kijoviae, 1706* (Cologne and Vienna, 1982); V. M. Zhivov, "Review of *Feofan Prokopovich: De arte rhetorica libri X . . . ,*" *Izvestiia AN SSSR: Seriia literatury i iazyka* 44 (1985): 3, 274–78.

37. For Matveev, see "Zapiski Andreia Artamonovicha grafa Matveeva," in *Zapiski russkikh liudei,* ed. I. P. Sakharov (St. Petersburg, 1841), 1–94. For love songs, see L. Maikov, *Ocherki iz istorii russkoi literatury XVII i XVIII stoletii* (St. Petersburg, 1889), 229–33.

E D W A R D   L .   K E E N A N

Afterword

ORTHODOXY AND HETERODOXY

THE ORIGINAL PLAN of our conference and the papers there presented (not all of which are included here) bore the mark of the organizers' original impulse to devote significant attention to problems of orthodoxy and heterodoxy in seventeenth-century East Slavic life. Religion, not surprisingly, played a central role in many of the contributions. I hope it may seem worthwhile to conclude these considerations with some thoughts on these subjects, thoughts that have been stimulated—or modified—by the conference and the rereading of the papers.

1. THE GENERAL CONFESSION

I think we should begin the next phase of our progress toward a better understanding of Russian religious history by admitting our manifold sins and wickedness: we (meaning, in varying degree, all students of the subject) probably have not yet established a sufficient base of textual/factual knowledge about Russian religious practice, culture, "spirituality," and ecclesiastical history to warrant comparison with anything at all—or any very confident pronouncements about these subjects, in the light of newer theories, or older theories, or whatever might be the current vogue in abstraction or representation.

Having thus acknowledged our limitations, we should next take account of the reasons why we abide in ignorance.[1] These reasons are worth listing, if only so that we may one day (God willing) be conscious of having overcome their consequences. (I rank them in what seems to me their order of importance; some stand in complex causal relation to one or several others):

A. The general disinclination of Russians, in the seventeenth century and later, to delineate and maintain boundaries between the ecclesiastical sphere and the secular realm (note here my disagreement with Professor Zhivov).

This is hardly a new subject; my objective here is to point out the difficulties this disinclination has created for our retrospective study of "Seventeenth-Century Orthodoxy and Heterodoxy." If, as I think we should, we define the seventeenth century for present purposes as the period of the first patriarchate, the matter becomes clear: the patriarchate, which had no precedent in Russian ecclesiastical life and little or no support among the larger community of believers, was created in 1589 as a political act of the secular power, which then "uncreated" it four generations later without notable public outcry. The majority of patriarchs were appointed and removed by the secular power, and so on and so forth.

Now it does not really matter much, from our cognitive vantage point, whether this behavior was the articulation of a deeply imbedded Caesaropapist tradition, whereby in the eyes of Russians the tsar was beatific and the patriarch a national leader (Michael Cherniavsky), or the result of the grand-princely court's general habit of simply pushing clerics around, as it did everyone else. The problem is: What do we mean by "the Russian Church" in this period? Is it an autonomous and single-minded rational actor? If, as I suspect, it is not but is instead self-sustaining (but not autonomous, like, for example, the great clans or the *prikaz* bureaucracy), can we really frame sentences that begin "The Russian Church . . ." without pointing out the facts at every turn?

B. The growing Russian seventeenth-century tendency, stimulated in no insignificant measure by the behavior of non-Russians, to identify religious affiliation with national self-conception.

Here we have a peculiarly seventeenth-century phenomenon. Europe was sorting itself out according to the principle *cuius regio, eius religio.* Protestants and Catholics were challenging Russians to defend Orthodoxy on the basis of the nominally shared doctrinal texts. Even the Greek and Ukrainian and Arab Orthodox, like Makarios, were scolding Russians for catechistic deficiencies or liturgical deviance. Meanwhile, it became increasingly clear not only that the native ecclesiastical establishment was in no position to debate, for example, the question of the moment of the Transubstantiation, but also that it did not really feel it was obliged to: the Russians knew what Orthodoxy meant for them (namely, the Russian Way), and they really didn't care all that much what foreigners thought about the details.

Now this time-saving reduction—which was later condemned by serious Russian church historians, including P. S. Smirnov, as *bukvo-obriado-verie* (which can be translated as "literal ritualism") but seen as a virtue by anti-*khitrost'* (anti-artifice) Slavophiles—is not for us to praise or condemn. But it decidedly makes it more difficult for us to get to the bottom of what seventeenth-century Russians were thinking about religion, as opposed to what they were thinking about themselves.

C. The remarkable reluctance of Russians to put to paper authentic description or analysis of either the institutional life of the church or the inner life of believers.

Here I do not mean to imply ignorance of the sermons, *oblicheniia* (polemical, theological reproach), conciliar protocols, and other texts that excoriate Orthodox clergy and believers for sins of commission and omission. But sermons are questionable testimony, much as, at another level, vocatives and imperatives are not subject to verification. And doubtless, as Alexander Strakhov has demonstrated, fulminations against, for example, *dvoeverie* all too often go back to Byzantine (or even Old Testament) originals. What seems to me to be wanting—yet vital for the interpretation of what we do have—is the candid, confidential, confessional, vernacular text, whether ecclesiastical or devotional, that would open for us the real world of these people on the threshold of modernity. Seventeenth-century Russian bishops did not, I believe, keep diaries; Russian believers, so far as I am aware, did not write mystical lyric poetry. And Russia had no Inquisition. (But see below.)

However fortunate Russians may have been in missing this challenging experience, the consequence for us is that we still have relatively little evidence about the quotidian beliefs of Russian laymen. Were they, as it has been argued, still becoming Christians in this period? Was their Christian belief system something we would recognize as such? Can we ever know?

D. The archaism and provincialism of "scholarship" on these subjects.

These insufficiencies derive in no small measure from A, B, and C, above. For the most part, Russian church history is grievously underdeveloped. One can, of course, list a handful of major exceptions, typically written by representatives of two generations born between 1850 and 1900. These exceptions, however (with the idiosyncratic exception of Georges Florovsky's *Puti*), tend to be limited to narrowly confined subjects (a biography, a controversy) and typically represent the first scholarly study of a subject that has not been studied since. There is no other major aspect of Russia's history that is so dependent on century-old work as is religious history. And there are many subjects that the Druzhinins and Belokurovs and Kharlampovskiis never got around to. It may be hoped, on the basis of some recent work, that this problem will be alleviated, but the currents are decidedly crossed.

E. The scrappiness of the written record.

Note that I say "scrappiness" here, not paucity. By "scrappiness" I mean that the generally calamitous history of religious institutions, from the patriarchate itself down to the lowliest monastery, has produced a situation in which almost no significant archival collections are integral and preserved in situ. The activities of cultural and administrative centers were typically episodic and periodically interrupted. Enormous work must be done simply to establish what we have and what shape it is in.

Certainly there seems to be plenty of it: for the *Raskol* alone, the massive publications of T. V. Barsov, V. G. Druzhinin, Ia. L. Barskov, V. G. Rumiantseva, and others are probably dwarfed by the poorly documented archives of the bishoprics, and so on. But these, too, are often scattered, poorly described, heterogeneous in any given repository. Moreover, many of these sources have been perversely edited and interpreted. Similarly, the nonadministrative, devotional texts are misidentified, poorly dated and attributed, hardly studied from the point of view of originality, and so on.

F. The relative primitiveness of Russian religious life in the seventeenth century.

Russians as a speech community, including the monastic and parish clergy, were only dimly aware of the vast and complex liturgical, hagiographic, patristic, and canonical literature of Christianity as it existed in the seventeenth century. As a consequence, it is no easy matter for a modern church historian—even a noncomparativist—to meet them on their own terrain.

2. RESOLUTION TO SIN NO MORE.

It seems to me that in framing our separate tasks as we undertake to remedy our lamentable ignorance, we should proceed upward from the bottom of this list, as follows:

F. There is no present-day remedy for the primitiveness of Russian Christian belief and practice in the seventeenth century. What we have at our disposal is a helpful conceptual predisposition: we should borrow from the literature of the cultural anthropologists and sociologists of religion who have studied arguably comparable Christian societies (rural Greece and Sicily, Ethiopia, Catholic Africa). Great benefit can be derived from the constant realization that, although we must learn a great deal simply in order to understand what they did not fully grasp, only a small group of Russians in the seventeenth century had even the knowledge and understanding of Ginzburg's Menocchio. Once we realize this fact and apply corresponding methods, the considerable written record will, I suspect, yield up all manner of helpful new evidence.

At the same time, we should not underestimate the complexity and regularity of certain aspects of Russian church life; before we can make confident judgments about any Russian religious text, we must establish the working canon of the time and locale in which it was produced, and its relation to that canon. We all need to learn more about seventeenth-century catechism and liturgics.

E. I have just called the written record "considerable"; above I characterized it as "scrappy." In fact (as we all know), whereas the statements I have made above describe our predicament, there does in fact exist an ocean of paper that can be used to study the religious behaviors of Russians in the seventeenth century. I have in mind not only the innumerable miscellanies *(sborniki),* but also the intra-hierarchical administrative and disciplinary paper trail. What we must undertake here is a concerted and massive effort to describe, classify, publish, and attribute this documentation, separating internal administrative paper (probably the greater portion of the original material) from devotional texts, dividing devotional texts into liturgical, hagiographic, and so on, and making careful distinctions between original and translated. Even the first cut at these tasks could take us a lifetime—at which point we would find ourselves roughly where students of the Western church were . . . in the seventeenth century. But this task is by far the most immediate and important. I frankly think that it makes little sense to write a syllable about "spirituality"—a perfectly legitimate subject in principle—until we have some minimal agreed corpus of authentic, original, dated, and attributed texts on which to base our generalizations. We can confidently leave *dukhovnost'* to our Russian colleagues—a prudent policy, from any point of view.

D. As a part of the same undertaking, we should retrieve, through systematic bibliographic search, reprints, and retrospective critique, the best of the serious scholarship of the generation I have referred to (N. K. Nikol'skii, S. A. Belokurov, K. V. Kharlampovich, N. A. Gibbenet, Aleksander Golubtsov, V. G. Druzhinin, A. Ia. Shpakov et al.) and attempt to place similar building blocks of solid, perhaps old-fashioned, text-based, logical-positivist scholarship alongside their contributions.

C. In saying above that Russians in the seventeenth century were not likely to provide authentic description or analysis of either the institutional life of the church or the inner life of believers, I had in mind conscious attempts at more-or-less objective description and analysis. In fact, in the bureaucratic paper of the episcopal and monastic establishments (and in secular documents like the denunciation for lèse-majesté *[slovo i delo gosudarevy]* materials and provincial files of all kinds), one can find rich material about the "superstitions" of average Russians, as some of our colleagues have demonstrated. For if Russia had no Inquisition, it may be because it had a surrogate: an intrusive and authoritarian political system that demanded submission above all and, indeed, was capable of construing any act or utterance as a symbol of disobedience.

What one must do, however, after a sufficient amount of this material has been identified and systematized (a lot is already published, here and there) is to compose a list of hard-headed forensic questions:

1. In each individual case, was the unlucky soul who became the victim of prosecutorial wrath actually guilty of heretical, blasphemous, sordid, or unspeakable acts, as charged?
2. If so, does he or she appear to have been sane, within generous definitional bounds?
3. If so, did his or her perseverance (recidivism is almost always an aggravating factor in the documentation) arise from conscientious belief or from an impulse of defiance, or both?
4. If from belief, can one derive from the facts of the case some notion of what these beliefs were?

Only after this procedure has been repeated for a large number of cases, it seems, can we begin to ask the larger questions: Can these beliefs be so arranged as to reveal what we might call a "belief system"? Where might this system or systems be placed in relation to other, better-known systems (vernacular syncretic Western Christianity, Indo-European paganism, Eurasian animism, and so on)? Is it individual? local? or, by contrast, shared widely? Is there anything "Russian" about it? If so, what?

B. Which brings us back to the seventeenth-century process of progressive religious isolation and the increasing identification of nation and church (but not necessarily belief) in the context of major intrusions and influences by non-Russians. (To rephrase the periodization suggested above, the Orthodox seventeenth century begins with a posse of renegade Greeks setting up a patriarchate in Moscow and ends with Iavorskii, Prokopovich, and Tuptalenko-Rostovskii in charge of closing it down—the last establishing, while he was about it, the "traditional" Russian hagiographic canon, his famous *Zhitiia,* for all time on the basis of . . . Polish and Bollandist vitae.)

Here, perhaps because the texts are better known and less problematical (although misconstrued no less frequently), a research agenda suggests itself, which is somewhat more traditional in form, if revisionist in content. We should explore the following questions:

1. What was the intellectual-confessional significance of the controlling presence—for the first time—of a cohort of engaged and au courant Greek clerical politicians (Arsenii Elassonskii, Patriarch Ignatii, et al.) in the patriarchate?
2. What is the influence of early anti-Protestant (but perhaps not precisely Counter-Reformation) polemical texts produced in the Ruthenian lands upon Russian clerical—and ultimately popular—thinking?
3. What, if any, were the doctrinal and ecclesiological positions of the otherwise crucially influential patriarchate of Filaret, in particular in regard to points 1 and 2?
4. How, in modern terms, can one describe the intellectual history of the several centers of native religious culture in the seventeenth century—the Trinity–St. Sergii Lavra under Dionisii and at mid-century; the Typography *(Tipografskii dvor)*, the patriarchate, and perhaps others, in the last decades?

A. These last questions bring us to our starting point: the interaction of the secular and religious institutions, and some paradoxes that are generated by the sui generis Möbius strip of the secular/religious relation:

1. Why, in view of the fact that from Godunov through Filaret and to Peter the secular political elite effectively controlled the church, were its representatives so little (practically not at all) interested in becoming "princes of the church," religious intellectuals, worldly bishops, or even comfortable curates?
2. Why, similarly, were individuals from the same elite (when they did become interested in religion) so likely to be attracted by Protestantism or Catholicism?
3. Why, given the domination of the church by the state and the growing identification of Orthodoxy with Russianness, did nativist movements tend to be either anti-clerical but loyal to the tsar (Avvakum) or anti-regime but indifferent to religion (revolts of 1648–1649)?

3. PENANCE

Once we have taken these and associated matters into account, it remains to decide just which comparative context will shed the most reflected light upon Russians' religious behaviors in the seventeenth century. In addition to the obvious juxtaposition with Orthodoxy (and consequently Reformation and Counter-Reformation trends) in the Ruthenian lands, I think one should probably think about the Balkan Orthodox communities, Slavic and non-Slavic, which were in certain respects more nearly comparable.

As concerns the connection between religion and national (or communal) self-definition, I suspect that the history of any of a number of groups might provide comparative insights. Here again, juxtaposition with the Serb/Croat/Muslim speech community could be fruitful—as might, in a more theoretical plane, the study of East European Jewry in the two centuries or so before the Holocaust, or the Ismaili Muslims in the nineteenth and twentieth centuries. The inherent problems of comparison, however (the learning of two or more languages and cultures, and so on), will be complicated because by and large such communities have been no less mythopoetic than the Russians about such matters, and the scholarship only slightly more modern.

I am aware that all of this may seem just a bit too Cartesian for some of my colleagues, and perhaps in purely practical terms it is not what we need to get the ball rolling, but I should be happy if we could discuss some of these notions.

NOTE

1. It should perhaps be said here that the suppression of Russian Orthodoxy in the middle decades of the twentieth century occupies only a modest place among these reasons; as a consequence, its replacement by the suppression of positivist atheism promises only very modest intellectual gains.

INDEX

Agricultural practices, 19–33 (*see also* Peasantry); chronology and, 24; crop rotation vs. field rotation, 28; efficiency and, 24–30; labor intensity and, 25–30; long fallow methods of, 20, 22, 26; nonagricultural community and, 28; population and, 22–30; slash-and-burn method of, 20, 22, 26, 31n. 7; state policies and, 29; success of, 20; technology and, 23; territorial expansion and, 29; three-field rotation method of, 20–22

Almazov, A. I., 97

Amico, B., 84

Anisim (deacon), 121–22

Anna from Kolomna, 126

Annales school historians, 7

Apocalypse, 75

Aquinas, T., 157

Armenian communities, 57

Army, 59, 60, 61

Arsenii Sukhanov, 81, 83, 93n. 21

Arsenios the Greek, 80

Art, 169–81; baroque, 179; naturalism in, 170. *See also* Icons

Associations, 59–64

Authorship, 194

Avraamii, 11, 132, 134, 135; "Christian's Secure Shield of Faith," 136; "Petition," 136; "Question and Answer," 136

Avvakum, 135, 141, 170, 188, 193, 197n. 22, 198n. 31; autobiography of, 140–41

Balyka family, 64

Bandini, O., 156, 157

Baron, S., 3

Baroque art, 179

Basil (saint), 125

Beauty prayer, 103

Begichev, I.: "On the Visible Image of God," 192

Begriffsgeschichte, 10

Belokurov, S., 73

Belz palantinate, 67

Bila Tserkva, 58

Binary opposites. *See* Polarities

Biography, 190, 195

Blum, J., 24

Bogoliubtsy. See Zealots of Piety

"Border crossings," 156. *See also* Peripheries

Borderlands, 11. *See also* Peripheries

Borec'kyj, J., 163

Boris (saint), 185, 186

Boserup, E., 10, 25–26, 28, 29

Boyars, 55–56, 67

Braudel, F., 21, 22, 23, 25

Bubnov, N. Iu., 135

Budny, S., 158

Bullinger, H., 158

Bureaucracy, 29, 39, 204

Burghers, 57, 67

Burke, P., 97

Bushkovitch, P., 3, 4, 8, 134, 141

Buturlin, Vasil'evich V., 163, 164

Bynum, C. W., 141

Byzantinism, Russian culture and, 169, 179–81, 185

Cathedral of the Annunciation, 172

Cathedral of the Dormition, 74–90, 171, 173

Cathedral of the Holy Sophia, 177

Chaadaev, P. Ia., 6

Chaianov, A. V., 24, 25, 26, 28

Chancellery School, 194

Chanter, P., 43

Charms, 97–98, 109n. 1

Cherniavsky, M., 200

Church of Ascension, 84

Church of the Forty Martyrs, 80

Church of Gregory of Neocaesarea, 173

Church of the Holy Sepulcher, 83, 171

Church of the Intercession in Fili, 179

Church of the Intercession on the Moat, 92n. 10

Church of Saint Zosima and Savvatii, 117

Church of the Trinity, 171, 173

Cipolla, Carlo, 21, 23
Clerics, 36
Collective assemblies, 39–40
Commemoration, 90, 91n. 4
Constantine-Cyril (saint), 186
Corporate orders, 53–59
Cossacks, 52–68
Court ceremony, 73–90
Crummey, R., 8, 11, 132
Cults, 124–25, 185; centralization of,
    117; types of, 121
Culture: behavior as, 8; Geertz's defini-
    tion of, 142n. 2; history of, 149–68;
    miracle stories and, 120–27

Damian (saint), 100, 103
Danilov, S., 106
Danilov Monastery, 119
Davis, N. Z., 155
Dekorum-Retorik, 194
Demons, 98, 104, 106, 118
Denisov, S., 137
Dichotomies. See Polarities
Diminutives, 35–36
Discourse, historical vs. current, 12–13
Dissimulation. See Rhetorical masks
Dmitriev, L. A., 118
Dmitrievskii, A., 73
Dmitrii Prilutskii, 123
Dnieper Basin, 58, 60, 61, 62, 64
Dobroklonskii, A. P., 5
Dobroliubov, N. A., 43
Don Monastery, 172
Donskaia, E., 121
Drama, 89–90
Dvoever'e, 13n. 1

Emigrés, 6
Epifanii, autobiography of, 140–41
Epiphany ritual, 74–76
Erasmus, 167n. 17
Evfrosiniia of Suzdal', 121
Exorcism, 104

Family, treaties between kinsmen, 46n.
    18. See also Identity issues
Fedor (deacon), 135
Fedorovich, Mikhail (tsar), 118
Fedotov, G., 3, 6–7
Filaret (patriarch), 117, 118, 161, 191,
    205

Finucane, R. C., 116
Flavius, J.: History of the Judaic Wars,
    The, 186
Flier, M., 9, 73, 169
Florishchevo Monastery, 177
Florovsky, G., 6, 187–88, 189, 201
Foley, J., 97
Folk healers, 106
Form-critical method of analysis,
    115–20, 122, 126–27
Fortune telling, 102, 112n. 32
Free will, 153
French, R. A., 20, 23, 25
Frick, D., 9, 11, 149

Game theory analysis, 155
Geertz, C., 7, 11
Gender issues: miracle stories and,
    120–31; visionary experience and,
    131n. 47
Gentryman, 5
George (saint), 103
Gernet, J., 165
Ginzburg, C., 7, 155
Gleb (saint), 185, 186
Godunov, Boris, 189
Goffman, E., 155
Golubinskii, E. E., 5
Gombrowicz, W., 149
Great Chain of Being, 43
Greek orthodox. See Orthodox religion,
    Greek
Grigorii (saint), 121, 122, 124
Guilds, 59, 62

Hagia Sophia, 80
Hagiography, 7, 8, 11, 190 (see also
    Saints); miracle stories and,
    115–31; Old Belief and, 132–45;
    source-critical problem and,
    116–17
Halpern, B., 97
Healing. See Illness
Herbals, 108
Heterodoxy, 199–206
Historical Museum, 177
Historicism, 171–81
Historiography, 3–13; American, 6, 7;
    continuity and, 166n. 6; diachronic
    approach to, 116–20; European, 6,
    7; firsthand accounts and, 45n. 1;

form-critical method of analysis of, 115–20, 122, 126–27; functional approach to, 116–20; inquest records and, 118; methodology vs. strategies of, 154–65; micro vs. macro, 13, 155; miracle stories and, 116–20; morphology and, 165; new cultural method of, 7–8; official church, 3; postmodernism and, 166n. 6; rhetorical masks and, 156–65; secularism and, 3, 192–97; sources and, 115–16, 154, 201–3; Soviet, 5–6, 13n. 2, 14n. 12; structuralism and, 151–54, 166n. 6; synchronic approach to, 116–20; twentieth century, 5
Holy Cross Monastery, 171
"Holy fools," 13n. 1
Holy Land, 81–83, 93n. 21
Holy water, 102
Homeric poetry, 110n. 6

Iakhontov, I., 119
Iaroslav Vasil'evich Sevastian of Pskov, 123
Icons, 9, 125, 133, 169–81; Cretan, 173, 177, 179; historicism and, 171–81
Identity issues, 9, 200–1, 204; Christian, 98; family and, 37; rank and, 37–38; region and, 37–38; social, 34–44
Illness: blindess, 124–26; men vs. women, 125; miracle cures for, 118–26; prayer and, 100–1, 106–8
Indicopleustes, C.: Christian Topography, 186
Individualism, 10, 12, 189–96; authorship and, 194; protagonists and, 194
Inquisition records, 45n. 1
Ioann and Loggin of Iarenga, 117, 118
Iosaf (patriarch), 118, 125
Iov (patriarch), 125
Iverian Mother of God, 171
Iz glubiny, 6
Izmaragd, 7

Jerusalem, 81–83, 93n. 21; as image, 9
Jerusalem Chapel of the Intercession, 76
Jesuits, 158
Jewish communities, 57–58, 60, 63

Kabasilas, N., 82; Commentary on the Divine Liturgy, 82
Kalita, Ivan, 171
Kamenskii, Ioasaf, 124
Kapterev, N., 73
Kassian of Avnega (saint), 121, 122, 124
Kazan Cathedral, 14n. 11
Kazan' Tatars, 75
Keenan, E. L., 8, 9, 199
Khmel'nyts'kyi uprising, 52, 159
Khodyka family, 64
Khutynskii, V., 126
Kiev, 57, 62–64, 185
Kievan Caves Monastery, 175
Kievan Rus', 75
Kingdom of Poland, 54
Kliuchevskii, V. O., 3, 115
Kollmann, N. Shields, 3, 8, 10, 34
Kosoi, F., 117
Koziol, G., 35
Kozma (saint), 100, 103
Krypetskii, S., 125
Kurbskii-Groznyi correspondence, 35
Kushtskii, A., 124

Lachmann, R., 194
Ladurie, E. Le Roy, 7
Land, concept of, 41, 42
Lavrentii Zyzanii, 160–63
Lenhoff, G., 8
Levin, E., 8, 10, 96
Lies. See Rhetorical masks
Likhachev, D., 185
Likhachev, D. S., 6, 188
Linguistics, 167n. 29, 187
Literacy, 110n. 7
Literature, 184–96 (see also Text); boundary fixing and, 192–93; genres and, 186, 193–95; reform and, 184–96
Lithuania, Grand Duchy of, 54, 55, 158
Liturgical reform, 73–90; drama and, 85, 89–90; Mark vs. Matthew, books of, 85–87; transcendence and, 91n. 4
"Lived experience," 7, 8, 11
Livestock, 21–23
Livonian war, 27
Lotman, I., 12, 153
Lubomirski, S., 65
Lukaris, C., 156, 161

Lviv, 57, 62–63
Lyzlov, A.: *History of the Scythians, A,* 193

Magic: sympathetic, 99–102, 108; term
    of, 111n. 10
Magnates, 65–66
Makarii, M., 5
Makarii-Rhetoric, 194
Makarii of Zheltye Vody and Unzha
    (saint), 117
Makarios of Antioch, 81
Mansvetov, I., 73
Margins. *See* Peripheries
Mariia (wife of deacon), 121–22
Mark vs. Matthew, books of, 85–87
Markarios of Antioch (patriarch), 76, 79
Marker, G., 110n. 7
Markov, E., 106
Martin, J., 10, 19
Martinian (monk), 117
Martyrdom, 132–45; concept of, 144n.
    14; term of, 134
Matveev, A. A., 195
Mazowsze, 56, 61
Mazunin, A. I., 137
Memling, Hans, 179
Metropolitan Peter, 171
Meyendorff, P., 73
Mikhailovich, A. (tsar), 163–65, 169,
    171, 192
Miliutin, Mikhail, 172
Miloslavskaia, M., 192
Minstrels, 13n. 1
Miracle, term of, 134
Miracle stories, 115–31, 140; authors of,
    117; form of, 120; historical reality
    and, 119; inquest records and, 118;
    literary borrowings compared to,
    119–20; redactions of, 117, 118,
    119; sources of, 115, 118; testi-
    monies and, 118–19
Miscellanies, 96, 101, 187, 203
Misogyny. *See* Gender issues
Monastery of the Apocalypse on Pat-
    mos, 177
Monastic code, 123–27, 130n. 32
Monographs, 6, 73
Morozova, B., 11, 137–39 (*see also Tale
    of Boiarynia Morozova, The*); chari-
    table acts and, 145n. 34; passive re-
    sistance of, 139

Municipal institutions, 64
Muscovy: cultural history of, 149–68
Musin-Pushkin, A., 172
Musketeer rebellion, 195
Myth: Christian, 99–102; Finno-Ugric,
    99; folk, 101; Slavic, 99

Nasedka, I.: "Exposition against the
    Lutherans," 194
Nathanail, Ioannis, 80, 82
Nechaev, V., 170
Neronov, I., 188, 190–91
New Convent of the Virgin in Moscow,
    172
New Jerusalem Monastery, 171, 190
Nicoleta, Nicholas, 179
Nikita of Novgorod (saint), 117, 119,
    125, 126
Nikolo-Ugresha Monastery, 177
Nikon (patriarch), 9, 73–90, 132, 133,
    188; advisors of, 91n. 3; as *imitatio
    Christi,* 85, 88, 94n. 38; prayer
    books and, 98, 109; reforms of,
    73–90, 138, 170–71, 188; "Refuta-
    tion," 88, 94n. 38; "Refutation or
    Excoriation of the Boyar Simeon
    Streshnev's Questions," 190
Nobles, 53–59, 67
Novgorod, 8, 37, 81

Obolensky, D., 185
Old Belief, 5, 8, 109, 142n. 1, 188, 193;
    hagiography and, 132–45
Oprichnina, 27
Orphan, 36, 46n. 16
Orthodox brotherhood, 61
Orthodox religion (*see also* Religion; *specific
    topics):* gender and, 121–27; Greek,
    48n. 37, 73–74, 80–81, 93n. 21; hesy-
    chasm and, 90; heterodoxy and,
    199–206; popular prayer and, 96–109;
    reform and, 73–90, 155, 184–96; rit-
    ual change and (*see* Ritual); Russian,
    39, 55, 61, 63–64, 73–90, 132–33;
    Slavs and, 9, 150–51, 155, 159
Ortner, Sherry, 8
Ostrih, 62
Otenskii, Z., 117

Pacifism, 191
Paganism, 121–22

Paisios (patriarch), 81, 83
Palitsyn, A.: "Skazanie," 189
Palm Sunday ritual, 73–90; 1655 vs. 1656, 78
Panov, I., 118
Parry, M., 110n. 6
Patriarch (church leader): as *imitatio Christi,* 85, 88, 94n. 38
Patriarchy, 36, 46n. 16
Patron-client networks, 64–66
Paul of Aleppo, 76
Peasantry, 10, 11, 19–33; enserfment of, 20, 29, 56; equilibrium and, 24–30; flexibility of, 21; migrations and, 28–30; population issues and, 22–30; prayer and, 96–109, 110n. 2; Ukrainian, 56, 67. *See also* Agricultural practices
Pereiaslav, 58
Perestroika, 14n. 11
Peripheries, 11, 149–65; secondariness vs. uniqueness, 155
Personality, 189. *See also* Individualism
Peter I (tsar), 170
Peter the Great, 184
Petitions, 35–44; collective, 39–41; formulaic, 35
Pimen of Novgorod (archbishop), 125
Podlachia, 61
Podolia, 55
Poetry, 193–94
Polacki, S., 160
Poland, 149–65
Polarities, 11–12, 16n. 27, 150–52, 167n. 29
Polish-Lithuanian Commonwealth, 53–59, 151, 163
Polotskii, S., 42
Population, 32–33n. 25; agriculture and, 22–30
Potocki, A., 160
"Praxis," 8
Prayer, 10; addressing evil in, 98; alcohol and, 105; "apocryphal," 97–98; beauty and, 103; earthly forces and, 104–5, 109; ecclesiastical, 106–7; illness and, 100–1, 106–8; lay authorship of, 97; mediators of, 97; origins of, 97; outsiders and, 105; saints and, 100–1; sources of, 96, 109n. 2; supplicatory, 96–109

Prayer books, 112n. 24; Eastern Orthodox service books, 98; Gospelbooks, 85; parish service books, 96; standardization of, 98; *Trebnik,* 92n. 14
Primers, 110n. 7
Prince, title of, 55
Procession on the Ass, 76
Procheiron, 185
Pronskoi, I. V. (prince), 35

Quaremius, F., 80, 84
Quarter Army, 59–61

Raeff, M., 7
Reforms. *See* Liturgical reform; Orthodox religion
Religion: as cultural system, 11; gender and, 115–31; high vs. low culture and, 111n. 13; popular, 96–109. *See also* Orthodox religion
Religious scholarship. *See* Historiography
Reservatio mentalis, 156
Revolt of 1637–1638, 61
Rhetoric, 194–95
Rhetorical masks, 156–65; silences and, 163–65
Ritual, 12, 73–90; 1655 vs. 1656, 78; change and, 75, 79; commemoration and, 90, 91n. 4; Mark vs. Matthew, books of, 85–87; repetition and, 75; theater and, 89–90
Roman Catholicism, 63, 65, 114n. 49, 155, 158
Roman Vladimirovich of Uglich (prince), 125
Romanov, Mikhail (Tsar), 117
Rublev, Andrei, 179
Rurikid dynasty, 75
Rus': cultural history of, 149–68. *See also* Russia
Russia *(see also specific topics):* change in, 11, 153; England compared to, 111n. 9; periods of history in, 184–85; population of, 32–33n. 25; westernization of, 19, 177–78, 187
Russian historiography. *See* Historiography
Russian language, 39
Russian Museum, 172

Russian Religious Life (Geertz), 7
Ruthenian palatinate, 62, 67

Saburova, S., 121
Saint George's Day, 103
Saints: hostility toward females and,
123–27; male disbelief of, 131n.
40; male vs. female, 141; martyr-
dom and, 132–45; miracle stories
of, 115–31; pagans and, 121–22;
prayer and, 100–1. *See also* Hagiog-
raphy
Savva (saint), 123
Savvatii (saint), 121
Schultz, T., 24, 25, 26
Secreta secretorum, 35
Secularism, 3, 192–96, 200
Self, 10; family and, 37; referents to,
36–44; social identity and, 34–44.
See also Identity issues
Self-criticism, 9
Semiotics, 9
Serfs, 20, 29
Sergiev Posad Museum, 172, 175
Sergii of Obnora (saint), 121
"Servitors," 5
Shelonskii, S., 117, 118
Shevyrev, S. P., 5
Shuiskii, V. (tsar), 41
Sigal, P. A., 116
Silences, 163–65
Skomorokhi, 187
Skrizhal', 79–83
Slavynets'kyi, E., 160
Slobody, 56, 61
Sluzhebnik, 79–80, 84
Smirnov, P. S., 201
Smirnov collection, 48n. 35
Smirnova, E., 9, 169
Smith, R. E. F., 23, 24
Smotryts'kyi, M., 11, 155, 156, 158,
163
Sobieski, J., 65
Social terminology, 42–43, 50n. 58
Society: concepts of, 34–44; conflict vs.
cohesion in, 43–44, 59–64
Solomoniia, 124
Solov'ev, V., 6
Southern steppe frontier, 37–38
State: centralization of, 50n. 59; term of,41
Steppe, 62

Stevens, C. B., 37
Stolbenskii, N., 125
Strakhov, A., 201
Streshnev boyer family, 106
"Stroganov School," 172, 177
Structuralism, 151–54, 166n. 6
Suárez, F., 157
Subbotin, N., 135
Svirskii, A., 125
Symeon of Thessalonike, 82
Sysyn, F., 9, 52
Szlachta. See Nobles

Tale of Boiarynia Morozova, The, 132,
134, 135, 137; classification of,
138–40; redactions of, 137–38,
140
Tale of Frol Skobeev, The, 188–89
Tale of Savva Grudtsyn, The, 188, 191
Tartu-Moscow School of Semiotics, 6,
7, 8, 14n. 13
Tax-payers, 36, 37
Taxation, 56, 62
Text, 201, 204; classification of,
138–40; dating of, 135; elitist, 96;
genres and, 186; Greek, 80, 161,
173; life as, 154; sacred vs. secular,
11, 187, 192–96, 200; Slavonic,
161; testimony as, 154
Theater, 89–90
Theissen, G., 8
Theophanic, term of, 91n. 4
Thomson, J., 185
Three orders, 49n. 41
Thyrêt, I., 8, 10, 115
Tikhonravov, S., 89
Time of Troubles, 10, 27, 41, 42, 75,
188
Torture, concept of, 144n. 14
Treaty of Pereiaslav, 164
Tree of Life, 84
Tret'iakov Gallery, 171, 172, 173, 176
Trinity–St. Sergii Lavra, 175, 189, 194
Trubetskoi, N., 185
True Cross, 171
Tsar: petitions to, 35–44; wills of, 46n. 18
Tulupov, G., 117

Ukraine, 52–70, 158, 160, 163; associations, 59–64; corporate orders,
53–59; patron-client networks,

64–66; regional ties, 59–64
Uliianiia of Murom, 141
Umilenie, 124, 126
Uniate church, 156, 158, 160
Union of Lublin, 57
Urban VIII (pope), 156, 157
Ushakov, S., 11, 169–81; *Blachernae Mother of God,* 172; *Don Mother of God,* 172; *Dormition,* 174, 175, 176–77; historicism and, 171–81; *Kazan' Mother of God,* 172; *Kykko Mother of God,* 173, 174; Mandylion icons, 173, 177, 179; *Pantocrators,* 177, 178, 180; *In Praise of the Vladimir Mother of God,* 171–72, 179; *Savior of the Golden Robe,* 177; Savior Not-Made-by-Hands, 173; *Spas Emmanuil,* 172; *Trinity,* 179
Uspenskii, B., 12, 153

van der Weyden, Rogier, 179
Varlaam (saint), 125
Varlaam / Vasilii, 117, 119
Vatas, Thomas, 177
Vekhi, 6
Villages, 61–62

Visionary experience: male vs. female, 131n. 47. *See also* Miracle stories
Vladimirov, I., 170
Vlasii (saint), 100
Volhynia, 56, 61, 62, 67
Volodimer, 75
Vologodskii, Ignatii, 124
Voloka reform, 56
Vonifat'ev, S., 192

Wisniowrecki, J., 65
Witchcraft, 106–7, 114n. 48; spells of, 106; trials, 96, 114n. 51
Wojsko Kwarciane. See Quarter Army
Women, role of, 8, 11, 36
Wood, I., 120

Zagovory. See Charms
Zaklinanaiia, 98
Zamoyski, T., 65
Zaporozhian Host, 61
Zealots of Piety, 10, 79, 187–89, 192
Zguta, R., 106
Zhivov, V., 9, 12, 184
Zosima (saint), 121
Zyzanii, L. *See* Lavrentii Zyzanii